Have *the* Faith *of* Jesus

David H. Thiele

TEACH Services, Inc.
P U B L I S H I N G
www.TEACHServices.com • (800) 367-1844

Copyright © 2014 David H. Thiele
Copyright © 2014 TEACH Services, Inc.
ISBN-13: 978-1-4796-0361-9 (Paperback)
ISBN-13: 978-1-4796-0362-6 (ePub)
ISBN-13: 978-1-4796-0363-3 (Mobi)
Library of Congress Control Number: 2014944641

Published by

TEACH Services, Inc.
P U B L I S H I N G
www.TEACHServices.com • (800) 367-1844

Table of Contents

Introduction

Sometimes referred to as Frank Lloyd Wright's "Ninth Symphony," the Johnson Wax Headquarters was completed in 1939. Located in Racine, Wisconsin, admirers continue to tour the facility and gaze in wonder at the beautiful symmetry of the structure. One of the most impressive features of the architecture involves the dendriform, or tree-like, concrete columns in the Great Workroom. These columns are nine inches in diameter at the bottom and eighteen feet across at the top—looking very much like a subliminal invitation to skip work for a round of golf.

The whole idea of the "lily pad" columns, as Wright called them, was to provide more space for office secretaries and clerks to move freely from one part of this spacious room to another. Although innovative and new, the dendriform columns were controversial. Building inspectors informed Wright that each column had to be capable of bearing a minimum of twelve tons. Wright was confident that the column could bear that amount and more. The inspectors weren't so certain, and, without their permission, construction could not be completed.

Unwilling to concede without a test, Wright made arrangements to physically prove the concept. A column was erected. With all vested parties present, including the press and an orchestra, the order was given to commence placing the minimum weight on top of the eighteen-foot wide expanse. Upon reaching the regulatory minimum, and to the astonishment of the building inspectors, Wright ordered the crane operator to continue placing weight upon the dendriform. Twenty, thirty, forty, fifty, and finally over sixty tons of sand rested on the pad before the calyx—the part of the column that meets the pad—began to crack and collapse. The weight of the falling material as it hit the ground reportedly broke a water main buried thirty feet beneath the earth, but Wright got his building permit.

This story begs the question, Why did Frank Lloyd Wright have faith in his new idea and the building inspectors did not? Could it be that his knowledge and understanding of building exceeded that of the inspectors? Remember, however, that neither Wright nor the inspectors had ever seen the capabilities of the dendriform before!

Have you ever been in a situation that called for all the confidence of an expert, and you had no help but your own ignorance?

Consider this story. One night an overconfident teenage driver is startled by a cat running across the road. Concerned for someone else's pet, the teenager makes a split-second decision and swerves, sending the vehicle racing across someone else's lawn, hitting some trash cans in the process. A friend in the passenger seat, yells, "Let's get out of here!" The impressionable youth, yielding to peer pressure, stomps on the accelerator. Moments later, feeling guilty, the penitent teen returns on foot, rings the doorbell, and confesses to the deed. The homeowner forgives the teen and simply asks that he pick up the scattered trash.

Unfortunately, the neighbor across the street had already phoned the police, and an all-points-bulletin had already been issued to find the culprit. Of course, the search concludes when police find the driver cleaning up the mess. They proceed to issue him a ticket for reckless driving. What does a teenager, who has never before committed such an indiscretion, know about getting out of this kind of a fix?

Any loving parent would procure the services of a reputable attorney. So, phone calls result in consultations where details are related, and a lawyer is hired. The parents have confidence in the applied knowledge of the expert—who sadly disappoints because the prosecutor refuses to negotiate down the charges. Now the lawyer attempts to console by giving advice on how to respond to the judge: "Plead guilty, and say nothing more. Hope the judge is merciful. Bye." Talk about disappointed faith!

Twice victimized, the parents have nowhere to turn. The father decides to talk to the prosecutor moments before the preliminary hearing begins. No mercy there. The prosecutor is going to make political hay over the incident because two years earlier a young girl was killed in the same neighborhood by a drunk driver. Addressing the teen, the father says, "If you trust me, say nothing in your own defense. Leave it to me." The child obeys. At the right moment, the father begins a defense by telling what he knows of the teen and giving the facts in a manner so as not to lessen the guilt of the driver, but to show that the charges are too harsh in light of the circumstances. The judge knows the prosecutor and the political reasons behind the decision not to negotiate down the charges. Since it is the youth's first offense, and because of the father's plea, the judge extends mercy.

Why did the child submit? What was the basis for the teenager's confidence in the father's plea? Could the answer be found in the concept that the substance of abstract faith is an applied understanding firmly grounded in the knowledge of the person or thing in which faith is placed?

Some may not see the faith of Jesus in this illustration as it ought to be grasped and exercised by those choosing to accept Jesus as their Savior. They may balk at its apparent emphasis on works. But the simple fact is that the faith of Jesus works by love.[1] For those who accept Jesus as Savior, He becomes an Advocate.[2] As Advocate,

> Jesus does not excuse their sins, but shows their penitence and faith, and, claiming for them forgiveness, he lifts his wounded hands before the Father and the holy angels, saying, "I know them by name. I have graven them on the palms of my hands. 'The sacrifices of God are a broken spirit; a broken and a contrite heart, O God, thou wilt not despise.'" [Psalm 51:17.] And to the accuser of his people he declares, "The Lord rebuke thee, O Satan; even the Lord that hath chosen Jerusalem rebuke thee. Is not this a brand plucked out of the fire?" [Zechariah 3:2.] Christ will place his own signet upon his faithful ones, that he may present them to his Father "a glorious church, not having spot, or wrinkle, or any such thing." Their names stand enrolled in the book of life, and concerning them it is written, "They shall walk with me in white; for they are worthy."[3]

Penitence is more than an emotion. It is demonstrated by restoration, so far as possible, of that which was stolen or destroyed. This is consistent with the spirit by which Zacchaeus said, "Behold, Lord, the half of my goods I give to the poor; and if I have taken any thing from any man by false accusation, I restore him fourfold." Jesus acknowledged this spirit of penitence by His response: "This day is salvation come to this house, forsomuch as he also is a son of Abraham. For the Son of man is come to seek and to save that which was lost."[4]

Many have preached or written about faith, often referencing Hebrews 11:1, which tells us, "Now faith is the substance of things hoped for, the evidence of things not seen." But the focus of the discourse is upon your faith, my faith, or the faith of others. Not much is said about the faith of Jesus. Things remain largely unchanged from the time Ellen White wrote the following insightful words: "The faith of Jesus

> *"The faith of Jesus has been overlooked and treated in an indifferent, careless manner."*

has been overlooked and treated in an indifferent, careless manner.... Faith in Christ as the sinner's only hope has been largely left out, not only of the discourses given but of the religious experience of very many who claim to believe the third angel's message."[5] "The faith of Jesus is not comprehended."[6] "Many who claim to believe the truth have no knowledge of faith in Christ by experience. It is this neglected part of the ministry which will be found the great instrument in

---

1   Galatians 5:6 tells us "but faith which worketh by love."
2   1 John 2:1
3   White, *Spirit of Prophecy*, vol. 4, p. 310.
4   Luke 19:8–10
5   White, *Selected Messages*, book 3, p. 168.
6   White, *Reflecting Christ*, p. 82.

the conversion of souls and in leading to the high standard of holiness which every church needs to become a living church."[7] What does it mean to "keep the commandments of God, and [have] the faith of Jesus"?[8]

We don't often think of God as needing or having faith. Yet Paul summed up the faith of God in these words to the Christians of Rome: "God, who … calleth those things which be not as though they were."[9] Can we safely conclude that the faith of Jesus is merely a New Testament phenomenon? Or can we find evidence of this faith in the Old Testament as well?

When I was young, I voraciously read every book I could find on the frontier legends of American lore—Daniel Boone, Davy Crockett, Lewis and Clark, Jedidiah Smith, Kit Carson. You name them, I read about them. I didn't go so far as to wear coonskin caps or fire black powder rifles and pistols, but I conscientiously tried to leave as little a trail as possible when I walked in the woods. I tried to teach myself to understand how various animals might move through the forest. And when I read Louis L'Amour's stories of the West, I learned techniques to improve my self-taught tracking skills.

The Bible works the same way, if only we were motivated to learn how it interprets itself. For example, Isaiah wrote, "And he saw that there was no man, and wondered that there was no intercessor: therefore his arm brought salvation unto him; and his righteousness, it sustained him. For he put on righteousness as a breastplate, and an helmet of salvation upon his head; and he put on the garments of vengeance for clothing, and was clad with zeal as a cloak."[10] From this context, we know that Isaiah is writing about God. Further study on the word breastplate shows us how Paul interprets this symbol. "Stand therefore, having your loins girt about with truth, and having on the breastplate of righteousness"[11]; "But let us, who are of the day, be sober, putting on the breastplate of faith and love; and for an helmet, the hope of salvation."[12] So, by this process of tracking symbolism in the Bible, we see how, even in the Old Testament, faith and love are character traits that God puts on like a breastplate.

God does not intend for us to be faithless, rather He shows us our great need so that we might realize our lack of faith and come to Him for the faith we need. And since He is more willing to give us faith than we are to receive it, we must also take note of important warnings for those who doubt. "[For] the scripture hath concluded all under sin, that the promise by faith of Jesus Christ might be given to them that believe,"[13] "according as God hath dealt to every man the measure of faith."[14] "Now the just shall live by faith: but if any man draw back, my soul shall

7   White, *The Ellen G. White 1888 Materials*, p. 843.
8   Revelation 14:12
9   Romans 4:17
10 Isaiah 59:16, 17
11 Ephesians 6:14
12 1 Thessalonians 5:8
13 Galatians 3:22
14 Romans 12:3

have no pleasure in him."[15] "And he that doubteth is damned … for whatsoever is not of faith is sin."[16] The seriousness of the topic should compel us to "seek … the Lord while he may be found, [and to] call … upon him while he is near."[17] How are we to seek that we may find? By "looking unto Jesus the author and finisher of faith; who for the joy that was set before him endured the cross, despising the shame, and is set down at the right hand of the throne of God."[18]

Looking at the progress mankind has made in the last three hundred years or so, we see a transition in human philosophy from classical renaissance to modernism to post-modernism. Most will admit that we have increased in knowledge, which in turn has produced many goods and services unknown to the great minds of the Renaissance. Yet it could truly be said that this generation is especially challenged when it comes to having the faith of Jesus. Confidence in the power of self-actualization has transcended a need to rely upon menial means of achieving our objectives. As the conveniences of our generation have practically eradicated the privations of much earlier generations, we have become less self-sufficient and more reliant upon experts in their individual fields of accomplishments. Computer proficiency has replaced the three R's that once defined and measured literacy.

> *Yet it could truly be said that this generation is especially challenged when it comes to having the faith of Jesus.*

But that doesn't matter to the post-modern mind because we have progressed from energy to synergy. The social creature has become so withdrawn that many do not know those who live in their apartment building, much less those who live on their block. It is, after all, more convenient to sit on the couch and watch television, or surf the Internet, than to visit on the front porch as our forefathers once did.

So it is no wonder that the Omniscient One would declare the last of the seven churches "lukewarm" with the greatest accuracy. We think we have great wealth, and yet we are poor in spirit. We think we are fashionably dressed, and yet we are naked for lack of Christ's righteousness. And, becoming wise in our own eyes, we do not see that we are worse than a fool because we do not see our true condition. Our greatest want is the love and faith of Christ. If we obeyed by faith, motivated by love, we would have His righteousness. And if we hid His Word in our hearts, so that we might not sin against God, then we would have infinite wisdom to discern between what is right and what is wrong. Then we would be properly motivated to do what is right and glorify our Father in heaven.

We have a solemn warning to consider:

---

15   Hebrews 10:38
16   Romans 14:23
17   Isaiah 55:6
18   Hebrews 12:2

Let the solemn question come home to every one who is a member of our churches, How am I standing before God as a professed follower of Christ? Is my light shining forth to the world in clear, steady rays? Have we as a people who have taken vows of dedication to God, preserved our union with the Source of all light? Are not the symptoms to declension and decay painfully visible among the Christian churches of today? Spiritual death has come upon many who should be examples of zeal, purity, and consecration. Their practices speak more loudly than their professions, and witness to the fact that some power has cut the cable that anchored them to the eternal Rock, and they are drifting without chart or compass.

The True Witness desires to remedy the perilous condition in which his professed people are placed, and he says: "I have somewhat against thee, because thou hast left thy first love. Remember therefore from whence thou art fallen, and repent, and do the first works; or else I will come unto thee quickly, and will remove thy candlestick out of his place, except thou repent." *Christ will cease to take the names of those who fail to turn to him and do their first works, and will no longer make intercession for them before the Father.* He says, "I know thy works, that thou art neither cold nor hot; I would thou wert cold or hot. So then because thou art lukewarm, and neither cold nor hot, I will spue thee out of my mouth. Because thou sayest, I am rich, and increased with goods, and have need of nothing; and knowest not that thou art wretched, and miserable, and poor, and blind, and naked." *Yet the case of those who are rebuked is not a hopeless one; it is not beyond the power of the great Mediator.* He says: "I counsel thee to buy of me gold tried in the fire, that thou mayest be rich; and white raiment, that thou mayest be clothed, and that the shame of thy nakedness do not appear; and anoint thine eyes with eye-salve, that thou mayest see." *Though the professed followers of Christ are in a deplorable condition, they are not yet in so desperate a strait as were the foolish virgins whose lamps were going out, and there was no time in which to replenish their vessels with oil.* When the bridegroom came, those that were ready went in with him to the wedding; but when the foolish virgins came, the door was shut, and they were too late to obtain an entrance. But the counsel of the True Witness does not represent those who are lukewarm as in a hopeless case. *There is yet a chance to remedy their state, and the Laodicean message is full of encouragement; for the backslidden church may yet buy the gold of faith and love, may yet have the white robe of the righteousness of Christ, that the shame of their nakedness need not appear.* Purity of heart, purity of motive, may yet characterize those who are half-hearted and who are striving to serve God and Mammon. They may yet wash their robes of character and make them white in the blood of the Lamb.

Today the question is to come home to every heart, Do you believe in the Son of God? The question is not, Do you admit that Jesus is the Redeemer of the world?

and that you should repeat to your soul and to others, "Believe, believe, all you have to do is to believe;" but, *Do you have practical faith in the Son of God, so that you bring him into your life and character until you are one with him*? Many accept of the theory of Christ, but they make it manifest by their works that they do not know him as the Saviour who died for the sins of men, who bore the penalty of their transgression, in order that they might be brought back to their loyalty to God, and through the merits of a crucified and risen Saviour, might find acceptance with God in their obedience to his law. *Christ died to make it possible for you to cease to sin, and sin is the transgression of the law.*[19]

It is not enough to keep the commandments of God. We must also have the faith of Jesus. To acknowledge that God has a law, and to attempt to keep it in our own strength, is nothing more than a feeble confirmation that we deserve the death penalty that the broken law demands. We must comprehend the value of faith and the right relationship it has to the law. Then we must desire to obtain that faith from the only Source—Jesus Christ.

As we look at the world around us, we cannot help but have concern for our future. The world economy, the social unrest, and the increase in natural disasters should awaken us to the nearness of Christ's return. How appropriate then, is this counsel to us?

In this season of conflict and trial we need all the support and consolation we can derive from righteous principles, from fixed religious convictions, from the abiding assurance of the love of Christ, and from a rich experience in divine things. We shall attain to the full stature of men and women in Christ Jesus only as the result of a steady growth in grace.

Oh, what can I say to open blind eyes, to enlighten the spiritual understanding! Sin must be crucified. A complete moral renovation must be wrought by the Holy Spirit. We must have the love of God, with living, abiding faith. This is the gold tried in the fire. We can obtain it only of Christ. Every sincere and earnest seeker will become a partaker of the divine nature. His soul will be filled with intense longing to know the fullness of that love which passes knowledge; as he advances in the divine life he will be better able to grasp the elevated, ennobling truths of the word of God, until by beholding he becomes changed and is enabled to reflect the likeness of his Redeemer.[20]

I am a Laodicean. You are a Laodicean. The Laodicean church of Revelation 3 should be significant to us because the name Laodicea means "judging of the people." Due to the

---

19   White, "The Obedient Approved of God," *The Review and Herald*, August 28, 1894, emphasis added.
20   White, *Testimonies for the Church*, vol. 5, p. 105.

characteristics of the city, it could also be called "the City of Compromise."[21] So whether we are stagnant Christians, or zealously repenting Christians, we are Laodiceans.

When I was first cognizant of my own lack of the faith of Jesus, I knew I didn't want to remain poor while thinking I was rich. These words had a real power of persuasion in my heart:

> Genuine faith in Jesus leads to denial of self; but *however high the profession may be, if self is exalted and indulged, the faith of Jesus is not in the heart.* The true Christian manifests by a life of daily consecration that he is bought with a price, and is not his own. He realizes that an infinite sacrifice has been made for him, and that his life is of inestimable value, through the merits of Jesus' blood, intercession, and righteousness. But while he comprehends the exalted privileges of the sons of God, his soul is filled with humility. There is no boasting of holiness from the lips of those who walk in the shadow of Calvary's cross. They feel that it was their sin which caused the agony that broke the heart of the Son of God, and their comeliness is turned to corruption. Those who live nearest to Jesus, feel most deeply their own unworthiness, and their only hope is in the merits of a crucified and risen Saviour. Like Moses, they have had a view of the awful majesty of holiness, and they see their own insufficiency in contrast with the purity and exalted loveliness of Jesus.[22]

I began asking God to give me that precious gold refined in the fire. I knew I had to enter into the sufferings of Jesus in order to learn obedience and strengthen my faith, yet my flesh was weak. I felt that Peter was writing to me when he stated in his epistle, "[You] who are kept by the power of God through faith unto salvation ready to be revealed in the last time. Wherein ye greatly rejoice, though now for a season, if need be, ye are in heaviness through manifold temptations: That the trial of your faith, being much more precious than of gold that perisheth, though it be tried with fire, might be found unto praise and honour and glory at the appearing of Jesus Christ."[23] I found myself asking how I might have the faith of Jesus, and I determined to begin a study on how Jesus practiced and strengthened faith in His life here on earth. And I want to share with you what I have learned so that you, too, may walk as Jesus, our Lord and Savior, walked—by faith.

Of course, nothing in this book is intended to be the end of all wisdom. What you are about to read is a collection of signposts along my journey through this study of faith. So, "prove all things; hold fast that which is good"[24] and right. And God bless as you obtain for yourself that gold which never perishes.

---

21   Anderson, *Unfolding the Revelation*, p. 41.
22   White, "Evidences of Genuine Faith," *The Review and Herald,* March 6, 1888, emphasis added.
23   1 Peter 1:5–7
24   1 Thessalonians 5:21

Chapter 1

By Faith Jesus Offered Himself

In 2007 we went to Japan to visit my wife's family and to show our sons something of their Japanese ancestry. While visiting several cities, we noticed a peculiar pattern at the entrance to all the temples and shrines. On each side of the gate would be an image of a demon or a lion-like dog. The one on the left had its mouth closed, whereas the one on the right had its mouth opened. My wife finally asked one of the monks the meaning behind the symbolism. His answer somewhat surprised us. The image on the right with the open mouth symbolized the pronunciation of the first character in the Japanese alphabet. The one on the left with a closed mouth symbolized the pronunciation of the last character, typifying that their religion was all-sufficient—from the beginning of life to the end of life.

Jesus, of course, is the only true Alpha and Omega. He is the Beginning and the End, the Author and Finisher of our faith. And as commandment-keeping people of God, He calls us to have the faith of Jesus. But when we meditate upon the life—the very existence—of the Captain of our salvation, do we even begin to contemplate, much less comprehend, where the faith of Jesus begins and where it ends?

Scripture tells us that "faith is the substance [or understanding] of things hoped for, the evidence of things not seen."[1] Yet when Jesus asked Peter the third time if he loved Him, Peter responded, "Lord, thou knowest all things."[2] Herein lies a great theological paradox: Jesus' faith as well as His omniscience. One stream of reason tells us the two concepts are divergent. Yet deeper study of the plan of salvation reveals parallelism when we recognize that the understanding "of things hoped for" and infinite knowledge are indeed complementary.

---

1   Hebrews 11:1
2   John 21:17. See also John 2:23–25 and *The Desire of Ages*, page 326, for more about the extent of Christ's knowledge.

Before creation, endless possibilities existed regarding the direction of God's kingdom. We are told that God knows both good and evil.[3] Desiring only good, all sentient created beings were to know only good, the consciousness of evil withheld, until disobedience gained entrance. Still, with infinite wisdom and foresight, God established a contingency plan whereby slighted and abused love might further reveal mercy and grace without compromising or abolishing justice. Therefore, by faith Jesus offered to represent any individual or group of free moral agents, atone for the emergence of evil at any level of creation, restore the fallen individual or race, and vindicate God's government before the universe. By faith Jesus offered Himself as an atoning sacrifice, model disciple, divine teacher, servant, shepherd, and our empathetic intercessor.

The history of the fall of Lucifer is well documented in Scripture. Revelation 12 tells us about the deception of one-third of the angels and the war in heaven that ensued. Isaiah 14 describes the motivation for the deception and the war. Ezekiel 28 reveals the position of Lucifer and the condition and the results of sin and violence following his rebellion. The culture of covetousness, the pampering of pride, the fostering of fiction inundated with infectious innuendos, the manifestation of murder, and the vindictive violence are all outlined in such a manner as to show the extent of the great conflict both in heaven and on earth. What we will never know is how Lucifer would have been redeemed if he had repented.

> **By faith Jesus offered Himself as an atoning sacrifice, model disciple, divine teacher, servant, shepherd, and our empathetic intercessor.**

Shortly after his creation, God showed Adam two trees: the tree of life and the tree of knowledge of good and evil. Then God gave Adam a warning with all the power of a promise. Adam learned that death would result from eating fruit from the tree of knowledge of good and evil. Giving no hint that a plan of salvation even existed, God expected willing obedience from a simple trust in His Word and a genuine appreciation of His wisdom. No premature hope of redemption was granted. All the evidence necessary filled every sense of Adam's being. Every need was more than abundantly supplied. Faith that works by love, and not presumption, would be displayed by such obedience. Life was conditional in that compliance was required. Noncompliance could only result in death.

Yet the moment Adam sinned, there was a Savior. Jesus "presented himself as surety for the human race, with just as much power to avert the doom pronounced upon the guilty as when He died upon the cross of Calvary."[4] He "stood between the living and the dead, saying, 'Let the punishment fall on Me. I will stand in man's place. He shall have another chance.'"[5] "The divine

---

3   Genesis 3:22
4   White, "Lessons from the Christ-Life," *The Review and Herald*, March 12, 1901.
5   White, *The SDA Bible Commentary*, vol. 1, p. 1085.

Son of God saw that no arm but his own could save fallen man. He determined to help man. He left the fallen angels to perish in their rebellion, but stretched forth his hand to rescue perishing man."[6]

Even though, long before Creation, the Godhead had formulated the plan to save any who fell, the immediate intercession of Christ resulted in a genuine struggle of will to implement the contingency. Sin was so offensive that it must separate the Father and the Son.[7] Such a separation would be infinitely painful. But the wonder of God's love for a world that no longer loved Him is revealed in the consent, the acceptance of Christ's substitution, and the execution of that sentence of death demanded by the law of love.

How our hearts should swell with gratitude and praise as we consider Christ's expressions of faith as He explained to the angels that which had before now remained hidden from their understanding!

> The angels could not rejoice as Christ opened before them the plan of redemption, for they saw that man's salvation must cost their loved Commander unutterable woe. In grief and wonder they listened to His words as He told them how He must descend from heaven's purity and peace, its joy and glory and immortal life, and come in contact with the degradation of earth, to endure its sorrow, shame, and death. He was to stand between the sinner and the penalty of sin; yet few would receive Him as the Son of God. He would leave His high position as the Majesty of heaven, appear upon earth and humble Himself as a man, and by His own experience become acquainted with the sorrows and temptations which man would have to endure. All this would be necessary in order that He might be able to succor them that should be tempted. Hebrews 2:18. When His mission as a teacher should be ended, He must be delivered into the hands of wicked men and be subjected to every insult and torture that Satan could inspire them to inflict. He must die the cruelest of deaths, lifted up between the heavens and the earth as a guilty sinner. He must pass long hours of agony so terrible that angels could not look upon it, but would veil their faces from the sight. He must endure anguish of soul, the hiding of His Father's face, while the guilt of transgression—the weight of the sins of the whole world—should be upon Him....
>
> Christ assured the angels that by His death He would ransom many, and would destroy him who had the power of death. He would recover the kingdom which man had lost by transgression, and the redeemed were to inherit it with Him, and dwell therein forever. Sin and sinners would be blotted out, nevermore to disturb the peace of heaven or earth. He bade the angelic host to be in accord with the plan

---

6   White, "Redemption—No. 1," *The Review and Herald*, February 24, 1874.
7   White, *Patriarchs and Prophets*, p. 63.

that His Father had accepted, and rejoice that, through His death, fallen man could be reconciled to God.[8]

So great was Christ's faith that He willingly offered Himself even if only one individual were to accept salvation. "Christ would have died for one soul in order that that one might live through the eternal ages."[9] But more important than the redemption, recovery, and restoration of the sinner is the vindication of God's character that is accomplished by the plan of salvation. His dealings with the unrepentant rebel and those who choose to cherish sin and selfishness more than purity and holiness are justified. Satan "charged upon God a lack of wisdom and love" by requiring obedience to divine law.[10] This charge would be forever revealed as baseless and unfounded in Christ's submission and obedience to the law.

Imagine, then, the rejoicing of the unfallen angels when they grasped Christ's faith even as He opened to them the conditions He must fulfill in order to remove the separation that sin caused by severing the sinner from God. Already Christ was sharing His faith in instructing the angels concerning their role in the plan of salvation. Truly, obedience and cooperation were expected of them. They were not to interfere or interpose on behalf of Christ without God's expressed command to intervene. They would be instrumental in teaching and guiding fallen humanity through the unveiling of Christ's faith so that the penitent sinner might receive and accept Christ's faith even as the angels had. The reality of angelic ministry was shared with Jacob in a dream, when Christ, by faith, proffered Himself as a ladder to bridge the expansive gulf between heaven and earth.[11] The whole of the gospel of salvation is rooted in the measure of faith given to every free moral agent.[12] With the acceptance of that gift of faith comes the call to exercise it "till we all come in the unity of the faith, and of the knowledge of the Son of God, unto a perfect man, unto the measure of the stature of the fulness of Christ."[13]

Just as Christ, by faith, offered Himself as our atoning sacrifice, we must, by faith, offer ourselves. Keeping the faith of Jesus means offering ourselves as living sacrifices.[14] We must comprehend and understand the central act of daily taking up our cross and following Jesus.[15] Only then can we say with Paul, "I am crucified with Christ: nevertheless I live; yet not I, but Christ liveth in me: and the life which I now live in the flesh I live by the faith of the Son of God, who loved me, and gave himself for me."[16]

---

8   Ibid., pp. 64, 65.
9   White, *Testimonies for the Church*, vol. 8, p. 73.
10   White, "Sin Condemned in the Flesh," *The Signs of the Times*, January 16, 1896.
11   Genesis 28:12
12   Romans 12:3
13   Ephesians 4:13
14   Romans 12:1
15   Luke 9:23
16   Galatians 2:20

For the moment, let us journey through time from the first revelations of Jesus—to Adam and Eve as the serpent crusher, to Abraham as the Lamb of God, to Jacob as the Lion of Judah, to Simeon as the stone of stumbling—down to His manifestation. His relatives and neighbors perceived Him as only a child—no different than any other child. His earthly parents taught Him. But more importantly, He was taught by God through Scripture and the great lesson book of nature. Do we comprehend His faith as He offered Himself as the model disciple? The time spent communing with His heavenly Father in meditation and prayer reveals to us that even in this time period of His life "the Son can do nothing of himself, but what he seeth the Father do: for what things soever he doeth, these also doeth the Son likewise."[17] Should we not also comprehend that without Him we can do nothing?[18]

Next, let us contemplate His ministry as the divine teacher. By faith Jesus educated the fallen human race, much as He had taught the unfallen angels shortly after Adam's transgression. Note the contrast between heavenly selflessness and earthly self-interest! Unfallen angels volunteered to go in Christ's stead when told of His infinite suffering and impending death upon the cross.[19] Such is the selfless nature of heavenly harmony with the law of God, which is best described as love. But when Jesus began preparing His disciples for the disappointment of their fondest hopes—being greatest in the kingdom, sitting on either side of Christ's throne, and all that goes with such expectations of self-exaltation—Peter chided Him, saying, "Be it far from thee, Lord: this shall not be unto thee."[20] Jesus proceeded to sternly rebuke him for clinging to the things of men rather than the will of God. Do we also lack understanding for the very same reason? Could this be the cause of our failure to keep the faith of Jesus?

Shortly after rebuking Peter, Jesus left the nine disciples at the foot of a mountain while Peter, James, and John accompanied Him to the summit. Jesus wanted His disciples to see Him in His glory and strengthen their faith in the divine plan of salvation.[21] However, because they still harbored thoughts of exaltation, they misunderstood the lessons God wished them to learn regarding the nature of Christ's kingdom. He wanted them to understand that much suffering would precede the future glory, suffering of which they had only tasted. True glory cannot exist without a selfless, willing humility found only among the meekest of the meek. If only they had received the imparted insights to the faith of Christ and joined with Him in His self-sacrifice! Would they not have avoided great sorrow of heart?

From the glory of the mountaintop, they next beheld the depravity of demon possession. A father had brought his son to the disciples for healing from demonic torment. But the nine remaining disciples could not help, much to their humiliation. They harbored resentment at being left behind. And they cherished thoughts of self-exaltation, of being the chief of ministers.

17　John 5:19
18　John 15:5
19　White, *Patriarchs and Prophets*, p. 64.
20　Matthew 16:22
21　White, *The Desire of Ages*, pp. 419, 420.

All this robbed them of God's faith and power during Christ's absence. And now they suffered as they began to comprehend that their inability had brought shame upon their Master. They longed for His presence and power and were much relieved when He arrived. Jesus cast out the demon by faith, commanding, "Thou dumb and deaf spirit, I charge thee, come out of him, and enter no more into him."[22] The power of Jesus' faith—that the devil would enter no more into this liberated soul! The disciples' lack of faith and lack of connection with the godly mission set before them made them powerless against the devil.

> Their unbelief, that shut them out from deeper sympathy with Christ, and the carelessness with which they regarded the sacred work committed to them, had caused their failure in the conflict with the powers of darkness.
>
> The words of Christ pointing to His death had brought sadness and doubt. And the selection of the three disciples to accompany Jesus to the mountain had excited the jealousy of the nine. Instead of strengthening their faith by prayer and meditation on the words of Christ, they had been dwelling on their discouragements and personal grievances. In this state of darkness they had undertaken the conflict with Satan.
>
> In order to succeed in such a conflict they must come to the work in a different spirit. Their faith must be strengthened by fervent prayer and fasting, and humiliation of heart. They must be emptied of self, and be filled with the Spirit and power of God. Earnest, persevering supplication to God in faith—faith that leads to entire dependence upon God, and unreserved consecration to His work—can alone avail to bring men the Holy Spirit's aid in the battle against principalities and powers, the rulers of the darkness of this world, and wicked spirits in high places.[23]

As we review our own spiritual condition, can we see that our own failures result from unbelief rooted in soil rife with the tare seeds of self-exaltation? Oh that we might learn well the lessons that prepare us for what otherwise would be overwhelming disappointment!

Patiently Jesus tried to correct their faulty thoughts and feelings. By faith He taught them by example that the greatest person needs be the servant of all. "The heavenly intelligences can co-operate with him who is seeking, not to exalt self, but to save souls. He who feels most deeply his need of divine aid will plead for it; and the Holy Spirit will give unto him glimpses of Jesus that will strengthen and uplift the soul. From communion with Christ he will go

"In this state of darkness they had undertaken the conflict with Satan."

22   Mark 9:25
23   White, *The Desire of Ages*, pp. 430, 431.

forth to work for those who are perishing in their sins. He is anointed for his mission; and he succeeds where many of the learned and intellectually wise would fail."[24]

The disciples eventually embraced the teachings of Jesus as He meant for them to. But what disappointment they had to experience, what repentance they had to learn, because they failed to understand! And what comforting joy and peace they experienced as they realized Jesus offered Himself by faith as an empathetic intercessor! Peter especially never forgot the prophetic intercession: "Satan hath desired to have you, that he may sift you as wheat: But I have prayed for thee, that thy faith fail not."[25] Surely John understood the significance of keeping the faith of Jesus when he wrote, "My little children, these things write I unto you, that ye sin not. And if any man sin, we have an advocate with the Father, Jesus Christ the righteous."[26]

What more assurance do we need? Those who comprehend what it means to keep the faith of Jesus will be found approaching the throne of grace with boldness, covered by the blood of Christ, seeking mercy in time of need, declaring, "The Lord is my helper, and I will not fear what man shall do unto me."[27]

Yes, Jesus, by faith, offered Himself for us. And just as He loved us, we ought to love one another, encouraging one another to keep the faith of the Captain of our salvation as we see the day fast approaching.[28]

---

24 Ibid., p. 436.
25 Luke 22:31, 32
26 1 John 2:1
27 Hebrews 13:6; see also Hebrews 4:16; 10:19
28 John 13:34, 35; Hebrews 10:24, 25

Chapter 2

By Faith Jesus Submitted to the Great Law of Heredity

My maternal grandmother was quite a character. One of my fondest memories of her somewhat warped sense of humor, which I inherited, involved comments about her money—how much it was and who would get it when she died. She would look me right in the eye, with a hint of gleam in her own, and say, "When I die, you will get my millions." At the time, I was young enough to be both greedy and gullible. But then I would glance at Papa, who, with a twinkle in his eye, would playfully say in a mournful tone, "If she doesn't spend it all first." As I got older, the joke wore a little thin because I began to understand that one cannot inherit what the deceased does not have. And, as I matured, I learned that money and things are never more important than good health and relationships.

How true, then, is Job's remark concerning birth and death. "Naked came I out of my mother's womb, and naked shall I return thither: the Lord gave, and the Lord hath taken away; blessed be the name of the Lord."[1] Those familiar with the story of Job will recall the great wealth he had and how Satan claimed Job's loyalty to God would last as long as his earthly possessions were intact.[2] However, after losing all but his own life and wife, Job maintained his integrity and faith in God. True, he asked the question common to all who suffer—Why? Why me? Why now? Why have my family and friends forsaken me? Why do strangers avoid me? Why has God forsaken me? He never got an answer to his query, but in the end, Job had more than at the beginning!

So, why is this story in the Bible, and what does it have to do with possessing the faith of Jesus? The example given by Job's experience is similar to that of Christ living by faith amongst

---

1   Job 1:21
2   Job 1:9–11; 2:4, 5

poverty, loneliness, and woe. Jesus left heaven where He was adored and worshiped by count-less unfallen angels and sentient beings on other worlds. By coming to this sinful planet, Jesus essentially risked everything and potentially could have lost everything.

Recalling my early collegiate years, theology professors and students held lengthy discus-sions about the nature of Christ, with two opposing camps: pre-fall and post-fall human nature. At that time, I didn't pay attention to the ongoing debate. My personal conclusion was, "Jesus died for me. He is my personal Savior, as well as the world's Redeemer, so what difference does it make?" As I gained knowledge and understanding of this issue, I remembered my grand-mother's teasing, and I began to ponder the thought that since I could not inherit what Adam could not pass on to me genetically—perfect obedience—it must matter somewhat regarding the makeup of Christ's nature.

Not long after I came to this conclusion, church leaders called for an end to the debate, mak-ing it clear that exhibiting a united Christlike spirit to the world should be of greater importance. The Biblical Research Institute of our denomination published an article in August 1989 that opined, "The world church has never viewed these subjects (nature of Christ, nature of sin) as essential to salvation nor to the mission of the remnant church… There can be no strong unity within the world church of God's remnant people so long as segments who hold these views vo-calize and agitate them both in North America and in overseas divisions. These topics need to be laid aside and not urged upon our people as necessary issues."[3]

Now here is the rub: If it is essential to the makeup of Christ's faith, then isn't it essential to salvation? Christ is the Author and Finisher of faith. This is a complete faith we should be longing to have for ourselves. This is the faith that, along with the power of God's Word, will ul-timately perfect us so "that the man of God may be perfect, thoroughly furnished unto all good works."[4]

We must learn from Jesus, our Captain, just as many soldiers learn valor from their com-manding officers. One of my favorite military stories is of an officer who ordered a private to go into a known Viet Cong tunnel with a satchel of explosives so they could blow the concealed en-emy therein to bits. The private grabbed the satchel, scurried down the entrance of the tunnel and secured the explosives in place, set the charges, and departed. But the explosives did not go off as expected. Now the officer commands another private to check it out and come back with the reason for their disappointment. The second private is somewhat reluctant to obey because the enemy may be ready this time to shoot and kill, or maybe they even rearranged the explosives to their advantage, and the private has reasons to live. Without a moment to lose, the officer jumps into the opening himself, goes to where the satchel should have been, discovers it is

---

3   Priebe, "Is It Essential or Nonessential?" Dennis Priebe Seminars, http://1ref.us/4. For additional understanding of this important issue, read Jean Rudolf Zurcher's book *Touched With Our Feelings* (Hagerstown, MD: Review and Herald Publishing Association, 1999).

4   2 Timothy 3:17; verse 15 mentions being "wise unto salvation through faith which is in Jesus Christ."

missing, and hurries back to order his men to leave the area. After the second private witnessed the officer's willingness to do the very deadly job he had been commanded to do, and with a deeper respect for his officer, that private never again hesitated to put his life on the line for duty.

Could Christ have done any less? What does Inspiration reveal to us about this important point on the completeness of Christ's faith?

The psalmist wrote of the activity leading up to the incarnation when he penned, also of which Paul expounded, "Wherefore when he cometh into the world, he saith, Sacrifice and offering thou wouldest not, but a body hast thou prepared me: In burnt offerings and sac-

At the heart of discussion on the nature of Christ is this phrase, "a body hast thou prepared me."

rifices for sin thou hast had no pleasure. Then said I, Lo, I come (in the volume of the book it is written of me,) to do thy will, O God: yea, thy law is within my heart."[5] At the heart of discussion on the nature of Christ is this phrase, "a body hast thou prepared me." Does this body consist of sinful or sinless flesh, fallen or unfallen flesh? The Bible leaves a trail of hints:

- **Genesis 3:15** – "And I will put enmity between thee and the woman, and between thy seed and her seed; it shall bruise thy head, and thou shalt bruise his heel."
- **Genesis 17:7** – "And I will establish my covenant between me and thee and thy seed after thee in their generations for an everlasting covenant, to be a God unto thee, and to thy seed after thee."
- **Psalm 132:11** – "The Lord hath sworn in truth unto David; he will not turn from it; Of the fruit of thy body will I set upon thy throne."
- **Isaiah 7:14** – "Therefore the Lord himself shall give you a sign; Behold, a virgin shall conceive, and bear a son, and shall call his name Immanuel."
- **Isaiah 49:1, 5** – "Listen, O isles, unto me; and hearken, ye people, from far; The Lord hath called me from the womb; from the bowels of my mother hath he made mention of my name…. And now, saith the Lord that formed me from the womb to be his servant, to bring Jacob again to him, Though Israel be not gathered, yet shall I be glorious in the eyes of the Lord, and my God shall be my strength."
- **Galatians 4:1–5** – "Now I say, That the heir, as long as he is a child, differeth nothing from a servant, though he be lord of all; But is under tutors and governors until the time appointed of the father. Even so we, when we were children, were in bondage under the elements of the world: But when the fulness of the time was come, God sent forth his Son, made of a woman, made under the law, To redeem them that were under the law, that we might receive the adoption of sons."

---

5   Hebrews 10:5–7; Paul is quoting from Psalm 40:6–8, in which verse 8 says, "I delight to do thy will, O my God: yea, thy law is within my heart."

- **Romans 8:3, 22** – "For what the law could not do, in that it was weak through the flesh, God sending his own Son in the likeness of sinful flesh, and for sin, condemned sin in the flesh…. For we know that the whole creation groaneth and travaileth in pain together until now."

- **Romans 5:14, 18** – "Nevertheless death reigned from Adam to Moses, even over them that had not sinned after the similitude of Adam's transgression, who is the figure of him that was to come…. Therefore as by the offence of one judgment came upon all men to condemnation; even so by the righteousness of one the free gift came upon all men unto justification of life."

- **Daniel 9:26** – "And after threescore and two weeks shall Messiah be cut off, but not for himself …"

- **Romans 6:4–7** – "Therefore we are buried with him by baptism into death: that like as Christ was raised up from the dead by the glory of the Father, even so we also should walk in newness of life. For if we have been planted together in the likeness of his death, we shall be also in the likeness of his resurrection: Knowing this, that our old man is crucified with him, that the body of sin might be destroyed, that henceforth we should not serve sin. For he that is dead is freed from sin."

- **1 Corinthians 15:22, 45, 46** – "For as in Adam all die, even so in Christ shall all be made alive…. The first man Adam was made a living soul; the last Adam was made a quickening spirit. Howbeit that was not first which is spiritual, but that which is natural; and afterward that which is spiritual."

- **Hebrews 2:17, 18** – "Wherefore in all things it behoved him to be made like unto his brethren, that he might be a merciful and faithful high priest in things pertaining to God, to make reconciliation for the sins of the people. For in that he himself hath suffered being tempted, he is able to succour them that are tempted."

- **Hebrews 5:7–9** – "Who in the days of his flesh, when he had offered up prayers and supplications with strong crying and tears unto him that was able to save him from death, and was heard in that he feared; Though he were a Son, yet learned he obedience by the things which he suffered; And being made perfect, he became the author of eternal salvation unto all them that obey him."

- **1 Peter 4:1, 2** – "Forasmuch then as Christ hath suffered for us in the flesh, arm yourselves likewise with the same mind: for he that hath suffered in the flesh hath ceased from sin; That he no longer should live the rest of his time in the flesh to the lusts of men, but to the will of God."

While this list is not comprehensive, one gets enough information to begin to sort out how the issue impacts faith. The premise, however, must begin with the law of heredity.

Just as I could not inherit my grandmother's millions because she did not have it, Cain and all his brothers and sisters could not inherit from fallen Adam and Eve any goodness, self-control, or perfect obedience. Without the intervention of God, by His promised placement of enmity between the dominion of sin and the authority of righteousness, Adam and Eve, along with all their descendants, would have no hope of breaking the power that the law of sin now had. The law of righteousness has no power to strengthen the fallen, weakened flesh, but the faith of Jesus and the power from an uncorrupted, quickening spiritual nature provided the necessary elements whereby the Savior in fallen flesh could condemn sin in the flesh by the trials and temptations He suffered while practicing perfect obedience by faith.

Some raise the objection that any savior with fallen flesh would be in need of a savior; therefore, Christ must have unfallen flesh. They somehow believe that being born with fallen flesh makes one a participant of sin. However, there are several problems with such a position. First, if Christ had unfallen flesh, then where did it come from? Mary—His virgin mother? If so, how did she obtain something that no other sinner has unless she never had sinful flesh? If she never had sinful flesh, then did she get it from her mother? If so, where did her mother get it? From her mother? Well, the mother of all flesh is Eve, and we know from Paul's writings that she was the first transgressor of the human race, "being deceived."[6] That leaves only one other option: Mary received by miracle what no other human has received since before Adam and Eve were created—sinless, unfallen flesh. Such is the position that the Roman Catholic Church takes when defending the doctrine of "Immaculate Conception."

This position is not new to me. It is not some fanciful thought only recently communicated. At least one church leader, E. J. Waggoner, preached it at the 1901 General Conference.

> Suppose we start with the idea for a moment that Jesus was so separate from us, that is, so different from us that he did not have in his flesh anything to contend with. It was sinless flesh. Then, of course, you see how the Roman Catholic dogma of the immaculate conception necessarily follows. But why stop there? Mary being born sinless, then, of course, her mother also had sinless flesh. But you can not stop there. You must go back to her mother, and in turn her mother, and her mother, and her parents, and so back until you come to Adam; and the result—there never was a fall; Adam never sinned; and thus, you see, by that tracing of it, we find the essential identity of Roman Catholicism and Spiritualism and all other false doctrines – evolutions also – which claim that there never has been any fall, but only an ascent: – the Spiritualistic idea that everything in man is right, and man is God himself. You see it comes to that when you trace it back.[7]

---

6   1 Timothy 2:14
7   Waggoner, *General Conference Bulletin*, vol. 4, p. 404.

Pope Pius IX spoke of this on December 8, 1854, asserting what ought to be the faith of all Roman Catholics:

> By the authority of our Lord Jesus Christ, of the blessed apostles Peter and Paul, and by our own authority, we declare, pronounce, and define that the doctrine which holds that the most blessed Virgin Mary, in the first instant of her conception, by a special grace and privilege of Almighty God, in view of the merits of Jesus Christ, the Saviour of mankind, was preserved free from all stain of original sin, has been revealed by God, and, therefore is to be firmly and steadfastly believed by all the faithful.
>
> Wherefore, if any shall presume, which may God avert, to think in their heart otherwise than has been defined by us, let them know, and moreover understand, that they are condemned by their own judgment, that they have made shipwreck as regards the faith, and have fallen away from the unity of the Church.[8]

Cardinal Gibbons wrote this about the Catholic position, thereby confirming this different position of faith:

> We affirm that the Second Person of the Blessed Trinity, the Word of God, who in His divine nature is, from all eternity, begotten of the Father, consubstantial with Him, was in the fullness of time again begotten, by being born of the virgin, thus taking to himself from her maternal womb a human nature of the same substance with hers.
>
> As far as the sublime mystery of the incarnation can be reflected in the natural order, the blessed Virgin, under the overshadowing of the Holy Ghost, by communicating to the Second Person of the adorable Trinity, as mothers do, a true human nature of the same substance with her own, is thereby really and truly His mother.[9]

Early Adventist pioneer A. T. Jones responded to the Roman Catholic position of faith:

> Such is the Roman Catholic doctrine concerning the human nature of Christ. The Catholic doctrine of the human nature of Christ is simply that that nature is not human nature at all, but divine: "more sublime and glorious than all natures." It is that in His human nature Christ was so far separated from mankind as to be utterly unlike that of mankind, that His was a nature in which He could have no sort of fellow-feeling with mankind....

---

8   Di Bruno, *Catholic Belief*, 3rd ed,, pp. 188, 189.

9   Gibbons, *Faith of Our Fathers*, p. 167.

> The faith of Rome as to the human nature of Christ and Mary and of ourselves springs from that idea of the natural mind that God is too pure and too holy to dwell with us and in us in our sinful human nature; that sinful as we are, we are too far off for Him in His purity and holiness to come to us just as we are.[10]

If Jones is correct in his analysis of the Catholic position, then Catholicism denies that Jesus, as God, was manifested in the flesh. It denies that we can be purified bodily temples of God. But if the Catholic position were truth, then why hasn't God given such a condition to all descended from Adam and Eve? The answer is simple enough: If God merely performed a miracle to give all who are born to the human race a sinless, unfallen flesh, then sin would never be condemned in the flesh. Other problems would arise, resulting in continued chaos for as long as condemnation is postponed. But Mary, like Nicodemus, and like all who are born of human parents, needed the rebirth experience in order to see the kingdom of God.

Still, some hedge their conclusion as to the truth about whether or not Jesus was born with a fallen flesh precisely categorized as post-fall flesh. They don't want to be seen as Catholics, but they can't bring themselves to believe that Jesus could be born with sinful flesh—yet without the propensity to sin—and not need a savior for Himself. Perhaps this is because of the temptation to believe, somehow, that Christ must inherit by natural generation the guilt for original sin if He should accept a body that might suffer from the effects of sin.

To get at the very heart of the matter, we need to focus on two premises that might help us get past the barriers apparently erected between those holding the pre-fall and post-fall positions: 1) Jesus was unique from us in that He was a blend of fully human and fully divine natures, and 2) Jesus was similar to us in that being born to the human race He had a nature weakened by the passing millennia without actually participating in sin. In other words, He could feel the strength of our temptations though He remained unyielding to them. Yet, on the other hand, those temptations were actually amplified by the simple fact that He did not have a sinful character. His character was pure, holy, and perfectly righteous. One author writes that "[t]he character of Jesus stands alone in its revelation of our heavenly Father…. So if we desire to know what God is like in His nature and character, the presence and person of Jesus is just that. The Father is no different from the Son, and Jesus is no different from the Father."[11]

Another author further delineates that "… Jesus was neither completely pre-Fall nor post-Fall—as such terns would imply. On the one hand, He was pre-Fall in the sense that His humanity was not 'infected' with sinful, corrupt tendencies, or propensities to sin, such as we are born with. On the other hand, He was post-Fall in the sense that His humanity was 'affected' by sin, in

---

10   Jones, *The Consecrated Way to Christian Perfection*, pp. 38, 39.
11   Heppenstall, *The Man Who Is God: A Study of the Person and Nature of Jesus, Son of God and Son of Man*, pp. 175, 176.

which He never indulged."[12] This infection is precisely how the reformer John Calvin described our carnal, fallen nature. "Adam, by sinning, not only took upon himself misfortune and ruin, but also plunged our nature into like destruction. This was not due to the guilt of himself alone, which would not pertain to us at all, but was because he infected all his posterity with that corruption into which he had fallen."[13] Yet the body prepared for Jesus is such that "… Christ took flesh as it had been affected by sin for four thousand years…. For Jesus Christ this was only an *assumed* condition."[14] So we see the corruption having more to do with wrong *being* than wrong *doing*. The corruption is inherent selfishness, which is enmity with God's unselfish, righteous character. And the body prepared for Christ would not see that fatal corruption of character.

> Sin is a spiritual thing caused by the alienation of the whole person from God. We cannot apply this alienated condition to Christ. He was not born as we are, separate from God. He was God Himself. He could inherit from Mary only what could be transmitted genetically. This means He inherited the weakened human physical constitution, the results of sin upon the body, that we all inherit. As concerning all other men, they are born without God. All men need regeneration. Christ did not. Here lies the great difference between Christ and ourselves…. Christ was conceived of the Holy Spirit. We are not.[15]

So, let us return to the realities of the laws of genetics established at creation, for surely, by faith, Jesus submitted to the great law of heredity as it relates to His "assumed condition." In the list of Scriptures provided earlier in the chapter, we read that Abraham received the covenant on behalf of his seed. The record provided by Matthew 1 shows that Jesus is descended from Abraham. Was Abraham a sinner? Again, we read that King David was promised "of the fruit of thy body will I set upon thy throne."[16] The record shows that Jesus is descended from David. Was David a sinner? Both Abraham and David had the fallen flesh they inherited from Adam. What then is the only difference between Christ and His fallen ancestors? He did not have a human father. When Gabriel visited Mary and announced the blessing she would receive, she asked, "How shall this be, seeing I know not a man?"[17] The explanation continues to be a mystery that we will search out for all eternity, because this was the miracle that God chose to perform in providing His Son a body in which to do the Father's will.

---

12   Whidden II, *Ellen White on the Humanity of Christ*, p. 15.
13   Heppenstall, *The Man Who Is God: A Study of the Person and Nature of Jesus, Son of God and Son of Man*, p. 114. In using this quote, Heppenstall also observes that "Calvin fails to clear God of the responsibility for making sin possible" (Ibid., p. 116).
14   Ibid., pp. 136, 137, emphasis original.
15   Ibid., pp. 126, 127.
16   Psalm 132:11
17   Luke 1:34

Ellen White wrote extensively on this issue. So let us ponder some comments that should shed light on Christ's nature while here on this earth. "Christ is called the second Adam. In purity and holiness, connected with God and beloved by God, *he began where the first Adam began.* Willingly he passed over the ground where Adam fell, and redeemed Adam's failure."[18]

Many would like to believe that this statement is proof positive that Christ was born with unfallen flesh. Is this really so? Perhaps we should compare how Christ began with how Adam began.

Christ willingly submitted to the learning curve of infants born four thousand years after Adam's failure.

Adam began as the representative of mankind. He was created pure and holy—sinless and unfallen. This is reference to the state of his character as well as his flesh. Christ, too, by virtue of His birth, began as the representative of mankind. But unlike Adam, who was formed from the dust, Christ was formed in the womb of a virgin who inherited the capacity, the propensity, to sin. As far as His birth is concerned, Christ began where Cain, Abel, Seth, and all other children begin. Adam began as a fairly cognizant creature from the moment God breathed into his nostrils. Adam didn't have to learn how to walk or talk as babies do. But Christ willingly submitted to the learning curve of infants born four thousand years after Adam's failure. When I think of the Son of God growing up as a child, overcoming temptation and sin, and compare His perfect character with my childhood character, I give thanks to God that Jesus willingly passed over the ground where I fell and redeemed my failure!

Ellen White's other quotes help us to see the consistency in the Scriptures earlier quoted:

> It would have been an almost infinite humiliation for the Son of God to take man's nature, even when Adam stood in his innocence in Eden. But Jesus accepted humanity when the race had been weakened by four thousand years of sin. *Like every child of Adam He accepted the results of the working of the great law of heredity.* What these results were is shown in the history of His earthly ancestors. He came with such a heredity to share our sorrows and temptations, and to give us the example of a sinless life.[19]

> Christ took our nature, *fallen* but not corrupted, and would not be corrupted unless He received the words of Satan in the place of the words of God.[20]

---

18   White, "The Second Adam," *The Youth's Instructor*, June 2, 1898, emphasis added.
19   White, *The Desire of Ages*, p. 49, emphasis added.
20   White, *Manuscript Releases*, vol. 16, pp. 182, 183, emphasis original.

But our Saviour took humanity, *with all its liabilities*. He took the nature of man, with the possibility of yielding to temptation. We have nothing to bear which He has not endured.[21]

Christ *bore the sins and infirmities of the race as they existed* when he came to the earth to help man. In behalf of the race, *with the weaknesses of fallen man upon him*, he was to stand the temptations of Satan upon all points wherewith man would be assailed.[22]

The human nature of Christ was like unto ours, and suffering was more keenly felt by him; for *his spiritual nature was free from every taint of sin*. Therefore his desire for the removal of suffering was stronger than human beings can experience.[23]

In order to elevate fallen man, Christ must reach him where he was. He took human nature, and bore the infirmities and degeneracy of the race. *He who knew no sin became sin for us*. He humiliated Himself to the lowest depths of human woe, that He might be qualified to reach man and bring him up from the degradation in which sin had plunged him.[24]

He [Christ] had clothed His divinity with humanity, and in every period of His life, through infancy, childhood, youth, and manhood, He *had suffered every phase of trial and temptation with which humanity is beset*.[25]

By taking upon Himself man's nature in its fallen condition *Christ did not in the least participate in its sin*. He was subject to the infirmities and weaknesses of the flesh with which humanity is encompassed ... He was touched with the feeling of our infirmities, and was in all points tempted like as we are. And yet He was without a spot.

There should not be the faintest misgiving in regard to the perfect freedom from sinfulness in the human nature of Christ.[26]

---

21   White, *The Desire of Ages*, p. 117, emphasis added.
22   White, "The Temptation of Christ," *The Review and Herald*, July 28, 1874, emphasis added.
23   White, "In Gethsemane," *The Signs of the Times*, December 9, 1897, emphasis added.
24   White, *Confrontation*, p. 33, emphasis added.
25   White, *Manuscript Releases*, vol. 17, p. 25, emphasis added.
26   Ibid., pp. 25, 26, emphasis added.

We are compassed with the infirmities of humanity. So also was Christ. *That He might by His own example condemn sin in the flesh, He took upon Himself the likeness of sinful flesh.*[27]

The Saviour took upon Himself the infirmities of humanity, and on this earth lived a sinless life that men should have no fear that because of the weakness of human nature they would not be able to overcome.[28]

The work of redemption is called a mystery, and it is indeed the mystery by which everlasting righteousness is brought to all who believe. The race in consequence of sin was at enmity with God. Christ, at an infinite cost, by a painful process, mysterious to angels as well as to men, assumed humanity. Hiding His divinity, laying aside His glory, He was born a babe in Bethlehem. *In human flesh He lived the law of God, that He might condemn sin in the flesh, and bear witness to heavenly intelligences that the law was ordained to life and to ensure the happiness, peace, and eternal good of all who obey.* But the same infinite sacrifice that is life to those who believe is a testimony of condemnation to the disobedient, speaking death and not life.[29]

Now, not only did the nature of faith impact the salvific mission of Christ toward mankind, but the nature of God's love was revealed through the conditions Jesus met in order to be declared a success. "Though sin has been accumulating for ages, God's love has never ceased to flow earthward. It was only restrained till a suitable channel was provided for it. Christ, the only begotten Son of God, left the royal courts and came to this world, and through him God poured forth the healing flood of his grace."[30] Furthermore, one must consider the necessity of hope and how it comes into play, which is evident in the following quotes.

> *"God's love has never ceased to flow earthward. It was only restrained till a suitable channel was provided for it."*

Christ would never have left the royal courts and taken humanity, and become sin for the race, had he not seen that man might, with his help, become infinitely happy, and attain durable riches, and a life that would run parallel with the life of God. He knew that without his help sinful man could not attain these things.[31]

---

27 Ibid., p. 28, emphasis added.
28 Ibid., p. 29.
29 White, *The SDA Bible Commentary*, vol. 7, p. 915, emphasis added.
30 White, "The Resurrection of Lazarus," *The Youth's Instructor*, March 30, 1899.
31 White, "The Spirit of Christ," *The Review and Herald,* June 22, 1886.

Christ would never have given His life for the human race if He had not confidence in the souls for whom He died. He knew that a large number would respond to the love He had expressed for humanity. It is not every heart that responds, but every heart may, and can, if it will, respond to that love that is without a parallel.[32]

Christ was the one who consented to meet the conditions necessary for man's salvation. No angel, no man, was sufficient for the great work to be wrought. The Son of man alone must be lifted up; for only an infinite nature could undertake the redemptive process. Christ consented to connect himself with the disloyal and sinful, to partake of the nature of man, to give his own blood, and to make his soul an offering for sin. In the counsels of heaven, the guilt of man was measured, the wrath for sin was estimated, and yet Christ announced his decision that he would take upon himself the responsibility of meeting the conditions whereby hope should be extended to a fallen race.[33]

If Christ had come with unfallen flesh, then we might reasonably question if His faith is sufficient for us because He would not have proven that we can keep the law of God by reason of our fallen flesh. But from Inspiration we have no more room for doubts regarding the faith of Jesus. He came to a condemned world to offer His faith, His spiritual nature, and character to us while living a life of obedience to His Father in our fallen flesh. Knowing the sufferings we rightly experience from the consequences of our own sins, we ought to have, not only great sorrow for the sufferings He didn't deserve, but great joy for the richness of God's grace we don't deserve.

No room for controversy exists when we acknowledge the tremendous faith of Christ exercised on our behalf. His pain and sufferings began with His incarnation, and His obedient faith in His heavenly Father was the only balm for His soul. Reader, His balm is ours if we will only believe on Him and receive His faith as our own. Christ's faith is a free gift to all who will receive it by God's grace.

32   White, "Sufficiency in Christ," *The Signs of the Times*, March 17, 1898.
33   White, "Divinity in Humanity," *The Signs of the Times*, March 5, 1896.

Chapter 3

By Faith Jesus Memorized Scripture

For many weeks the Germans had been preparing a defense against a presumed invasion of Western Europe by the Allied forces. Diligently their officers compelled soldiers and civilians alike to fortify their defensive positions. The risks were very high, but French Resistance fighters deliberately infiltrated the Nazi efforts and, with vital information photographed or memorized, recorded the defensive positions on maps that they passed on to Allied commanders.

In October of 1944 American troops focused their military might on a city mapped by the French freedom fighters. The smuggled information was given to a concerned captain. Not wanting to write many letters of condolence to the families of potential casualties, he impressed upon the men in his unit the need to memorize copies of the map. After each soldier had an opportunity to commit the map to memory, the captain tested them. Not until each man passed the test could they proceed to the battle. They passed on their first attempt. His method of leadership proved successful, since, in this instance, few American casualties resulted.

Decades later an Army researcher decided to replicate this method as a comparative study on motivation and leadership methods and how they relate to successful outcomes. Approaching American tourists, he gave them a copy of the same map and asked them to study it as the soldiers had been instructed. They were given the same test, but they failed miserably. The obvious difference between the soldiers' success and the tourists' failure is grounded in the motivational factor as influenced by the urgency of war and the leisure of peace. When reality is rightfully perceived as a choice between life or death, the intensity of motivation to succeed is much higher.[1]

As I look back on my childhood in relation to memorizing scriptures, I can see how I was like those tourists who failed to memorize the military positions and installations. But as miserable a failure as our personal experiences may be in memorizing Scripture, we are not without hope.

---

1   Smalley and Trent, *The Gift of Honor*, pp. 9–11. In Smalley and Trent's book, they cited a study that appeared in the *Journal of Comparative Physiological Psychology* titled "Response and Reaction to Motivation."

Jesus came to take our place and encourage us to follow Him in His example. Memorization of Scripture becomes very important to us as we grasp its importance to Christ and His faith.

Perhaps some are puzzled about the connection between faith and the memorization of Scripture. How do the two tie together? In Romans 10:8, 17, we read, "But what saith it? The word is nigh thee, even in thy mouth, and in thy heart: that is, *the word of faith*, which we preach…. So then faith cometh by hearing, and hearing by the word of God." When we internalize Scripture, first by memorization, and then by practice in our lives, we preach the faith of Jesus louder than any amplified sound system. We become connected to Christ through the Word of God by faith. And by virtue of that connection, we are living sermons, witnesses to the re-creative power of God.

In light of eternity, the risks are much greater because of the spiritual conflict we face every day. We are in warfare against something greater than the weapons any human can devise and aim at us. Yet how many of us comprehend the faith of Jesus as applying to the memorization of Scripture—our map for eternal survival and life? First, let's

> *When we internalize Scripture, first by memorization, and then by practice in our lives, we preach the faith of Jesus louder than any amplified sound system.*

delve into the life of Christ and His experiential relationship with Scripture. Next, we will learn a little about the history of the Bible. Finally, we must comprehend the symbols in Scripture so we might accept His faith for our very own and follow wherever He leads us with the utmost confidence of success.

From the time Jesus was old enough to remember, Mary taught Him from Scripture. His education was never entrusted to the teachers of the period, for they had corrupted the pure doctrines of God with the vain philosophies of man. Tradition, elevated above the laws of God as handed down to the people from Moses, became paramount. "The priests and Pharisees thought they were doing great things as teachers by putting their own interpretation upon the word of God," but all they did was "darkened that which they tried to make clear."[2] Many are just as guilty today as they "falsely interpret the divine oracles, and souls are brought into perplexity and shrouded in darkness because of their misconception of divine truth."[3]

Independent learning, that is, separation from the rabbinical schools of Christ's day, proved to be a blessing despite the daily conflict arising from the line of distinction made between Scripture and traditions. The peace and wisdom of God sustained Jesus because of the living connection maintained by His knowledge and understanding of Scripture. He was able to keep

---

2   White, *Christ's Object Lessons*, p. 110.
3   Ibid., p. 111.

every circumstance of His life in perspective because each of the guiding principles found in Scripture was directly linked to His faith and trust in His heavenly Father.

The question asked during the Saviour's ministry, "How knoweth this man letters, having never learned?" does not indicate that Jesus was unable to read, but merely that He had not received a rabbinical education. John 7:15. *Since He gained knowledge as we may do, His intimate acquaintance with the Scriptures shows how diligently His early years were given to the study of God's word.* And spread out before Him was the great library of God's created works. He who had made all things studied the lessons which His own hand had written in earth and sea and sky. Apart from the unholy ways of the world, He gathered stores of scientific knowledge from nature. He studied the life of plants and animals, and the life of man. From His earliest years He was possessed of one purpose; He lived to bless others. For this He found resources in nature; new ideas of ways and means flashed into His mind as He studied plant life and animal life. Continually He was seeking to draw from things seen illustrations by which to present the living oracles of God. The parables by which, during His ministry, He loved to teach His lessons of truth show how open His spirit was to the influences of nature, and how He had gathered the spiritual teaching from the surroundings of His daily life.

Thus to Jesus the significance of the word and the works of God was unfolded, as He was trying to understand the reason of things. Heavenly beings were His attendants, and the culture of holy thoughts and communings was His. From the first dawning of intelligence He was constantly growing in spiritual grace and knowledge of truth.[4]

From childhood He acted independently of the rabbinical laws. The Scriptures of the Old Testament were His constant study, and the words, "Thus saith the Lord," were ever upon His lips….

… when reproved for His own simple habits, He presented the word of God in justification of His conduct….

Jesus seemed to know the Scriptures from beginning to end, and He presented them in their true import. The rabbis were ashamed to be instructed by a child. They claimed that it was their office to explain the Scriptures, and that it was His place to accept their interpretation. They were indignant that He should stand in opposition to their word….

4   White, *The Desire of Ages*, p. 70, emphasis added.

His brothers, as the sons of Joseph were called, … insisted that the traditions must be heeded, as if they were the requirements of God. They even regarded the precepts of men more highly than the word of God, and they were greatly annoyed at the clear penetration of Jesus in distinguishing between the false and the true. His strict obedience to the law of God they condemned as stubbornness. They were surprised at the knowledge and wisdom He showed in answering the rabbis. They knew that He had not received instruction from the wise men, yet they could not but see that He was an instructor to them. They recognized that His education was of a higher type than their own. But they did not discern that He had access to the tree of life, a source of knowledge of which they were ignorant.[5]

How important is it for us to spend time memorizing Scripture? Ellen White wrote that:

The mind must be restrained, and not allowed to wander. It should be trained to dwell upon the Scriptures, and upon noble, elevating themes. Portions of Scripture, even whole chapters, may be committed to memory, to be repeated when Satan comes in with his temptations. The fifty-eighth chapter of Isaiah is a profitable one for this purpose. Wall the soul in with the restrictions and instructions given by inspiration of the Spirit of God. When Satan would lead the mind to dwell upon earthly and sensual things, he is most effectually resisted with "It is written." When he suggests doubts as to whether we are really the people whom God is leading, whom by tests and provings he is preparing to stand in the great day, be ready to meet his insinuations by presenting the clear evidence from the word of God that this is the remnant people who are keeping the commandments of God and the faith of Jesus.[6]

Today we have great access to the Bible. Not only can we easily obtain Scripture published and bound in book form, but we can surf the Internet and look up any number of translations in just about every language known to humanity. However, a right understanding of the history of the Bible can help us avoid some serious pitfalls as we attempt to hold fast to the Word of God. Two snares still remain that existed in Christ's time: 1) subtle changes and omissions that are used to entice us to let go of our integrity just as Jesus was tempted to do upon that temple pinnacle, and 2) the pressures applied by learned ministers and scholars that we should accept their interpretations and traditions. Should we be so careless in our Bible knowledge and understanding as to fall into either snare, it would be for no other reason than because we relinquished our

5   Ibid., pp. 84–86, emphasis added.
6   White, "Humility and Faithfulness in Laborers," *The Review and Herald*, April 8, 1884.

personal responsibility to memorize Scripture and obtain a right understanding of God's will as revealed in His Word.

One must accept the premise established by the Scriptures as to the reason why the Bible even exists in order to properly sort out the importance of this issue: "All scripture is given by inspiration of God, and is profitable for doctrine, for reproof, for correction, for instruction in righteousness: That the man of God may be perfect, thoroughly furnished unto all good works."[7] Each individual must acknowledge this as the sole purpose for Scripture memorization, or be lost by the deceptive changes and omissions that tend to ensnare the individual will of conscience into the bondage of sin from which Christ, by His faith, sought to deliver us. No need exists for Scriptures to instruct us on correct doctrine unless the danger of deceptive doctrines is real. Each one of us must acknowledge that the forces of evil desire to break the Scriptures because therein is revealed the power of the Word of God. It is imperative that we rest in the faith of Jesus even as He proclaimed that "the scripture cannot be broken"[8]—another way of saying, "For ever, O Lord, thy word is settled in heaven."[9] "Have not I written to thee excellent things in counsels and knowledge, That I might make thee know the certainty of the words of truth; that thou mightest answer the words of truth to them that send unto thee?"[10]

The Old Testament, consisting of the Hebrew Scriptures, has come down through the ages in a more or less settled condition because of the unrivaled methods of transmission established by the Jews. However, from the time it was translated from the Hebrew and Aramaic into Greek, it has been subjected to less rigid standards. True, "God had especially guarded the Bible, yet learned men, when the copies were few, had changed the words in some instances, thinking that they were making it more plain, when they were mystifying that which was plain, in causing it to lean to their established views, governed by tradition."[11]

> ### *No need exists for Scriptures to instruct us on correct doctrine unless the danger of deceptive doctrines is real.*

Foremost of the early instigators of change were Justin Martyr, Tatian, Clement of Alexandria, and Origen. Justin Martyr's pagan influence on Scripture is most noted in Tatian's authorship of the Diatessaron, supposedly intended to harmonize the four Gospels, which was so terribly corrupted by word changes and deleted passages that in later years a bishop of Syria was obliged to throw no less than two hundred copies out of his churches because his members were confusing them with the true Gospels.

---

7   2 Timothy 3:16, 17
8   John 10:35
9   Psalm 119:89
10   Proverbs 22:20, 21
11   White, *Spiritual Gifts*, vol. 1, p. 117.

Clement of Alexandria went even further than his teacher, Tatian, declaring that rather than handing down unadulterated Christian teachings, he would dress them up with the precepts of pagan philosophies. And Origen further mystified the events of the Bible by turning each one into an allegory, claiming, "The Scriptures are of little use to those who understand them as they are written."[12]

The Latin Vulgate of Jerome is largely based upon the foundational work of these four men. So it should be of no surprise that the worst corruptions to the Gospels occurred within a hundred years of the originals as written by the apostles, or that we now have two streams of Bible manuscripts competing for the souls of men. Those two streams became more clearly divergent as further corruptions occurred in the fourth century with the alleged conversion of Constantine to Christianity. "The nominal conversion of Constantine, in the early part of the fourth century, caused great rejoicing; and the world, cloaked with a form of righteousness, walked into the church. Now the work of corruption rapidly progressed. Paganism, while appearing to be vanquished, became the conqueror. Her spirit controlled the church. Her doctrines, ceremonies, and superstitions were incorporated into the faith and worship of the professed followers of Christ."[13]

George Burnside, former ministerial secretary of the Australasian Division of Seventh-day Adventists, wrote:

> One of Constantine's acts was to have the Catholic bishop Eusebius make copies of fifty bibles for use in the churches....
>
> The evidence is overwhelming in favour of the fact that the Vatican and Sinai manuscripts were two of Constantine's fifty bibles. Sidney Collett in his "The Scripture of Truth" when writing about the Sinaitic manuscript that was found by Dr. Tischendorf stated:
>
>> Dr. Tischendorf believed that this and the Vatican manuscript were two of the fifty copies of the Bible which were made in Greek by command of the Emperor Constantine, about the year A.D. 331, under the supervision of Bishop Eusebius, the historian of Caesarea. p. 28.[14]

Burnside also points out, "Dr. Robinson on page 80 of his book entitled 'Introduction to Textual Criticism' states: 'Constantine himself ordered fifty Greek Bibles from Eusebius, Bishop of Caesarea, for the churches in Constantinople. It is quite possible that Aleph and B are two of these fifty.'"[15] Eusebius is described by Ellen G. White as "a bishop who sought the favor of

12   Wilkinson, *Our Authorized Bible Vindicated,* pp. 16, 17.
13   White, *The Great Controversy*, pp. 49, 50.
14   Burnside, *The New International Version or The King James Version*, p. 50.
15   Ibid., p. 123.

princes, and who was the special friend and flatterer of Constantine."[16] What significance does this have to us, given what she also wrote concerning the forgeries of that time period and that "ancient writings were forged by monks"[17]? Would this forgery not only apply to the attempts at establishing church authority but also church doctrines such as Sunday worship?

For centuries the Bible was removed from common men. In most of Europe the New Testament in the original Greek was virtually unknown during the Dark Ages. In 1382 John Wycliffe made a small breach in the walls of secrecy when he completed translation of the New Testament from the Latin Vulgate into English and his followers hand-copied the Scriptures in order to get the Bible into the hands of the people. But the time came at last when the Greek manuscripts made their way to the universities of Europe from pressures caused by the Muslim Turks' military successes in the East. Erasmus of Holland "was ever on the wing, ransacking libraries and every nook and corner where ancient manuscripts might be found. He divided all Greek New Testament manuscripts into two classes: those which followed the Received Text, edited by Lucian; and those which followed the Vaticanus manuscript, the pride of the Vatican library. He specified the positive grounds on which he rejected the Vaticanus while receiving the other. And when he brought forth his edition of the Greek New Testament, a new day dawned."[18] "In 1516, a year before the appearance of Luther's theses, Erasmus had published his Greek and Latin version of the New Testament. Now for the first time the word of God was printed in the original tongue. In this work many errors of former versions were corrected, and the sense was more clearly rendered. It led many among the educated classes to a better knowledge of the truth, and gave a new impetus to the work of reform. But the common people were still, to a great extent, debarred from God's word."[19]

From 1525 to 1530, William Tyndale worked on his English translation from the Hebrew, as well as Erasmus' Greek compilation. Printing the first Bible in English, Tyndale accomplished what Wycliffe set out to do in opening the truths of the Gospel to the common people in their own language. Others were to follow in his footsteps: Myles Coverdale (1535); Thomas Cranmer (1539); Edward Whytchurche (1540); Thomas Matthew (1549); Bishop's Bible (1568); and the Geneva Bible (1587), to name a few. These translations fueled the Reformation, causing the papacy great concern. The pope determined that the Jesuits should also produce an English translation from "the authentic Latin"—at first called the Rheims (1582), better known as the Douay-Rheims (1610), but also known as the Challoner-Rheims (1752).

The Great Schism commenced because the "ever-growing power of the gospel truth was exalting the Bible above the church. [But] the Papacy refused to surrender its claim that the church was above the Bible."[20] In an attempt to reconcile the reformers to Roman Catholicism, Pope

16 White, *The Great Controversy*, p. 574.
17 Ibid., p. 56.
18 Wilkinson, *Truth Triumphant*, p. 384.
19 White, *The Great Controversy*, p. 245.
20 Wilkinson, *Truth Triumphant*, pp. 384, 385.

Paul III called for a special ecumenical council to be held in the northern Italian city of Trent starting in May of 1542. However, because of war between Francis I and Charles V, the council was unable to commence until December of 1545. At that time the council was politicized by two opposing groups—the curialists and the ultramontanes—those who wished for stronger centralized control by the pope, and those who wished to assert the rights of the individual bishops to govern their dioceses. Ultimately the council decided in favor of the centralized power and authority of the pope, eliminated some prominent abuses, established Catholic orthodoxy in the strongest possible terms, and confirmed the Latin Vulgate as the authentic version—with the church as the only institution that could interpret it.[21] "The Council of Trent had declared the Vulgate, 'not only better than all other Latin translations, but better than the Greek text itself in those places where they disagree.'"[22]

> The Council of Trent in 1546 had called the Vulgate the church's authentic version of the Bible. It alone was to be used in lectures, disputations, sermons. 'Authentic' means that Catholics can be sure it is free from doctrinal and moral error and substantially faithful to the originals. When the fathers of Trent commissioned a new edition of the Vulgate, they had no idea of the size of the task. Eleven popes lived and died, and nothing happened. Until Sixtus V.
>
> Three years into his pontificate, at the end of 1588, the scholars he had appointed to edit the Vulgate presented him with their final text. There was too much scholarship in it for the pope's liking; and they had put in too many variant readings. He shouted the president of the commission, Cardinal Carafa, out of his room, screaming he could do far better on his own. This astounding claim he set about trying to prove. In a 300-word sentence, he declared in a Bull that he, the pope, was the only proper person to decide the question of an authentic Bible for the church.[23]

Pope Sixtus V did such a terrible job that when he died the scholarly scandal had to be concluded as judiciously and quietly as possible. Robert Bellermine advised to cut the Gordian knot by submitting a lie—revise the Sixtus Bible with appropriate corrections, reprint it under Pope Sixtus' name, and uphold papal authority without admitting to the errors Pope Sixtus made in his Vulgate. In his autobiography, Bellermine told the truth about the cover-up:

> Some men, whose opinions had great weight, held that it [the Sixtus Vulgate] should be publicly prohibited. I did not think so, and I showed the Holy Father that, instead of forbidding the edition of the Bible in question, it would be better to correct it in

---

21   Clough, *European History in a World Perspective: Ancient Times to 1715*, 3rd ed., pp. 628–632.
22   Bobrick, *Wide as the Waters: The Story of the English Bible and the Revolution It Inspired*, pp. 89, 90.
23   De Rosa, *Vicars of Christ: The Dark Side of the Papacy*, p. 217.

such a manner that it could be published without detriment to the honour of Pope Sixtus. This result could be achieved by removing the inadvisable changes as quickly as possible, and then issuing the volume with Sixtus' name upon it, and a preface stating that owing to haste some errors had crept into the first edition through the fault of printers and other persons.[24]

History aside, a diligent comparison between the Bibles of the reformers and those produced by the Jesuits shows a clear divergence of meaning that influences the developmental understanding of doctrine. When one expands the historical evolution of English translations to include those versions published since the mid-nineteenth century, one can clearly see the work of Westcott and Hort—in reorganizing the Greek manuscripts—as more consistent with the work of the Jesuits than that of the reformers. Therefore, the work that Westcott and Hort did was in harmony with the decisions made by the counter-reformers at the Council of Trent. Of the Revision Movement, Cardinal Wiseman wrote, "When we consider the scorn cast by the reformers upon the Vulgate, and their recurrence, in consequence, to the Greek, as the only accurate standard, we cannot but rejoice at the silent triumph which truth has at length gained over clamorous error. For, in fact, the principal writers who have avenged the Vulgate, and obtained for it its critical preeminence, are Protestants."[25]

What about Ellen White's use of modern versions available to her throughout the extent of her ministry? The official response from the Ellen G. White Estate is, "While it was Ellen White's custom to use the King James Version, she made occasional use of the various English translations that were becoming available in her day. She does not, however, comment directly on the relative merits of these versions, but it is clear from her practice that she recognized the desirability of making use of the best in all versions of the Bible. For example, in her book *The Ministry of Healing,* Ellen White employed eight texts from the English Revised Version, 55 from the American Revised Version, two from Leeser's translation, and four from Noyes, in addition to seven marginal renderings."[26]

> "For, in fact, the principal writers who have avenged the Vulgate, and obtained for it its critical preeminence, are Protestants."

But truth be known, this answer is just a little misleading and incomplete at best. When one thoroughly studies out Ellen White's use of modern versions, one might come to the same conclusion as George Burnside who noticed these important facts:

24   Ibid., p. 218.
25   Wilkinson, *Our Authorized Bible Vindicated*, p. 227.
26   "Questions and Answers About Ellen G. White," The Ellen G. White Estate, Inc., http://1ref.us/6.

According to the index [the volumes indexing Ellen G. White's writings], there are listed 15,117 Scripture references in the 25 Volumes that are listed. 95% Of these references are from the King James Version (KJV) and 5% from all the other versions. The Revised Version came out in 1881. Since 1881 more than three quarters of Sister White's writings have been produced. Therefore several of the revised versions were available during most of Sister White's writing years.

In Testimonies Vol. 8

There are 666 quotations from the KJV, 53 from the American Revised Version, and 5 from the Revised Version. She quoted often from the Practical Psalms where the change was slight in the wording....

Testimonies Volume Nine.

This was the last Volume written by Sister White. Notice she never quoted from a Revised Version once in this volume. Sister White began with the King James Version and she finished the Volume with it. Our prophet used these modern versions less and less. It is a tragedy that too many Adventists are now using the modern Versions more and more. Inspiration used them less and less. Apostasy uses them more and more. May you follow the example of Sister White in her last volume of the Testimonies and drop out the so called revisions.[27]

We should also note that not once did Ellen White quote any passage from the modern versions that was in error. Furthermore, she quoted passages from the KJV that are omitted from the modern versions, and she wrote of them as inspired.

For the sake of interest, here is a list of her books (published while she was alive, so excluding the compilations, but including those about to be published at the time of her death) that include Scripture passages from modern versions: *Patriarchs and Prophets* (1890); *Steps to Christ* (1892, 1893); *Thoughts from the Mount of Blessing* (1896); *The Desire of Ages* (1898); *Christ's Object Lessons* (1900); *Testimonies for the Church*, volume 6 (1901); *Testimonies for the Church*, volume 7 (1902); *Education* (1903); *Testimonies for the Church*, volume 8 (1904); *The Ministry of Healing* (1905); *The Acts of the Apostles* (1911); *The Great Controversy* (1911); *Counsels to Parents, Teachers, and Students* (1913); and *Prophets and Kings* (1917).

Let us take a moment to examine several texts and see how the translators can influence doctrine, or how the doctrine of translators can influence Bible translation. In Paul's first letter to the Corinthians, we read in the Authorized Version (otherwise known as the King James Version), "The first man *is* of the earth, earthy: the second man *is* the Lord from heaven."[28] All the modern versions share virtually the same wording as the Rheims: "The first man of earth, earthly; the second man from heaven, heavenly." The missing key thought, which strongly

27 Burnside, *The New International Version or The King James Version*, pp. 48, 49.
28 1 Corinthians 15:47

impacts doctrine by its omission, is "the Lord." The translation is emasculated by that omission! Such a little thing, some might say, but when compared with other such key texts, the impact becomes exponentially enormous.

In Paul's letter to the Ephesians, we read in the Authorized Version, "And to make all *men* see what *is* the fellowship of the mystery, which from the beginning of the world hath been hid in God, who created all things by Jesus Christ."[29] Again, modern versions omit the same phrase as did the Rheims: "And to illuminate all men what is the dispensation of the Sacrament hidden from the worlds in God, who created all things." Clearly, one version teaches the doctrine of Jesus Christ as Creator, while the others deny that doctrine by virtue of their omission. The only real difference between the Rheims and modern translations is that the Jesuits strongly emphasized the doctrine of the sacrament, or the host, as a part of the Roman Catholic liturgy, of which the New International Version hints by its rendering of the text: "and to make plain to everyone the administration of this mystery, which for ages past was kept hidden in God, who created all things." How does the word "administration" make it easier to understand "the fellowship of the mystery"? It is not for the purpose of making Scripture easier to understand, but for the purpose of giving strange doctrine, i.e. transubstantiation, mariology, the natural immortality of the soul of man, etc., the appearance of biblical support.

A quick study of Daniel 9:26, as translated in the NIV, exposes the desire of false teachers to make the power of Jesus nothing: "After the sixty-two 'sevens,' the Anointed One will be put to death and will have nothing." The KJV clearly teaches that "and after threescore and two weeks shall Messiah be cut off, but not for himself." Jesus, as the Anointed One—the Messiah—declared of Himself, "The Father loveth the Son, and hath given all things into his hand."[30] "All power is given unto me in heaven and in earth."[31] Daniel declared of Jesus, "I saw in the night visions, and, behold, *one* like the Son of man came with the clouds of heaven, and came to the Ancient of days, and they brought him near before him. And there was given him dominion, and glory, and a kingdom, that all people, nations, and languages, should serve him: his dominion *is* an everlasting dominion, which shall not pass away, and his kingdom *that* which shall not be destroyed."[32] Gabriel, the archangel sent to reveal God's purpose and will for Mary, plainly stated, "He shall be great, and shall be called the Son of the Highest: and the Lord God shall give unto him the throne of his father David: And he shall reign over the house of Jacob for ever; and of his kingdom there shall be no end."[33] Make no mistake about it, the modern versions are consistently promoting the same error in the translation of Daniel's vision recorded in chapter 9 verse 26, including the NASB, CEV, RSV, BBE, ASV, and the Darby translation.

---

29 Ephesians 3:9
30 John 3:35
31 Matthew 28:18
32 Daniel 7:13, 14
33 Luke 1:32, 33

In my study of the Scriptures from various translations, I can only conclude that there is indeed an agenda and that the counter-reformers are stealing a march on God's people who are being destroyed for lack of knowledge. In my discussions with others on this very topic, I have learned that people don't want to be in conflict or controversy on this issue. Yet our eternal destiny can be determined by a right understanding of the Word of God. Remember, the Roman Catholic Church claims supremacy over those Protestants who worship on Sunday because the Catholics claim to have the authority to change the sacred day from Saturday to Sunday. Are we then to think we can casually escape a similar charge if we accept as our biblical authority a version that is doctrinally aligned with the Latin Vulgate? After all, the Council of Trent established what Bible the Roman Catholics claim to be authentic, as well as the right to be sole interpreter of the Scriptures!

In 1849 John Cumming wrote regarding the blasphemies of the papal system, stating:

> I will now read to you a document which also conveys the same idea of blasphemies—for that is the Scripture epithet bestowed on the assumptions of the Pope. The quotation is authoritative, being from one of the symbolical books of the Church of Rome. It is entitled, Libri Symbolici Ecclesiae Catholicae editi a Streitwolf, Gotting. 1838.—The passage I now quote is to be found in vol. ii. p. 343, and it is called the Confession of the Catholic faith to be taken by all Protestants in Hungary, conforming to that faith. "First, we confess that we have been brought from heresy to the Roman faith, by the diligence of the Fathers of the Society of Jesus. Secondly, we confess that the Pope of Rome is head of the Church, and cannot err…. Fourthly, we confess that whatever new thing the Pope of Rome may have instituted, whether it be in Scripture or out of Scripture, is true, divine, and full of salvation, and therefore ought to be regarded as of higher value by lay-people than even the precepts of the living God. Fifthly, we confess that the most holy Pontiff ought to be honoured by all with divine honour, with more prostration than even what is due to Christ Himself." … And the 11th article of this document is, "We confess that the Pope has power of altering Scripture, or increasing or diminishing it according to his will."[34]

Read this astonishing testimony by the Abbate Jacopo Leone, a former Jesuit who escaped from that order upon learning their agenda while overhearing a secret meeting on this matter.

> We shall know how, by marvellous stories and gorgeous shows, to exorcise heresy from the heads and hearts of the multitude; we shall know how to nail their thoughts upon ours … so that they shall make no stir without our good pleasures.

---

34 Cumming, *Apocalyptic Sketches: Lectures on the Book of Revelation*, pp. 307, 308.

Then the Bible, that serpent which, with head erect and eyes flashing fire, threatens us with its venom whilst it trails along the ground, shall be changed again into a rod as soon as we are able to seize it; and what wounds will we not inflict with it upon these hardened Pharaohs and their cunning magicians! what miracles will we not work by its means! Oh, then, mysterious rod! we will not again suffer thee to escape from our hands, and fall to the earth![35]

So, one should understand why Paul strongly exhorted Timothy to "study to shew thyself approved unto God, a workman that needeth not to be ashamed, rightly dividing the word of truth."[36] When we read the Bible, we should, by careful comparative study, be led to a clearer understanding of what God has revealed in His Word. With so many differences of translation between the Protestant and Catholic Bibles, how can we come to an agreement of the truth as it is in Jesus Christ so that we may be of "one Lord, one faith, one baptism"?[37] How can we repeat in unison what we have memorized when the repeated verses of a multitude of translations don't even match?

One Sabbath morning we heard one of our Sabbath School superintendents reading Proverbs 26 from the New International Version. Those of us following in the Authorized Version got lost when she read verse ten: "Like an archer who wounds at random is one who hires a fool or any passer-by." We thought that a verse had been skipped, and we quickly searched throughout the rest of the chapter to find our place again. What caused the confusion? The AV reads: "The great *God* that formed all *things* both rewardeth the fool, and rewardeth transgressors." I immediately recognized that two doctrines were affected by this change. The first being reference to the creative power of God, and the second being the rewards granted by judgment. When I got home, I quickly researched other translations, and they were virtually the same as the NIV, with the exception of the Rheims, which reads, "Judgment determineth causes: and he that putteth a fool to silence, appeaseth anger." Then I read some interesting commentary by the translators of the NET Bible:

A similar rendering is given by ASV, NAB, NIV, NRSV, and NLT; it is the only one that makes sense out of a verse that most commentators consider hopelessly corrupt. That is not to say it is the correct rendering, only that it makes sense as a required negative statement in a proverb. The first line has רַב מְחוֹלֵל־כֹּל (rav mÿkholel-col). The first word, רַב (rav), can mean "archer," "master," or "much." The verb מְחוֹלֵל (mÿkholel) can mean "to wound" or "to bring forth." The possibilities are: "a master performs [or, produces] all," "a master injures all," "an archer wounds all,"

---

35   Leone, *The Jesuit Conspiracy: The Secret Plan of the Order*, p. 98.

36   2 Timothy 2:15

37   Ephesians 4:5

or "much produces all." The line probably should be stating something negative, so the idea of an archer injuring or wounding people [at random] is preferable. An undisciplined hireling will have the same effect as an archer shooting at anything and everything.[38]

Notice how the commentary is inconclusive based on the manuscripts. The basis for the translation made by the translators is that "most commentators consider [the manuscripts] hopelessly corrupt." But we are not told who these commentators are or upon what manuscripts they were relying. Furthermore, the translators assume they are correct based upon their own admission of conjecture that the "line probably should be stating something negative" as the sole basis for their preferred and foregone conclusion!

Perhaps there is something to Lewis Foster's advice regarding translations. He ought to know, since he was on the New International Version and New King James Version committees. "Study the translators as well as their translations … A change may be better understood by knowing the position of the translator … whether they are based upon … a shift in the theological beliefs of the translator."[39] Donald Arthur Carson, a Canadian-born evangelical theologian and professor of the New Testament, apparently concurs, succinctly stating, "Some modern translations tend toward the heretical by virtue of the force of the presuppositions that govern the translation."[40] But no stronger indication of what is happening to modern Bibles can be given than that by Dr. G. Vance Smith, a Unitarian minister who worked with Wescott and Hort on the Revised English Version: "It has been frequently said that the changes of translation … are of little importance from a doctrinal point of view … Any such statement appears … contrary to the facts."[41]

One translator from the New International Version translation committee, Dr. Virginia Mollenkott, wrote three articles that give strong indication where her theology is headed: "The Divine Feminine: The Biblical Imagery of God as Female;" "Sensuous Spirituality: Out from Fundamentalism;" and "Whore-ishly Implementing the Political Vision of the Christ-Sophia." Do we really want our understanding of God to be guided by the theology of those who refuse to acknowledge God's laws, precepts, statutes, and commandments governing the moral, spiritual, and social aspects of our lives?

When I was young, I occasionally watched the game show "To Tell the Truth." I was fascinated by the attempts of two impostors, by their fabrications, to confuse the panel of celebrities who asked questions of all three contestants in an effort to determine the identity of the one contestant sworn to tell the truth. Then, after the panel had placed their votes, the host would

38   "Proverbs 26:10," NET Bible Study Environment, http:/1ref.us/5.
39   Foster, *Selecting a Translation of the Bible*, pp. 77, 78, 48.
40   Carson, *The King James Version Debate: A Plea for Realism*, p. 65.
41   Smith, *Texts and Margins of the Revised New Testament*, p. 45.

ask, "Will the real [contestant's name] please stand up!" Sometimes the celebrity panel guessed correctly, and sometimes they didn't. In order to fool the panel, the impostors had to be able to answer in ambiguous, but plausible terms. Sometimes they dressed to impress, when the real contestant was clothed rather casually. If a celebrity on the panel knew the real contestant, he or she had to recuse himself or herself from voting, but we should never recuse ourselves from discovering or determining the truth about the Scriptures.

In Revelation 2:12, 14, 15, Jesus revealed to John the behavior of the Nicolaitans among them in Pergamos and God's hatred for their doctrine and practices. "These things saith he which hath the sharp sword with two edges ... But I have a few things against thee, because thou hast there them that hold the doctrine of Balaam, who taught Balac to cast a stumblingblock before the children of Israel, to eat things sacrificed unto idols, and to commit fornication. So hast thou also them that hold the doctrine of the Nicolaitanes, which thing I hate."

We know from Hebrews 4:12 that God's Word is like a two-edged sword and a capable "discerner of the thoughts and intents of the heart." So we should be able to discern between pure and adulterated doctrine. *The New Unger's Bible Dictionary* informs us that "the general voice of antiquity accuses them [the Nicolaitans] of holding the lawfulness of eating things offered to idols, and of mixing in and encouraging idolatrous worship; and as they are charged with denying God to be the creator of the world, and attributing its existence to other powers, they could unquestionably, on such grounds, permit themselves so to act, and thus far it is probable that the accusation is not ill-founded. The community of women was another doctrine which they are said to have adopted, and their conduct seems to have been in the highest degree licentious."[42] So, is it possible to find Nicolaitan doctrine inserted into the translations where the Greek manuscripts used contain pagan philosophy?

We have already seen how in Proverbs 26:10 the changes affecting doctrines of creation and judgment. The King James Version, in 1 Corinthians 8:4, reads, "As concerning therefore the eating of those things that are offered in sacrifice unto idols, we know that an idol is nothing in the world, and that there is none other God but one." Compared to the New American Standard Bible, we get a different meaning altogether. "Therefore concerning the eating of things sacrificed to idols, we know that there is no such thing as an idol in the world, and that there is no God but one." If there is "no such thing as an idol in the world," then we could very well understand why the Nicolaitans believed and taught that it was okay to eat food offered to idols. However, a larger context must be considered. So, how does Paul conclude his remarks two chapters later? 1 Corinthians 10:20-22 states, "But I say, that the things which the Gentiles sacrifice, they sacrifice to devils, and not to God: and I would not that ye should have fellowship with devils. Ye cannot

---

42   Unger, *The New Unger's Bible Dictionary*, p. 921.

drink the cup of the Lord, and the cup of devils: ye cannot be partakers of the Lord's table, and of the table of devils. Do we provoke the Lord to jealousy? are we stronger than he?"[43]

Scattered across the West are many abandoned gold mines. Some have tried to take advantage of the gullible by "salting" those mines—giving them the appearance that much gold is left to be extracted. The scam gains the appearance of legitimacy when the con artist melts down gold trinkets acquired from pawn shops or by theft, molds the molten mineral into bird-shot sized pellets, places these in shotgun shells, and then fires them into the rock formations in the mine shaft. The greedy gulper sees the gold and, led to believe the mine has more to offer, buys the property for much more than it is worth. Satan does the same thing to the truth. He devises methods and means to pervert pure doctrine while maintaining the appearance of truth. But in the end, the deceived get only the shaft!

No doubt should exist in the minds of all that doctrines are to be established by the Scriptures. And the Scriptures should be translated in such a manner that leaves in place every golden link in the chain of truth. Therefore, the words of Paul to Timothy are very important indeed: "But continue thou in the things which thou hast learned and hast been assured of, knowing of whom thou hast learned them; And that from a child thou hast known the holy scriptures, which are able to make thee wise unto salvation through faith which is in Christ Jesus."[44] We should also continue in what we have learned with assurance, knowing from whom we have learned through faith. Our confidence is from the Holy Spirit, the other Comforter, who is to guide us into all truth.[45]

Now that we have examined the history of the Scriptures and the importance of the unadulterated Word of God, let us further delve into Jesus' use of Scripture and the value He placed on God's Word. Throughout the Scriptures we find important symbols—word pictures—that help us comprehend the connection between the faith of Jesus and the discipline of Scripture memorization. Just as we learned earlier about the breastplate spoken of in Isaiah 59:16, 17, as being faith and love according to Paul in Ephesians 6:14 and 1 Thessalonians 5:8, we can see a connection through the symbols used to represent faith and God's Word.

Notice carefully the words of Jeremiah concerning the Scriptures, "Is not my word like as a fire? saith the Lord; and like a hammer that breaketh the rock in pieces?"[46] Let's build on this theme by looking at how the articles of gold for the tabernacle were to be fashioned. "And he made two cherubims of gold, beaten out of one piece made he them, on the two ends of the mercy seat … And he made the candlestick of pure gold: of beaten work made he the candlestick;

---

43 So much more could be written along these lines of thought that it would be a book. Several books are already available to help the diligent Bible student begin to understand the issues at stake. For further study, I recommend the following books: Benjamin G. Wilkinson, *Our Authorized Bible Vindicated*; D. A. Waite, *Defending the King James Bible*; and G. A. Riplinger, *New Age Bible Versions*.
44 2 Timothy 3:14, 15
45 John 16:13
46 Jeremiah 23:29

his shaft, and his branch, his bowls, his knops, and his flowers, were of the same … Their knops and their branches were of the same: all of it was one beaten work of pure gold. And he made his seven lamps, and his snuffers, and his snuffdishes, of pure gold."[47] Peter draws a comparison between faith and gold tried by fire.[48] And Ellen White wrote, "The gold is faith and love."[49] Contemplating these symbols, we then begin to comprehend that the fire and hammer of God's Word, when brought into contact with faith and love, results in the product of beaten gold—an article worthy of placement within the tabernacle of God. But the lesson doesn't end here.

Remember the apostasy at Mount Sinai? Scripture records that the Israelites fashioned a golden calf to bow down and worship. "And he received them at their hand, and fashioned it with a graving tool, after he had made it a molten calf: and they said, These be thy gods, O Israel, which brought thee up out of the land of Egypt."[50] The gold was melted by fire, but it was not beaten with a hammer. It was "fashioned with a graving tool." When we do not submit to the process ordained by God to prepare us for the place He has planned for us, we become unacceptable instruments of a false religion.

Another symbol representing God's Word is found in the olive tree. Found in both the Old and New Testaments, we can see amazing truths revealed about their importance to God, and to us. Zechariah relates a vision to us: "Then answered I, and said unto him, What are these two olive trees upon the right side of the candlestick and upon the left side thereof? And I answered again, and said unto him, What be these two olive branches which through the two golden pipes empty the golden oil out of themselves? And he answered me and said, Knowest thou not what these be? And I said, No, my lord. Then said he, These are the two anointed ones, that stand by the Lord of the whole earth."[51]

We learn more about the importance of this symbol in John's vision found in Revelation 11:

> These are the two olive trees, and the two candlesticks standing before the God of the earth. And if any man will hurt them, fire proceedeth out of their mouth, and devoureth their enemies: and if any man will hurt them, he must in this manner be killed. These have power to shut heaven, that it rain not in the days of their prophecy: and have power over waters to turn them to blood, and to smite the earth with all plagues, as often as they will. And when they shall have finished their testimony, the beast that ascendeth out of the bottomless pit shall make war against them, and shall overcome them, and kill them.… And after three days and an half the spirit of life from God entered into them, and they stood upon their feet; and great fear fell upon them which saw them. And they heard a great voice from heaven saying

47   Exodus 37:7, 17, 22, 23; this was in fulfillment of God's express command as recorded in Exodus 25:18, 31, 36
48   1 Peter 1:7
49   White, "Importance of Right Associations," *The Signs of the Times*, December 7, 1882.
50   Exodus 32:4
51   Zechariah 4:11–14

unto them, Come up hither. And they ascended up to heaven in a cloud; and their enemies beheld them.[52]

So significant is the relationship between faith and Scripture that the enemy of Christ made war against the Scriptures and overcame them for a period of time, but God has intervened by restoring them with the "Spirit of life" and giving them greater status than they previously possessed. And what better way for Satan to separate the golden oil from the candlesticks, fashioned in beaten gold, than to make changes to God's Word—a little here and a little there—which would inhibit a pure, simple faith capable of complete reliance upon God? After all, Paul wrote the Corinthians, "But I fear, *lest by any means*, as the serpent beguiled Eve through his subtilty, so your minds should be corrupted from the simplicity that is in Christ."[53]

I recall a fable about a lazy boy who somehow managed to catch a leprechaun. By methods of interrogation the sluggard pried from the leprechaun a promise to reveal his secret stash of treasure. Through the woods they hiked until, at last, they came to a great oak tree that marked the location of gold and precious jewels. But now the boy was in a quandary. In his greed for easy wealth, he had forgotten to bring a shovel with which to dig up the treasure. He took off his yellow scarf and tied it to the lowest branch of the stately oak. Then he forced from the leprechaun a promise not to remove the scarf. Upon obtaining the promise, he leisurely took his time retrieving the shovel. But when he returned to the place where he thought the treasure was, he discovered a yellow scarf hanging from every low branch on every tree in the woods.

"A silly story!" you might say. Perhaps. But just like the parable of the rich man and Lazarus, it is loaded with meaning consistent with Paul's counsel to Timothy or the words of John. While God desires to give us the treasure of heaven, which is found in His Word, Satan seeks to do everything possible to keep the treasure hidden. "Now the Spirit speaketh expressly, that in the latter times some shall depart from the faith, giving heed to seducing spirits, and doctrines of devils.... If thou put the brethren in remembrance of these things, thou shalt be a good minister of Jesus Christ, nourished up in the words of faith and of good doctrine, whereunto thou hast attained."[54] "Whosoever transgresseth, and abideth not in the doctrine of Christ, hath not God. He that abideth in the doctrine of Christ, he hath both the Father and the Son. If there come any unto you, and bring not this doctrine, receive him not into your house, neither bid him God speed."[55]

If we are to receive our eternal reward, we must first acknowledge our true condition. Ellen White gives us much to think about in this regards:

---

52 Revelation 11:4–7, 11, 12
53 2 Corinthians 11:3
54 1 Timothy 4:1, 6
55 2 John 1:9, 10

The gold of love and faith is wanting in our ranks. Christ declares, "I have somewhat against thee, because thou hast left thy first love." Many are holding on to the truth with only the tips of their fingers. They have had great light and many privileges. Like Capernaum, they have in this respect been exalted to heaven. But unless they put away their pride and self-confidence, in the time of trial that is approaching they will become apostates. Unless they have an entire transformation of character, they will never enter heaven.[56]

Who will heed the counsel of the True Witness, to seek the gold tried in the fire, the white raiment, and the eye-salve? The gold is faith and love, the white raiment is the righteousness of Christ, the eye-salve is that spiritual discernment which will enable us to see the wiles of Satan and shun them, to detect sin and abhor it, to see truth and obey it.[57]

Several times each day precious, golden moments should be consecrated to prayer and the study of the Scriptures, if it is only to commit a text to memory, that spiritual life may exist in the soul. The varied interests of the cause furnish us with food for reflection and inspiration for our prayers. Communion with God is highly essential for spiritual health, and here only may be obtained that wisdom and correct judgment so necessary in the performance of every duty.[58]

Build a wall of scriptures around you, and you will see that the world cannot break it down. Commit the Scriptures to memory, and then throw right back upon Satan when he comes with his temptations, "It is written." This is the way that our Lord met the temptations of Satan, and resisted them. Be determined that you will not live without the presence and light and love of Jesus, and then you will have precious victories, and will know who is the Source of your strength.[59]

May we desire to obtain the faith of Jesus. May we desire to feed upon His Word so that we might grow in grace, knowledge, and wisdom—just as He did. Only then will we be properly prepared to live with Him forever in the place He has prepared for us.

56 White, "The Need of Earnest Effort," *The Review and Herald*, February 11, 1904.
57 White, "Importance of Right Associations," *The Signs of the Times*, December 7, 1882.
58 White, *Testimonies for the Church*, vol. 4, p. 459.
59 White, "Missionaries for God," *The Review and Herald*, April 10, 1888.

Chapter 4

By Faith Jesus Was Baptized

While serving as a missionary in Japan, I befriended a young man who had been raised a Sabbath-keeping Christian. He had some knowledge of the Bible and seemed to love Jesus, but he had never been baptized. Our initial contacts involved the swapping of language lessons so that I could learn Japanese and he could brush up his already excellent social English. Eventually I asked him how he became a Christian. He explained that his father raised him to keep the commandments and have faith in Jesus. But I was amazed when he said his father did not believe that baptism was necessary.

I didn't understand then what I am learning now about the faith of Jesus, so I was unable to give reasons for baptism from the perspective of Christ's faith. At the time, I tried to convince my friend with proof-texts on the topic of baptism without success. I hope the seed was planted to bear fruit later, for not long afterward he moved away, and I never saw him again.

Everyone who is drawn to Christ by the Father should comprehend the faith of Christ in the ritual of baptism. Otherwise, the tremendous significance of the symbolism is lost, and baptism becomes to us what circumcision became to the Jews—salvation by works accomplished through meaningless, formal ceremonies.

Of course, nearly all professedly Christian sects embrace the concept of baptism. But differences regarding the practice abound as to the appropriate method, the appropriate age of the candidate, and the correctness of the words intoned moments prior to or during the commission of the rite. Crusades have been fought over differences in this and other doctrines. Pope Gregory I was rather emphatic about its necessity, writing that children who died unbaptized went directly to hell to stay there for all eternity. Popes Innocent I and Gelasius I both wrote that babies who were baptized but hadn't received the communion host were condemned to hell. The Council of Trent reversed these extreme positions.[1] Nevertheless, most believe that baptism ought not to be neglected on account of Jesus' conversation with Nicodemus: "Verily, verily, I say unto thee, Except a man be born of water and of the Spirit, he cannot enter into the kingdom of God."[2]

Some practice baptism by aspersion (sprinkling), while others baptize by affusion (pouring) water onto the head. Still others adhere to baptism by immersion, or even submersion, as the only proper symbolic act of death to self, burial, and resurrection with Christ to a new life of obedience. Many act upon the tradition of their church, not realizing that aspersion and affusion became officially "valid" or acceptable methods of baptism in AD 1311 at the Council of Ravenna.

> ## *"Sprinkling some dirt on that chicken didn't bury it!"*

Regarding Christ's baptism, which is to be our example, we are told that "Jesus, when he was baptized, went up straightway out of the water,"[3] which indicates that He was in deep enough water for immersion. We are told—after Jesus cleansed the temple—that "John also was baptizing in Aenon near to Salim, because there was much water there: and they came, and were baptized."[4]

I recall hearing a story about a young man who wished to be re-baptized by immersion despite his father's protests that his infant baptism by sprinkling was sufficient. Then one day, as his father drove up to the farmhouse, a chicken ran in front of the pickup. A direct hit with the front tire rendered the chicken inedible, so the father commanded his son to bury the dead chicken in the compost pile. Later, upon checking up on his son's compliance, he noticed the chicken on top of the pile with some dirt lightly sprinkled over it. Marching back to his son's room in a foul mood, the father scolded, "Why didn't you bury the chicken like I told you to?" The son softly answered, "But, Dad, I did. I took it to the compost pile and sprinkled some dirt on it." Red faced, the father retorted, "Sprinkling some dirt on that chicken didn't bury it!" Then the light began to dawn upon his reasoning, and his expression softened. "Okay, son, you can get re-baptized by immersion after you have truly buried that chicken."

Paul told the Roman Christians, "Know ye not, that so many of us as were baptized into Jesus Christ were baptized into his death? Therefore we are buried with him by baptism into death: that like as Christ was raised up from the dead by the glory of the Father, even so we also should walk in newness of life."[5]

The disciples followed Jesus for nearly three and a half years. Early in His ministry, they witnessed Christ's rejection by the religious leaders, by zealots, by His townspeople, and even the scorn His own step-brothers and step-sisters held for Him. The disciples had moments of doubt

---

1   De Rosa, *Vicars of Christ: The Dark Side of the Papacy*, p. 207.
2   John 3:5
3   Matthew 3:16
4   John 3:23
5   Romans 6:3, 4

regarding the outcome of Christ's earthly kingdom as a result of the evident rejection. They did not truly comprehend the nature of Christ's mission. But by reason of Jesus' many miracles and the depth of His teachings, they held fast to their misconceived hope that Jesus would soon be acknowledged as king of Israel, and they would obtain their expected reward in His kingdom.

For this eventuality, Mrs. Zebedee decided to improve her two sons' situation. Approaching Jesus with the request that Jesus would place her two sons in the cherished positions of the kingdom—one on His right and the other on His left—when He was enthroned, Jesus responded with these words: "Ye know not what ye ask. Are ye able to drink of the cup that I shall drink of, and to be baptized with the baptism that I am baptized with?"[6] If you think about it carefully, James and John were at the Jordan when Jesus was baptized. They probably had received John the Baptist's baptism after the same method as Christ had. So what was this cup and baptism that Christ now mentioned? What could He possibly mean by His response? Without second thought, they responded, "We are able."[7] Later they were to understand what Christ meant. Because we have opportunity to learn from their experiences, our joy can be perfected now as we comprehend how Christ exhibited His faith by His words and actions.

Nowhere in the Old Testament are the words baptize or its variants used, but clues exist in Scripture which indicate that the concept is present in various representations. Paul gives us one clue when writing to the Corinthians in his first epistle: "Moreover, brethren, I would not that ye should be ignorant, how that all our fathers were under the cloud, and all passed through the sea; And were all baptized unto Moses in the cloud and in the sea; And did all eat the same spiritual meat; And did all drink the same spiritual drink: for they drank of that spiritual Rock that followed them: and that Rock was Christ."[8] Paul is definitive about a two-fold baptism—one by cloud, the other by the crossing of the Red Sea. More could be said about the need for baptism by water and by the Holy Spirit, but right now we are looking for clues that ultimately will help us comprehend the faith of Jesus in this matter.

After the crossing of the sea, when in the shadow of Mount Sinai, the Israelites were given a copy of the heavenly tabernacle so that God might dwell with His chosen people. In the ceremonial rituals associated with the portable tabernacle, we see no less than three that fit the question Jesus posed to James and John—yes, even to the remaining ten disciples, and to us.

The first example regarded the burnt offering, the ram that was divided and washed before being placed upon the altar as a sweet savor to the Lord.[9] The second applied to the priests, that they wash their hands and feet before coming into the Lord's presence so they would not suffer death from uncleanness. Moses washed Aaron and his sons when they were dedicated to the priesthood. And on the Day of Atonement the high priest was to wash himself.[10] The parallelism

---

6   Matthew 20:22; see also Mark 10:38
7   Ibid.
8   1 Corinthians 10:1–4
9   Exodus 29:16–18
10   Exodus 30:18–21; Leviticus 8:6; 16:24

between Christ and the ram is striking as we consider Jesus as our sacrificial Lamb. Also, we note the comparison between Christ and the priests as we consider Jesus as our High Priest and Mediator before God. Here we begin to comprehend the suffering Sacrifice being washed or baptized, and the entering into His sufferings if we desire to be seated next to Him in His throne. We begin to understand the need for purity as we join Christ in His intercessory ministry on behalf of others for whom Christ died—in a kingdom of priests.

The third example has less to do with baptism than with drinking the cup that Christ drank. But the two are intertwined, since the baptismal vow is likened to the marriage vow. We can see the connection with the baptism of the Israelites at the Red Sea and their marriage to God at Mount Sinai in the covenant established there.

While at Mount Sinai, God made it clear that He was jealous for His uniqueness, His reputation, and His people. He told the Israelites His "name is Jealous"[11] and that He is "a jealous God."[12] And so we find the ceremony of jealousy recorded in Numbers 5. Nowhere in Scripture do we see an example of this ceremony carried out, but it relates to the spirit of jealousy that a man has for his wife—whether she be faithful, or unfaithful, to her marriage vows. Nothing happened if the wife was faithful, but a curse resulted from drinking the "bitter" water, which contained dust from the tabernacle floor and ink from the blotted scroll upon which the curse was written, if the woman had indeed been unfaithful.[13] However, there can be no doubt that both Isaiah and Jeremiah alluded to this passage when writing about the day of the Lord as a time of executed judgment.

The passage that Isaiah wrote applies directly to the unfaithful: "Howl ye; for the day of the Lord is at hand; it shall come as a destruction from the Almighty. Therefore shall all hands be faint, and every man's heart shall melt: And they shall be afraid: pangs and sorrows shall take hold of them; they shall be in pain as a woman that travaileth: they shall be amazed one at another; their faces shall be as flames. Behold, the day of the Lord cometh, cruel both with wrath and fierce anger, to lay the land desolate: and he shall destroy the sinners thereof out of it."[14]

Whereas Jeremiah describes the anguish of the faithful in that day: "For thus saith the Lord; We have heard a voice of trembling, of fear, and not of peace. Ask ye now, and see whether a man doth travail with child? wherefore do I see every man with his hands on his loins, as a woman in travail, and all faces are turned into paleness? Alas! for that day is great, so that none is like it: it is even the time of Jacob's trouble; but he shall be saved out of it."[15]

Examples using the concept of washing can be seen elsewhere. Isaiah 1:16–18 says, "Wash you, make you clean; put away the evil of your doings from before mine eyes; cease to do evil; Learn to do well; seek judgment, relieve the oppressed, judge the fatherless, plead for the widow.

---

11   Exodus 34:14
12   Exodus 20:5
13   Numbers 5:12–31
14   Isaiah 13:6–9
15   Jeremiah 30:5–7

Come now, and let us reason together, saith the Lord: though your sins be as scarlet, they shall be as white as snow; though they be red like crimson, they shall be as wool."

In Ezekiel 16, the prophet uses the same imagery associated with natural birth—the washing with water, the rubbing of salt, the cleansing from blood, anointing with oil, the swaddling clothes—and with the adornments found in the tabernacle—broidered work, badgers skins, fine linen, and silk. Zechariah 3 tells of the vision shown the prophet, of Joshua's filthy clothes taken away, his cleansing, and his being clothed again with a change of raiment and a fair mitre. Baptism is tied to all these symbols—cleansing from sin, clothed with the robes of Christ's righteousness, and a fair mitre with the words "holiness to the Lord" inscribed upon it.

Looking at Jesus' example, we see that He was led by the Holy Spirit. He recognized the appointed time had come, and He departed from Nazareth for the Jordan River. When John the Baptist saw Jesus before him, he recognized His purity of character and felt unworthy of the privilege. How could he, a sinner, baptize One who had never sinned? So Jesus responded, "Suffer it to be so now: for thus it becometh us to fulfill all righteousness."[16] Even this son of a priest had not fully comprehended the faith of Jesus! So Jesus was baptized by faith in order to fulfill righteousness, to renounce sin, even though He had never sinned, and to be anointed by the Holy Spirit at the beginning of His earthly ministry—He was washed as Sacrifice and Priest.[17]

Ellen White provides this insight into Jesus' baptism: "Jesus did not receive baptism as a confession of guilt on His own account. He identified Himself with sinners, taking the steps that we are to take, and doing the work that we must do. His life of suffering and patient endurance after His baptism was also an example to us."[18] He, who needed no regeneration of heart, illustrated to us through baptism the emblem of spiritual rebirth. And immediately after His water baptism He received the anointing baptism of the Holy Spirit. "A new and important era was opening before Him. He was now, upon a wider stage, entering on the conflict of His life."[19]

If we are a commandment-keeping people who also have the faith of Jesus, we will follow His example of baptism by immersion.

In baptism we are given to the Lord as a vessel to be used. Baptism is a most solemn renunciation of the world. Self is by profession dead to a life of sin. The waters cover the candidate, and in the presence of the whole heavenly universe the mutual pledge is made. In the name of the Father, the Son, and the Holy Spirit, man is laid in his watery grave, buried with Christ in baptism, and raised from the water to live the new life of loyalty to God. The three great powers in heaven are witnesses; they are invisible but present."[20]

---

16 White, *The Desire of Ages*, p. 111.
17 Matthew 3:6, 14, 15
18 White, *The Desire of Ages*, p. 111.
19 Ibid.
20 White, *The SDA Bible Commentary*, vol. 6, p. 1074.

In His words to Nicodemus, "Christ made baptism the entrance to His spiritual kingdom. He made this a positive condition with which all must comply who wish to be acknowledged as under the authority of the Father, the Son, and the Holy Ghost. Those who receive the ordinance of baptism thereby make a public declaration that they have renounced the world, and have become members of the royal family, children of the heavenly King."[21]

Nicodemus had no better comprehension than John the Baptist about the necessity of baptism as it related to Christ's faith. Unfortunately, many who have been baptized do not recognize their need for a greater understanding of their own condition and are worse off than Nicodemus in that they have given public display of renouncing sin, but do not repent by forsaking it. They have an intellectual assent, but lack the genuine rebirth. They are counted as the "generation that are pure in their own eyes, and yet is not washed from their filthiness."[22] Consider this thought: "The new birth is a rare experience in this age of the world. This is the reason why there are so many perplexities in the churches. Many, so many, who assume the name of Christ are unsanctified and unholy. They have been baptized, but they were buried alive. Self did not die, and therefore they did not rise to newness of life in Christ."[23]

Too often baptism is perceived as the end of the journey—a graduation of sorts—rather than the beginning of a new life aimed at selfless ministry on behalf of those who have yet to receive the everlasting gospel.

> Many, having learned a little in school, think they are ready to graduate. They think they know about all that is worth knowing. We are not to think that as soon as we are baptized we are ready to graduate from the school of Christ. When we have accepted Christ, and in the name of the Father, and of the Son, and of the Holy Spirit have pledged ourselves to serve God, the Father, Christ, and the Holy Spirit—the three dignitaries and powers of heaven—pledge themselves that every facility shall be given to us if we carry out our baptismal vows to "come out from among them, and be ... separate, ... and touch not the unclean thing." When we are true to our vows, He says, "I will receive you."[24]

When the great day of the Lord comes, we will be lost unless found faithful to our baptismal vows. "At our baptism we pledged ourselves to break all connection with Satan and his agencies, and to put heart and mind and soul into the work of extending the kingdom of God. All heaven is working for this object. The Father, the Son, and the Holy Spirit are pledged to co-operate with sanctified human instrumentalities. If we are true to our vow, there is opened to us a door of

---

21   Ibid., p. 1075. See also John 3:5.
22   Proverbs 30:12
23   White, *The SDA Bible Commentary*, vol. 6, p. 1075.
24   Ibid.

communication with heaven,—a door that no human hand or satanic agency can close."[25] How important then is the Savior's warning couched in the question, "Nevertheless when the Son of man cometh, shall he find faith on the earth?"[26]

Upon giving Jesus a positive response to His searching question about drinking the cup of Christ and baptism, James and John were both encouraged and rebuked.

> Ye shall drink indeed of my cup, and be baptized with the baptism that I am baptized with: but to sit on my right hand, and on my left, is not mine to give, but *it shall be given to them* for whom it is prepared of my Father.... Ye know that the princes of the Gentiles exercise dominion over them, and they that are great exercise authority upon them. But it shall not be so among you: but whosoever will be great among you, let him be your minister; And whosoever will be chief among you, let him be your servant: Even as the Son of man came not to be ministered unto, but to minister, and to give his life a ransom for many.[27]

The greatest travesties result from abuse of power rooted in a desire to control the bodies and minds of others. And all the disciples, guilty of desiring self-exaltation whereby great authority might be obtained for the purpose of exercising dominion over others, were in danger of yielding to the snare of power abuse. The evidence of this guilt is in the indignation expressed upon their overhearing Mrs. Zebedee's request. What the disciples should have realized is that the question posed to James and John was also addressed to them and all who desire to follow Christ. Christ says to you and to me, "Will you drink of the cup that I drink of? And will you be baptized with the baptism that I am baptized with?" It is more than a rhetorical question. The question must be carefully pondered and the answer carefully weighed before being rashly spoken. A review of Christ's teachings will help us comprehend the lessons Christ constantly taught in regards to His kingdom.

On earlier occasions Jesus spoke about the costs and rewards of being His disciples.

> And it came to pass, that, as they went in the way, a certain man said unto him, Lord, I will follow thee whithersoever thou goest. And Jesus said unto him, Foxes have holes, and birds of the air have nests; but the Son of man hath not

What the disciples should have realized is that the question posed to James and John was also addressed to them and all who desire to follow Christ.

25   White, "Filled With the Fruits of Righteousness," *The Review and Herald*, May 17, 1906.
26   Luke 18:8
27   Matthew 20:23, 25–28

where to lay his head. And he said unto another, Follow me. But he said, Lord, suffer me first to go and bury my father. Jesus said unto him, Let the dead bury their dead: but go thou and preach the kingdom of God. And another also said, Lord, I will follow thee; but let me first go bid them farewell, which are at home at my house. And Jesus said unto him, No man, having put his hand to the plough, and looking back, is fit for the kingdom of God.[28]

If any man come to me, and hate not his father, and mother, and wife, and children, and brethren, and sisters, yea, and his own life also, he cannot be my disciple. And whosoever doth not bear his cross, and come after me, cannot be my disciple. For which of you, intending to build a tower, sitteth not down first, and counteth the cost, whether he have sufficient to finish it? Lest haply, after he hath laid the foundation, and is not able to finish it, all that behold it begin to mock him, Saying, This man began to build, and was not able to finish. Or what king, going to make war against another king, sitteth not down first, and consulteth whether he be able with ten thousand to meet him that cometh against him with twenty thousand? Or else, while the other is yet a great way off, he sendeth an ambassage, and desireth conditions of peace. So likewise, whosoever he be of you that forsaketh not all that he hath, he cannot be my disciple.[29]

Here Jesus emphasized the great importance of properly prioritizing our relationships. This teaching is consistent with loving God supremely, and our neighbors as ourselves, and not, as some might think, that we should hate close relatives.

On the occasion Jesus was approached by the rich young ruler, who consequently refused to sell all that he had, take up his cross, and follow Jesus, the disciples were given plain utterances about the difficulties for the wealthy to enter into the kingdom of God. Peter was quick to respond to Jesus' instruction:

Behold, we have forsaken all, and followed thee; what shall we have therefore? And Jesus said unto them, Verily I say unto you, That ye which have followed me, in the regeneration when the Son of man shall sit in the throne of his glory, ye also shall sit upon twelve thrones, judging the twelve tribes of Israel. And every one that hath forsaken houses, or brethren, or sisters, or father, or mother, or wife, or children, or lands, for my name's sake, shall receive an hundredfold, and shall inherit everlasting life.[30]

28 Luke 9:57–62
29 Luke 14:26–33
30 Matthew 19:27–29

Yet it was not enough for the disciples to think of the reward of having a throne and judging the twelve tribes of Israel. The placement of those thrones, as though their positioning might give an order of exaltation, was a source of continual argument rooted in covetousness and pride! Right up to the time of the last Passover meal with His disciples, they quibbled over who was going to have the places of greatest honor in Jesus' kingdom—not yet realizing that the greatest position was one of selfless service, which Christ demonstrated by washing their feet.

The disciples' lack of faith and trust in God's divine plan is juxtaposed with the example of Capernaum's centurion who, desiring only that Jesus heal his servant, saw himself as unworthy of Christ's presence in his house and said, "Speak the word only, and my servant shall be healed. For I am a man under authority, having soldiers under me: and I say to this man, Go, and he goeth; and to another, Come, and he cometh; and to my servant, Do this, and he doeth it."[31] Jesus noted the centurion's faith as being greater than any in Israel. Does that mean it was greater than that of the disciples who had performed miracles in Christ's name? Yes. He recognized that Christ had authority because he himself was under authority. Therefore, he better understood Christ's work and faith than even the disciples did.

Patiently Jesus ministered to and taught His disciples until they fully comprehended at Pentecost the lessons He had intended for them to learn all along. At that point, His followers were prepared for the special outpouring of the Holy Spirit. Thousands gave their lives to Christ—being baptized of water and Spirit—to follow in His footsteps of self-denying service. Not too many years later, James was beheaded by King Herod. Each of the disciples experienced the cup and baptism that Christ experienced, until finally, on the lonely isle of Patmos, Jesus revealed to John the identity of those who would sit with Him in His throne. "To him that overcometh will I grant to sit with me in my throne, even as I also overcame, and am set down with my Father in his throne."[32]

Let us have the faith of Jesus as we follow His example in baptism.

---

31   Matthew 8:8, 9
32   Revelation 3:21

Chapter 5

By Faith Jesus Prayed

Driving a truck for a living has its moments of stress with its near misses, rude drivers, and deadlines. I cannot speak for other over-the-road drivers, but I found it especially stressful finding a place to park the rig for my ten-hour break after eleven hours of driving long into the night. In all the years I have driven commercially, I have always been able to park safely before I went to the sleeper bunk. But I attribute that success to prayer. When it looked like there was no safe place to park, I would pray, claiming the promise "nothing that in any way concerns our peace is too small for Him to notice,"[1] and God would direct me to a place of refuge.

Prayer, however, is more than a hastily uttered petition for a personal need. "Prayer is communion with God. It is the opening of the heart to God as to a friend. Not that it is necessary in order to make known to God what we are, but in order to enable us to receive Him. Prayer does not bring God down to us, but brings us up to Him."[2]

I have heard many sermons on prayer in my lifetime. Many were excellent in content and presentation. But few are unforgettable. In 1987 I attended a retreat for church youth leaders in Leoni Meadows, California. I shall never forget Elder Richard O'Ffill's sermon on prayer because he compared his prayer life to his married life. He shared how it seemed that nine times out of ten God answered his prayers with a no. But when he asked his wife for something, nine times out of ten she would say yes. The difference between results, he surmised, was that he knew his wife well enough not to ask her for things to which he knew she would say no! With this observation in mind, he changed his prayer requests, knowing that God would not say no to those things that are consistent with His character and purpose.

> *A right understanding of His holy character is the principal part of prayer uttered in faith.*

---

1   White, "Prayer," *The Signs of the Times*, June 18, 1902.
2   Ibid.

The beginning of wisdom is respect for God and His commandments. A right understanding of His holy character is the principal part of prayer uttered in faith.[3] When we know our petitions are consistent with God's character, we have great assurance that they are consistent with His will and that they will be answered in a timely fashion. Sometimes there is a waiting period. But we have the assurance that "the ear of the Lord is open to the cry of every suppliant. Even before the prayer is offered or the yearning desire of the soul made known, the Spirit of God goes forth to meet it. Never has there been a genuine desire, never a tear shed in contrition of soul, but grace from Christ has gone forth to meet [supplement] the grace working upon the human heart."[4]

The beauty of Christ's mission to this sinful planet is that He revealed, in a perfect and practical way, the Father's character. At the close of His earthly ministry, He said to Philip, "If ye had known me, ye should have known my Father also: and from henceforth ye know him, and have seen him…. Have I been so long time with you, and yet hast thou not known me, Philip? he that hath seen me hath seen the Father; and how sayest thou then, Show us the Father?"[5] He showed us the Father in a manner by which we might live as we behold. He showed us the Father while living out a life of perfect obedience in fallen flesh. Such an existence could only succeed by a living faith.

We must comprehend the faith of Jesus in His prayer life in order to, by the grace of God, emulate Him. We cannot begin to succeed unless we take up His yoke and learn of Him who is meek and lowly of heart.[6] By beholding His example and imitating Him with sincerity of heart, we will become like Him.

In an earlier chapter, we learned of the painful process Jesus subjected Himself to by being born of a woman, born under the law. Remember and consider that before Jesus was born of Mary He communed with His Father face to face. When Adam and Eve yielded to Satan's temptation and disobeyed God's Word, the wedge of sin was placed between humanity and God.

> Sorrow filled heaven, as it was realized that man was lost and that world which God had created was to be filled with mortals doomed to misery, sickness, and death, and there was no way of escape for the offender. The whole family of Adam must die. I saw the lovely Jesus and beheld an expression of sympathy and sorrow upon His countenance. Soon I saw Him approach the exceeding bright light which enshrouded the Father. Said my accompanying angel, He is in close converse with His Father. The anxiety of the angels seemed to be intense while Jesus was communing with His Father. Three times He was shut in by the glorious light about the Father,

---

3   Psalm 111:10; Proverbs 1:7; 9:10

4   White, "Prayer," *The Signs of the Times*, June 18, 1902.

5   John 14:7, 9

6   Matthew 11:29

and the third time He came out from the Father, His person could be seen. His countenance was calm, free from all perplexity and doubt, and shone with benevolence and loveliness, such as words cannot express.[7]

Here we see Christ's first act of intercessory prayer on behalf of fallen man. "The plan of salvation had been laid before the creation of the earth; for Christ is 'the Lamb slain from the foundation of the world' (Revelation 13:8); yet *it was a struggle, even with the King of the universe, to yield up His Son to die for the guilty race*."[8]

By expressed faith Christ prayed for, and obtained, the Father's blessing upon the implementation of the preplanned ministry of salvation. From the time of His birth in Bethlehem to His ascension shortly after His resurrection, Christ's communion with His Father was no longer done face to face. Instead, He had to spend time with Him through prayer, by faith, and not by sight. In this way, as in so many other ways, Jesus serves as our example, showing us how we can approach the Father in His name. "In Christ's name His followers are to stand before God. Through the value of the sacrifice made for them, they are of value in the Lord's sight. Because of the imputed righteousness of Christ, they are accounted precious. For Christ's sake the Lord pardons those that fear Him. He does not see in them the vileness of the sinner; He recognizes in them the likeness of His Son, in whom they believe."[9]

> *By expressed faith Christ prayed for, and obtained, the Father's blessing upon the implementation of the preplanned ministry of salvation.*

We have no record in the Bible that Jesus communed face to face with His Father. We have only three recorded occasions that the Father spoke directly to Christ so that others heard the Father's voice: at His baptism, at the transfiguration, and in the temple court when Jesus was speaking to the Greeks who had sought an audience with Him.[10] Some may differ on this point by bringing up Exodus 33:11 and Numbers 12:6–8; however, one must keep in mind what the Lord said to Moses upon his request to see the glory of God. "And he said, Thou canst not see my face: for there shall no man see me, and live.... And I will take away mine hand, and thou shalt see my back parts: but my face shall not be seen."[11]

Some may think that somehow it was different for Christ since He was God's Son. But we are told that "we should not think that Christ's need of prayer in His human life lessens His dignity as our Redeemer. He came to be our Example in all things. He identified Himself with our

---

7   White, *The Story of Redemption*, p. 42.
8   White, *Patriarchs and Prophets*, p. 63, emphasis added.
9   White, "Prayer," *The Signs of the Times*, June 18, 1902.
10   Matthew 3:17; 17:5; John 12:28
11   Exodus 33:20, 22

weakness that we might identify ourselves with His strength. He was tempted in all points like as we are, yet He did not yield in a single instance to the sins that were proving the ruin of the sons of men. Thru prayer and communion with God, we, like Him, are to come forth refreshed and strengthened for the battles of life."[12]

Surely prayer was a discipline Christ practiced all His childhood, but the first occasion recorded in Scripture was in His thirtieth year. Notice that immediately after being baptized by John at the Jordan, Jesus prayed:

> As Christ's ministry was about to begin, he received baptism at the hands of John. Coming up out of the water, he bowed on the banks of the Jordan, and offered to the Father such a prayer as heaven had never before listened to. That prayer penetrated the shadow of Satan, which surrounded the Saviour, and cleaved its way to the throne of God. The heavens were opened, and a dove, in appearance like burnished gold, rested upon Jesus; and from the lips of the Infinite God were heard the words, "This is my beloved Son, in whom I am well pleased."
>
> This visible answer to the prayer of God's Son is of deep significance to us. It assures us that humanity is accepted in Christ. The repenting cry of every sinner, the petition of every believing soul, will be heard, and the suppliant will receive grace and power. Christ has opened the way to the highest heavens for every bereaved heart. All may find rest and peace and assurance in sending their prayers to God in the name of his dear Son. As the heavens were open to Christ's prayer, so they will be opened to our prayers. The Holy Spirit will come to every son and daughter of Adam who looks to God for strength.[13]

I am encouraged to know that, just as Satan interposes himself between me and God, Christ also experienced the shadow of interposition, and Christ overcame by prayer. Such encouragement is needed if we are to overcome as Jesus overcame, which will result in the reward of sitting with Him in His throne.[14] We can have confidence that, because of Christ's righteous merits, our penitent prayers will ascend to heaven faster than the speed of thought and that God hears because of our great need!

As Jesus ascended at the close of His earthly ministry in view of the disciples, He said, "Go ye therefore, and teach all nations, baptizing them in the name of the Father, and of the Son, and of the Holy Ghost: *Teaching them to observe all things whatsoever I have commanded you*: and, lo, I am with you alway, even unto the end of the world."[15] If we are to teach others to be as Christ,

---

12   White, "Christ's Example in Prayer," *The Signs of the Times*, July 15, 1908.
13   White, "Tempted in All Points Like as We Are," *The Youth's Instructor*, December 21, 1899. See also Luke 3:21.
14   Revelation 3:21
15   Matthew 28:19, 20

we must practice those things for ourselves, which includes the discipline of prayer. To have the faith of Christ and pray as He did, we must observe His methods—what He prayed for and what He commanded His disciples to pray for.

"Search me, O God, and know my heart: try me, and know my thoughts: And see if there be any wicked way in me, and lead me in the way everlasting."[16] This must be the most difficult prayer for us to pray, for it appears that too few of us wait for God's reply before we are off our knees and running our mouths about the things we see wrong in the lives and characters of others. I am talking from my own personal Laodicean experience! We all need to submit to judgment before we point a condemning finger at others. We ought to give heed to this counsel: "Look to your own defects. You had better discover one of your own faults than ten of your brother's."[17]

Let's consider Jesus' position on judgment as recorded in the book of John: "For the Father judgeth no man, but hath committed all judgment unto the Son."[18] "Ye judge after the flesh; I judge no man. And yet if I judge, my judgment is true: for I am not alone, but I and the Father that sent me."[19] "And if any man hear my words, and believe not, I judge him not: for I came not to judge the world, but to save the world."[20]

> *"Look to your own defects. You had better discover one of your own faults than ten of your brother's."*

We are to pray that God will search our hearts so we may confess our own imperfections and be healed of our backsliding. Then we can teach others His way and pray to God to forgive and heal them of their backsliding. We, who need repentance, can then show them how to repent even as Christ, who needed no repentance, showed us how to repent! Otherwise, we are condemned as unchristian.

> Those who look for evil, who are ready to charge those who do not meet all their expectations by accommodating them and carrying out their ideas with evil, who feel at liberty to judge their brethren and misconstrue their motives, are not Christians. Those who encourage and sustain persons who are not walking in the ways of the Lord, are aiding Satan by doing his work…. Those whose tongues are so free to utter words of criticism, the adroit questioner, who draws out expressions and opinions which have been put into the minds by sowing seeds of alienation, are [Satan's] missionaries.[21]

---

16   Psalm 139:23, 24
17   White, *The Paulson Collection of Ellen G. White Letters*, p. 357.
18   John 5:22
19   John 8:15, 16
20   John 12:47
21   White, *The Paulson Collection of Ellen G. White Letters*, pp. 357, 358.

The foundational root of Satan's rebellion has been—and always will be—self-exaltation. When we put away all bitterness, envy, malice, and evil-surmising, self is crucified with Christ. Then we are free to do those things that God desires to empower us to do—works greater than what Christ performed.[22]

> It is natural for us to have much self-confidence and to follow our own ideas, and in so doing we separate from God; and we do not realize how far we are from him, until the sense of self-security is so firmly established that we are not afraid of failure. We should be much in prayer. We need Jesus as our counselor; at every step we need him as our guide and protector. If there was more praying, more pleading with God to work for us, there would be a greater dependence on him, and faith would be strengthened to take him at his word. It would be easier to believe that if we ask for grace or wisdom, we shall receive it; because his word says, "Ask, and it shall be given you; seek, and ye shall find; knock, and it shall be opened unto you." "If any of you lack wisdom, let him ask of God, that giveth to all men liberally, and upbraideth not; and it shall be given him."[23]

As we look back on the disciples' experience, and comprehend their faults to be our own, we can understand why we don't have power to do the works of Christ. In an earlier chapter we learned how the excited jealousies of the nine disciples prevented them from doing the work given them while Christ and the favored three went up the mountain to experience the transfiguration. We cannot afford to undertake conflict with Satan while harboring ill-will toward others. We "must come to the work in a different spirit. [Our] faith must be strengthened by fervent prayer and fasting, and humiliation of heart. [We] must be emptied of self, and be filled with the Spirit and power of God. Earnest, persevering supplication to God in faith—faith that leads to entire dependence upon God, and unreserved consecration to His work—can alone avail to bring men the Holy Spirit's aid in the battle against principalities and powers, the rulers of the darkness of this world, and wicked spirits in high places."[24] Until we learn this lesson, we will fail to have the faith and love of Jesus.

Christ tried to teach this lesson to the disciples early in His ministry when at Jacob's well just outside the village of Sychar. They treated the Samaritans with a disdain that

"But the union for which Christ prayed must exist among God's people before he can bestow on the church the enlargement and power that he longs to bestow on it."

---

22   John 14:12
23   White, "Humility and Faithfulness in Laborers," *The Review and Herald*, April 8, 1884.
24   White, *The Desire of Ages*, p. 430, 431.

prohibited them from doing His works and greater. But He said to them, "My meat is to do the will of him that sent me, and to finish his work. Say not ye, There are yet four months, and then cometh harvest? behold, I say unto you, Lift up your eyes, and look on the fields; for they are white already to harvest."[25] Not long afterward, He commanded as He sent out the seventy, "the harvest truly is great, but the labourers are few: pray ye therefore the Lord of the harvest, that he would send forth labourers into his harvest."[26] The seventy must have obeyed in all particulars, for when they returned, they declared that even the devils were subject to them through Christ's name. Jesus reminded them that He gives power to them to overcome, and that instead of rejoicing over the power exerted against Satan, they should rejoice that their names were written in heaven—in the book of life. By these words Jesus warned against self-exaltation so that the disciples would not forfeit what He had already gained for and had given to them.

Then Jesus gave a prayer of thanks: "I thank thee, O Father, Lord of heaven and earth, that thou hast hid these things from the wise and prudent, and hast revealed them unto babes: even so, Father; for so it seemed good in thy sight. All things are delivered to me of my Father: and no man knoweth who the Son is, but the Father; and who the Father is, but the Son, and he to whom the Son will reveal him."[27] How often have we withheld gratitude and praise from God because we have forgotten the One who, in giving us His only begotten Son, gave us all of heaven? By His example, Christ reminds us to give thanks unto God for all the blessings we receive.

Even in this prayer of gratitude we see the continuity of theme that was in all of Christ's prayers—oneness in purpose, unity in action, and solidarity in teamwork—being one with the Father. Only Christ could distinctly reveal the united relationship between Himself and the Father. This distinction was most poignantly demonstrated and manifested by His prayer life.

In the event of the transfiguration, Jesus removed Himself from the three disciples to pray:

> Stepping a little aside from them, the Man of Sorrows pours out His supplications with strong crying and tears. He prays for strength to endure the test in behalf of humanity. He must Himself gain a fresh hold on Omnipotence, for only thus can He contemplate the future. And He pours out His heart longings for His disciples, that in the hour of the power of darkness their faith may not fail…. Now the burden of His prayer is that they may be given a manifestation of the glory He had with the Father before the world was, that His kingdom may be revealed to human eyes, and that His disciples may be strengthened to behold it. He pleads that they may witness a manifestation of His divinity that will comfort them in the hour of His supreme

---

25   John 4:34, 35
26   Luke 10:2
27   Luke 10:17–22

agony with the knowledge that He is of a surety the Son of God and that His shameful death is a part of the plan of redemption.[28]

During His last meal with the disciples but before His severest agonies, we see Jesus praying again—and not for His disciples only but for all of His ambassadors. He prays for unity. We should take special note of this theme's importance to Christ and those who believe upon Him:

The last prayer that Christ offered for his disciples before his trial was that they might be one in him. Satan is determined that this oneness shall not be; for it is the strongest witness that can be borne that God gave his Son to reconcile the world to heaven. But the union for which Christ prayed must exist among God's people before he can bestow on the church the enlargement and power that he longs to bestow on it.

Unity should be recognized as the element of preservation in the church. Those who are united in church capacity have entered into a solemn covenant with God to obey his word, and to unite in an effort to strengthen the faith of one another. They are to be one in him, even though they are scattered the world over. This is God's purpose concerning them, and the heart of the Saviour is set upon his followers fulfilling this purpose. But God can not make them one with Christ and with one another unless they are willing to give up their way for his way.[29]

"When the union exists for which Christ prayed, his followers will be a holy and powerful people."

Christ prayed that his disciples might be one, even as he is one with the Father. Every one who claims to be a child of God should labor for this oneness. When the union exists for which Christ prayed, his followers will be a holy and powerful people. But if they let love die out of their souls, and accept the accusations of Satan's agents against the children of God, they will become servants of sin and allies of the adversary of God and of man. Let them heed the instruction of the apostle and cultivate the love of which he speaks.[30]

The believer in Christ should understand that dissension and division in the church are brought about through the working of the powers of darkness, in order that those who profess to be the children of God may not present the oneness for which

28 White, *The Desire of Ages*, pp. 419–421.
29 White, "The Ministry Is Ordained of God," *The Review and Herald*, May 12, 1903.
30 White, "Be Gentle Unto All Men," *The Review and Herald*, May 14, 1895.

Christ prayed. God's people greatly dishonor his name, and misrepresent his truth, when they manifest a lack of love one for another. As love for God grows cold, they lose the childlike simplicity that knits heart to heart in loving tenderness. Hardheartedness comes in, and there is a drawing away one from another. Many are saying by their actions, "I care not for the prayer of Christ." They feel under no special obligation to love others as Christ has loved them, and Jesus can do little for these souls, for his words and Spirit are not permitted to enter into the heart.[31]

After Jesus ascended to the Father, the disciples finally understood what He had tried to teach them all along. Obeying Christ's command to wait at Jerusalem for the outpouring of the Holy Spirit, they returned "unto Jerusalem from the mount called Olivet, which is from Jerusalem a sabbath day's journey. And when they were come in, they went up into an upper room, where abode both Peter, and James, and John, and Andrew, Philip, and Thomas, Bartholomew, and Matthew, James the son of Alphaeus, and Simon Zelotes, and Judas the brother of James. *These all continued with one accord in prayer and supplication*, with the women, and Mary the mother of Jesus, and with his brethren."[32] And when harmony was threatened by claims of ethnic bias, the apostles gave room for seven deacons—most of whom were Grecian, and one a proselyte—so that unity might be maintained. Here is the reason that Peter gave for this adjustment: "But we will give ourselves continually to prayer, and to the ministry of the word."[33]

As we contemplate what it means to have the faith of Jesus, we should ever keep in mind that Christ is our example.

His life was a life of prayer. Yes, Christ, the Son of God, equal with the Father, Himself all-sufficient, the storehouse of all blessings, He whose voice could rebuke disease, still the tempest, and call the dead to life, prayed with strong crying and many tears. He often spent whole nights in prayer. While the cities were hushed in slumber, angels listened to the pleadings of the Redeemer. See the Saviour bowed in prayer, His soul wrung with anguish. He is not praying for Himself, but for those whom He came to save. In the mountains of Galilee and in the groves of Olivet the Beloved of God prayed for sinners. Then He came forth to minister to them, His tongue touched anew with living fire.[34]

---

31   White, "The Living Testimony," *The Signs of the Times*, February 7, 1895.

32   Acts 1:12–14

33   Acts 6:4

34   White, "Ask, and It Shall Be Given You," *The Signs of the Times*, September 5, 1900.

After teaching throughout the entire day, He frequently devoted the night to prayer. He made His supplications to His Father with strong crying and tears. He prayed, not for Himself, but for those whom He came to redeem.

Few ministers pray all night, as did our Saviour, or devote hours in the day to prayer that they may be able ministers of the gospel and effectual in bringing men to see the beauties of the truth and to be saved through the merits of Christ. Daniel prayed three times a day, but many who make the most exalted profession do not humble their souls before God in prayer even once a day. Jesus, the dear Saviour, has given marked lessons in humility to all, but especially to the gospel minister.[35]

We should constantly think about what Christ prayed for and cried out for: ears to hear His word, eyes to see our duty, strength to perform it thoroughly, and love that unifies in faith. With the global events now taking place, the wars and rumors of wars, the increase in natural and man-made disasters, the fulfilling of the signs of prophecy, and the devaluation of moral values that even worldly minds observe, "is it not time we sought for the unity for which the Saviour prayed? Shall we not open our hearts to the melting love of Jesus? Shall we not let that love take the place of the coldness and hardness that have been too often revealed in the character? May the Lord have compassion upon us; may he forgive our perversity, heal our backslidings, and unite the hearts of all that believe the truth in that oneness for which Christ prayed, that we may be one even as he and the Father are one."[36]

My personal response is, "Yes!" My personal prayer is, "Lord, forgive me my trespasses as I forgive those who have trespassed against me. Heal me of my backslidings. Teach me to love others as Jesus has loved me. And give me the faith of Jesus until I am like Him in character. Unite Your people so we can manifest unity in faith and truth. Amen." Won't you join me?

---

35 White, *Testimonies for the Church*, vol. 4, p. 373.
36 White, "The Living Testimony," *The Signs of the Times*, February 7, 1895.

Chapter 6

By Faith Jesus Overcame Temptation

My mother didn't want me to suffer unnecessarily while in college, so she sat me down for a heart-to-heart discussion before I left home. She told me about the difficulties that would arise if I mixed the demands of family with academics; then she made me promise that I would not get married before I graduated from college. There were moments when I wished I hadn't made that vow. I nearly broke it on a couple of occasions. Once I yielded to temptation and proposed; however, I was turned down, and I found that I was actually relieved by the rejection because the promise remained intact. I didn't experience the challenges of married college life with a wife and small children while obtaining my first degree, but I did have to juggle family and studies when I returned to school to earn another degree after starting my family.

I cannot imagine what it was like for Adam to be tempted. Perhaps a few hours of loneliness followed by a perfect marriage would have made the loss of Eve seem quite unbearable. (I was lonely for more than a few hours before I met and married my Proverbs 31 wife, so I must avoid being too critical of Adam.) But whatever the case may be, as humans we have all yielded to temptation and sinned against God. The sad part is that we all sin because we don't trust the Word of God or implement it in our lives so that we can stand against the devil's attacks.

When we contemplate the life and faith of Jesus, we must review an important point by which Christ's faith—as tried by temptation—may be measured and found infinite. Which condition requires greater faith: a physique untainted by sin or one that has been degenerated by sin? Earlier we discussed the difference between having sinful flesh with a sinless spirit and character and having unfallen flesh with a sinless spirit and character. The ramifications are tremendous as we consider which condition took greater faith in order to redeem sinners and vindicate God's character. Now we must expand our understanding so that we might truly comprehend how Christ—being made sin for us, and being tempted in all points as we are—was victorious over sin and death. In pondering His temptations, where they came from, and how He overcame them, we shall receive a greater outpouring of the faith of Jesus for the purpose of overcoming temptation and sin in our own lives. In so doing, we shall overcome as He overcame.

Scripture does not record the specific temptations Jesus suffered as a child. However, we do have some insights into His developmental years that clearly indicate He was tempted.

The life of Jesus was a life in harmony with God. While He was a child, He thought and spoke as a child; but no trace of sin marred the image of God within Him. Yet He was not exempt from temptation. The inhabitants of Nazareth were proverbial for their wickedness. The low estimate in which they were generally held is shown by Nathanael's question, "Can there any good thing come out of Nazareth?" John 1:46. Jesus was placed where His character would be tested. It was necessary for Him to be constantly on guard in order to preserve His purity. He was subject to all the conflicts which we have to meet, that He might be an example to us in childhood, youth, and manhood.[1]

Young companions urged Him to do as they did. He was bright and cheerful; they enjoyed His presence, and welcomed His ready suggestions; but they were impatient at His scruples, and pronounced Him narrow and strait-laced.[2]

Of the bitterness that falls to the lot of humanity, there was no part which Christ did not taste. There were those who tried to cast contempt upon Him because of His birth, and even in His childhood He had to meet their scornful looks and evil whisperings. If He had responded by an impatient word or look, if He had conceded to His brothers by even one wrong act, He would have failed of being a perfect example. Thus He would have failed of carrying out the plan for our redemption. Had He even admitted that there could be an excuse for sin, Satan would have triumphed, and the world would have been lost. This is why the tempter worked to make His life as trying as possible, that He might be led to sin.[3]

But why would Satan even attempt to overthrow Jesus by temptation if there was truly no way possible for Christ to yield to temptation? "Unless there is a possibility of yielding, temptation is no temptation. Temptation is resisted when man is powerfully influenced to do a wrong action; and, knowing that he can do it, resists, by faith, with a firm hold upon divine power. This was the ordeal through which Christ passed."[4] And so, upon witnessing the baptism and

1   White, *The Desire of Ages*, p. 71.
2   Ibid., p. 89.
3   Ibid., p. 88.
4   White, "Sacrificed for Us," *The Youth's Instructor*, July 20, 1899.

anointing of Jesus—the first by John the Baptist, the second by the Holy Spirit—, and upon hearing the prayer of Christ after coming out of the water, Satan knew that he must do all in his power to overwhelm Christ with deceptive temptations as never before. He experienced an intense hatred for Christ as he considered the evidence before him.

For forty days and nights Christ's greatest adversary watched Him physically weaken from fasting. Would His prayers serve to strengthen Him by faith for the coming battle and more than compensate the loss of physical power? The test commenced with Satan appearing to our Lord as an angel of light.[5]

> *"He was subject to all the conflicts which we have to meet, that He might be an example to us in childhood, youth, and manhood."*

The outcome of the contest would be determined by the preparation for it. Christ had been prepared since childhood to be a disciple of His heavenly Father in the company of angels. The memorization of Scripture, the time spent in prayer, and the illustrations of God's grace and salvation found in nature and the sacrifices of the temple had prepared Him to withstand Satan's temptations. The token of God's love exhibited at His baptism upon the utterance of His prayer of dedication further supported Jesus as He continued to fast and pray. So when Satan confronted Jesus concerning His identity, and tempted Him to prove Himself to be the Son of God by turning stones into bread, Jesus did not parley with Satan. He did not entertain the temptation. "He repulsed Satan with the same scripture He had given Moses to repeat to rebellious Israel when their diet was restricted and they were clamoring for flesh meats in the wilderness, 'Man shall not live by bread alone, but by every word that proceedeth out of the mouth of God.' In this declaration, and also by His example, Christ would show man that hunger for temporal food was not the greatest calamity that could befall him."[6]

In the first temptation, Satan tried to take advantage of Christ's physical weakness and appearance by insinuating doubt that the Father could not love such a Being whose visage was marred beyond that of men.[7] Since God apparently could not love such an emaciated specimen so much as to provide food for Jesus, the temptation to exert personal power for selfish benefit—in order to remove Himself from suffering—was very great. But Jesus continued exercising self-control, and by faith He won the victory.

Failing in the first temptation, Satan tried to awe Christ by his power and take advantage of Jesus' trust in God to preserve Him. "In order to awe Christ with his superior strength he carried Him to Jerusalem and set Him on a pinnacle of the Temple, and continued to beset Him with temptations. He again demanded of Christ that, if He was indeed the Son of God, to give

---

5   White, *Confrontation*, pp. 29, 32, 38. See also 2 Corinthians 11:14..
6   Ibid., p. 43.
7   Isaiah 52:14

him evidence by casting Himself from the dizzy height upon which he had placed Him. He urged Christ to show His confidence in the preserving care of His Father by casting Himself down from the Temple."[8] And to give weight to his demand, Satan quoted from Scripture, only with deceptive editing, for "he omitted the words, 'to keep Thee in all Thy ways;' that is, in all the ways of God's choosing."[9]

Jesus did not need further demonstration of protection than that given by the experience of being carried by Satan to the temple heights. God allowed Satan this much control over His Son's person, but He protected Christ from Satan's hatred by preventing Satan from casting Christ down. So again, Jesus overcame temptation by relying upon Scripture as His undeniable weapon of defense and upon past exhibitions of God's favor as proof of love and protection.

Here we see the importance of memorizing Scripture so that we might overcome similar temptations. The Bible is its own expositor. Word associations lend to word studies that reveal to us what God would have us know and understand regarding our relationship and duty to Him. King David wrote, "I will meditate in they precepts, and have respect unto thy ways."[10] If we meditate on God's Word, it will "keep thee in all thy ways."[11] However, modern translations have changed the words to infer a different meaning about the power of God's Word. Psalm 91:11 is translated as such: "to keep you wherever you go" or "to protect you wherever you go."[12] Such renderings lead the mind away

> *Word associations lend to word studies that reveal to us what God would have us know and understand regarding our relationship and duty to Him.*

from the association drawn with Psalm 119:15, thereby diminishing the power God intends His Word to exert. We are instead led to presume that God will always protect us in the way of our own choosing. The inference is a submission of God's will to ours, instead of the proper relationship where we yield our will to God. So we see that the faith of Jesus had infinite strength because He rested upon Scripture, the memorization of which prepared Him for the great conflict.

We must learn a great lesson about the difference between faith and presumption.

> Faith is in no sense allied to presumption. Only he who has true faith is secure against presumption. For presumption is Satan's counterfeit of faith. Faith claims God's promises, and brings forth fruit in obedience. Presumption also claims the promises, but uses them as Satan did, to excuse transgression. Faith would have led

---

8   White, *Confrontation*, pp. 47, 48.
9   White, *The Desire of Ages*, p. 125.
10   Psalm 119:15
11   Psalm 91:11
12   Bible in Basic English; Contemporary English Version

our first parents to trust the love of God, and to obey His commands. Presumption led them to transgress His law, believing that His great love would save them from the consequence of their sin. It is not faith that claims the favor of Heaven without complying with the conditions on which mercy is to be granted. Genuine faith has its foundation in the promises and provisions of the Scriptures.[13]

Presumption promotes a type of sanctification by "will-worship" and leads to defeat. Faith promotes simple trust in God's Word, which results in yielding our wills to God—therein is the enduring victory.

Unable to tempt Christ any further while maintaining his disguise Satan then reveals his true identity—his true character. Once again he exerts a physical control over Christ's person by carrying Him to a high mountain. He presents to Jesus all the glories of the kingdoms of this earth—all traces of evil concealed—so that Jesus might be led to believe He would be gaining everything by simply bowing down and worshiping His foe. But "Christ's mission could be fulfilled only through suffering. Before Him was a life of sorrow, hardship, and conflict, and an ignominious death. He must bear the sins of the whole world. He must endure separation from His Father's love."[14] While Christ must be separated from His Father's love—a love maintaining conditions whereby such a separation may occur—that state of separation was not to exist because of Christ's personal participation in sin. Daniel, under the inspiration of the Holy Spirit foretold, "Messiah [shall] be cut off, but not for himself."[15]

> *The right worship of God cannot be separated from the right obedience to God's law.*

To worship Satan would have resulted in Satan gaining the victory. When the devil said, "All these things will I give thee, if thou wilt fall down and worship me,"[16] it served his purpose to pretend it was the whole truth. In truth, "Satan's dominion was that wrested from Adam, but Adam was the vicegerent of the Creator. His was not an independent rule. The earth is God's, and He has committed all things to His Son. Adam was to reign subject to Christ. When Adam betrayed his sovereignty into Satan's hands, Christ still remained the rightful King.... Satan can exercise his usurped authority only as God permits."[17] For God is "a great King over all the earth."[18]

The right worship of God cannot be separated from the right obedience to God's law. If Christ had bowed down and worshiped Satan, He would have been worshiping the creature

---

13   White, *The Desire of Ages*, p. 126.
14   Ibid., p. 129.
15   Daniel 9:26
16   Matthew 4:9
17   White, *The Desire of Ages*, pp. 129, 130.
18   Psalm 47:2.

rather than the Creator, thereby giving sanction to a whole system of idolatry established and practiced by the wicked. The Scripture plainly states, "They that forsake the law praise the wicked: but such as keep the law contend with them."[19] Jesus clearly understood the ramifications of yielding to this temptation, and without any hesitation He summoned His remaining strength to order Satan from His presence, "Get thee hence, Satan: for it is written, Thou shalt worship the Lord thy God, and him only shalt thou serve."[20]

For all the vaunted exhibition of strength Satan displayed by twice carrying Christ's person to where he wanted to go, he was powerless to disobey Christ's expressed command uttered by faith in the Word of God.

> Satan had questioned whether Jesus was the Son of God. In his summary dismissal he had proof that he could not gainsay. Divinity flashed through suffering humanity. Satan had no power to resist the command. Writhing with humiliation and rage, he was forced to withdraw from the presence of the world's Redeemer. Christ's victory was as complete as had been the failure of Adam.
>
> So we may resist temptation, and force Satan to depart from us. Jesus gained the victory through submission and faith in God, and by the apostle He says to us, "Submit yourselves therefore to God. Resist the devil, and he will flee from you. Draw nigh to God, and He will draw nigh to you." James 4:7, 8. We cannot save ourselves from the tempter's power; he has conquered humanity, and when we try to stand in our own strength, we shall become a prey to his devices; but "the name of the Lord is a strong tower: the righteous runneth into it, and is safe." Proverbs 18:10. Satan trembles and flees before the weakest soul who finds refuge in that mighty name."[21]

If we have the faith of Jesus, victory is assured!

This record of Christ's temptations in the wilderness is intended to teach us special lessons regarding our spiritual weaknesses. "The enticements which Christ resisted were those that we find it so difficult to withstand. They were urged upon Him in as much greater degree as His character is superior to ours. With the terrible weight of the sins of the world upon Him, Christ withstood the test upon appetite, upon the love of the world, and upon that love of display which leads to presumption. These were the temptations that overcame Adam and Eve, and that so readily overcome us."[22]

---

19   Proverbs 28:4
20   Matthew 4:10
21   White, *The Desire of Ages*, pp. 130, 131.
22   Ibid., pp. 116, 117, emphasis added.

We are tempted by Satan, and by our lustful desires, by taking to extremes our various appetites: "For all that is in the world, the lust of the flesh, and the lust of the eyes, and the pride of life."[23] In this way, the good and bountiful blessings of God are perverted, revealing that the source of resulting evil "is not of the Father, but is of the world."[24] The baneful results are seen in civil unrest, riots, conflicts, and wars. Instead of blaming God for the existence of these things, we need to begin confessing the truth about the strivings of men. "From whence come wars and fightings among you? come they not hence, even of your lusts that war in your members? Ye lust, and have not: ye kill, and desire to have, and cannot obtain: ye fight and war, yet ye have not, because ye ask not. Ye ask, and receive not, because ye ask amiss, that ye may consume it upon your lusts."[25] When we acknowledge our true condition, then we can seek, with single-mindedness, the power of God to overcome temptation through the faith of Jesus, which He will bestow upon us.

There is another class of temptations that seem to burst upon us at those times when we desire only purity of heart and soul. Of these occasions James counseled, "My brethren, count it all joy when ye fall into divers temptations; Knowing this, that the trying of your faith worketh patience. But let patience have her perfect work, that ye may be perfect and entire, wanting nothing. If any of you lack wisdom, let him ask of God, that giveth to all men liberally, and upbraideth not; and it shall be given him. But let him ask in faith, nothing wavering. For he that wavereth is like a wave of the sea driven with the wind and tossed. For let not that man think that he shall receive any thing of the Lord."[26]

Paul had this to say about temptations: "There hath no temptation taken you but such as is common to man: but God is faithful, who will not suffer you to be tempted above that ye are able; but will with the temptation also make a way to escape, that ye may be able to bear it."[27] When we can praise God for trying our faith by the temptations He allows for the purpose of testing and purifying our faith, then our eyes will be opened, and we will see the way of escape.

Christians are often surprised by the increase of temptations after they have accepted Jesus as their Savior. They think that God, who does not tempt,[28] would prevent all temptation since Jesus overcame temptation on our behalf. To the contrary, God allows temptations to come our way so that we will recognize our weakness and ask for wisdom.

> Temptation will come upon all the children of God…. The Word does not say that we are to count it all joy when we fall under temptation, but when we fall into temptation. It is not necessary to fall under temptation, for temptation comes upon us

---

23 1 John 2:16
24 Ibid.
25 James 4:1–3
26 James 1:2–7
27 1 Corinthians 10:13
28 James 1:13–15

for the trying of our faith. And the trying of our faith worketh patience, not fretfulness and murmuring. If we put our trust in Jesus, he will keep us at all times, and will be our strength and shield. We are to learn valuable lessons from our trials. Paul says: "We glory in tribulations also: knowing that tribulation worketh patience; and patience, experience; and experience, hope: and hope maketh not ashamed; because the love of God is shed abroad in our hearts by the Holy Ghost which is given unto us."…

Take courage, tempted soul, for the Lord knoweth them that are his…. Keep talking faith, and the victory is yours; for 'this is the victory that overcometh the world, even our faith.' Jesus has said we should not walk in darkness, but should have the light of life, and we believe it. We are to keep talking of the light, to keep praying and believing, and the light will break upon us when our faith has been tried and patience has had its perfect work.[29]

Every temptation is one of the Lord's means of establishing his people in the faith. They will obtain an experience if they will seek unto the Lord; or through the wiles of Satan, they may yield their faith. But if they will refuse to make any move until they seek counsel of God, if they will open the word to understand what is written therein, they will see where they are standing, and what is their peril. The disciples who forsook Jesus had entertained contention and unbelief. Unbelief had grown into a habit; and now had become a more distinct and startling opportunity to demonstrate that they were offended. The strife of the Jews over Christ's words, meeting them with questioning and doubt, gathered about the souls of these disciples the dark clouds of unbelief. Their faith had not been genuine, and the test revealed their weakness and unreliable position. These lessons were designed to give to all a knowledge of self, to show them the true position they sustained toward Christ. Temptation, working in darkness, was causing the weak and tempted ones to lose faith in Christ, because they could not understand the spiritual meaning of his words.[30]

A genuine faith will recognize and acknowledge the truth regarding our need for a righteousness we are powerless to attain by our own strength alone. We have fallen under the power of the law of sin by yielding to Satan's temptations and the temptations of our own lusts. In the effort of obtaining genuine faith, as a free gift, we accept Christ's righteousness in exchange for our unrighteousness. Christ established righteousness by the exercise of His faith while enduring

29 White, "Resisting Temptation," *The Review and Herald*, February 20, 1913.
30 White, "The Vine and the Branches—3," *The Review and Herald*, November 16, 1897.

temptation. Now He offers righteousness by imputing and imparting it to us if we will only take hold of His faith and overcome as He overcame.

> The thought that the righteousness of Christ is imputed to us, not because of any merit on our part, but as a free gift from God, is a precious thought. The enemy of God and man is not willing that this truth should be clearly presented; for he knows that if the people receive it fully, his power will be broken. If he can control minds, so that doubt and unbelief and darkness shall compose the experience of those who claim to be the children of God, he can overcome them with temptation. The simple faith that takes God at his word should be encouraged. God's people must have that faith which will lay hold of divine power; "for by grace are ye saved through faith; and that not of yourselves: it is the gift of God." Those who believe that God for Christ's sake has forgiven their sins should not, through temptation, fail to press on to fight the good fight of faith. Their faith should grow stronger until their Christian life, as well as their words, shall declare, "The blood of Jesus Christ his Son cleanseth us from all sin."
>
> Faith is trusting God,—believing that he loves us, and knows best what is for our good. Thus instead of our own way, it leads us to choose his way. In place of our ignorance, it accepts his wisdom; in place of our weakness, his strength; in place of our sinfulness, his righteousness. Our lives, ourselves, are already his; faith acknowledges his ownership and accepts its blessing. Truth, uprightness, purity, have been pointed out as secrets of life's success. It is faith that puts us in possession of these principles. Every good impulse or aspiration is the gift of God; faith receives from God the life that alone can produce true growth and efficiency.[31]

So, consider your ways. Take the time to ponder and weigh your choices and actions, and determine by close evaluation what advantage is gained if you yield to temptation—to do one's pleasure contrary to what pleases God. Until Christ abides in the heart by faith, you will have no strength to meet and overcome temptation. Christ prayed that we might be sanctified by the truth, and in that prayer He identified the truth as God's Word. With God's Word hidden in our hearts, we will realize its correcting influence upon the life. Our minds will be strengthened and invigorated to think God's thoughts, and our imagination will be sanctified to dwell upon God's desires and His will for our lives. We will not be found tarnishing "the truth by indulging in habits and practises that are inconsistent with its holy character, but hold it as a treasure of highest value."[32] Only when He dwells in the heart can we attempt to make Him our daily pattern, memorizing Scripture, praying righteous prayers, trusting our heavenly Father, and living His

---

31   White, "Grace and Faith the Gifts of God," *The Review and Herald*, December 24, 1908, emphasis added.
32   White, "The Character That God Approves," *The Youth's Instructor*, August 3, 1899. See also John 17:17.

virtues by selfless obedience. Then our characters will be transformed into His. We will become like Him.

Please understand the importance of this process of evaluating your condition. Many think they have faith. But do they truly have the faith of Jesus? Compare your experience with that of Moses, whom God used to deliver Israel from bondage in Egypt and whom God used to point forward to the work of Christ in delivering His children from the bondage of sin.

> Much of the faith which we see is merely nominal; the real, trusting, persevering faith is rare. Moses realized in his own experience the promise that God will be a rewarder of those who diligently seek Him. He had respect unto the recompense of the reward. Here is another point in regard to faith which we wish to study: God will reward the man of faith and obedience. If this faith is brought into the life experience, it will enable everyone who fears and loves God to endure trials. Moses was full of confidence in God because he had appropriating faith. He needed help, and he prayed for it, grasped it by faith, and wove into his experience the belief that God cared for him. He believed that God ruled his life in particular. He saw and acknowledged God in every detail of his life and felt that he was under the eye of the All-seeing One, who weighs motives, who tries the heart. He looked to God and trusted in Him for strength to carry him uncorrupted through every form of temptation. He knew that a special work had been assigned to him, and he desired as far as possible to make that work thoroughly successful. But he knew that he could not do this without divine aid, for he had a perverse people to deal with. The presence of God was sufficient to carry him through the most trying situations in which a man could be placed.
>
> Moses did not merely think of God; he saw Him. God was the constant vision before him; he never lost sight of His face. He saw Jesus as his Saviour, and he believed that the Saviour's merits would be imputed to him. This faith was to Moses no guesswork; it was a reality. This is the kind of faith we need, faith that will endure the test. Oh, how often we yield to temptation because we do not keep our eye upon Jesus! Our faith is not continuous because, through self-indulgence, we sin, and then we cannot endure "as seeing Him who is invisible."[33]

Again, we must ascertain the truth about the condition of our faith, because "the faith in Christ which saves the soul is not what it is represented to be by many. 'Believe, believe,' is their cry; 'only believe in Christ, and you will be saved. It is all you have to do.' While true faith trusts wholly in Christ for salvation, it will lead to perfect conformity to the law of God. Faith is

---

33   White, *Testimonies for the Church*, vol. 5, pp. 651, 652.

manifested by works. And the apostle John declares, 'He that saith, I know him, and keepeth not his commandments, is a liar, and the truth is not in him.' "[34]

As we conclude this chapter, I want to draw your attention to Scripture regarding what took place after the third temptation Jesus experienced in the wilderness. "And when the devil had ended all the temptation, he departed from him for a season."[35] Satan had to leave Jesus when commanded, but that didn't mean he stayed away. He devised means to make Christ's work as difficult as he could. He strategized and implemented further temptations by which to ensnare Jesus by the misconceived theology of the day, the misunderstanding of family, neighbors, disciples (Judas and Peter come foremost to mind), the religious leaders, and common folk that made up the multitudes following after Jesus. Satan was only gone for a "season."

Jesus faced temptation after feeding the five thousand from a few small loaves and fishes when the multitude determined to crown Him king. Jesus faced temptation when He said that He must go to Jerusalem to be crucified and raised to life on the third day and Peter objected, "Be it far from thee, Lord: this shall not be unto thee."[36] Jesus faced temptation while praying in the Garden of Gethsemane in the midst of His intense suffering. He faced temptation while hanging on the cross, hearing the snide jeering of an ungrateful nation saying, "He saved others; let him save himself, if he be Christ, the chosen of God."[37] But in every instance, He overcame by faith. He offers this faith to us. What will we do with it?

The time of the end is upon us, and we must obtain the assurance that we have the faith of Jesus. Without this assurance, we will succumb to temptation. Then we will discover our wretchedness—that while claiming to be clothed with righteousness we have neither kept God's commandments nor have the faith of Jesus. Because of the nearness of the time, we must recognize that a special temptation is upon us:

> But the day is coming, and it is close upon us, when every phase of character will be revealed by special temptation. Those who remain true to principle, who exercise faith to the end, will be those who have proved true under test and trial during the previous hours of their probation, and have formed characters after the likeness of Christ. It will be those who have cultivated close acquaintance with Christ, who, through his wisdom and grace, are partakers of the divine nature. But no human being can give to another, heart-devotion and noble qualities of mind, and supply his deficiencies with moral power. We can each do much for each other by giving to men a Christlike example, thus influencing them to go to Christ for the righteousness without which they cannot stand in the judgment. Men should prayerfully

---

34 White, "The Conference in Sweden," *The Review and Herald*, October 5, 1886.
35 Luke 4:13
36 Matthew 16:22
37 Luke 23:35

consider the important matter of character-building, and frame their characters after the divine model.[38]

My prayer is that God, who is able to keep us from falling through faith in His sanctifying Word, will preserve us in our time of temptation—our time of need—by the faith of Jesus demonstrated in our lives. Won't you lift up your heart by uniting with me in this prayer—in this determined purpose to obtain the gold purified by fire? We may always have the assurance that God will hear and answer such a prayer!

---

38   White, "Wise or Foolish, Which?" *The Youth's Instructor*, January 16, 1896.

Chapter 7

By Faith Jesus Preached the Kingdom of God

Timing is everything. Even someone who hasn't bulked up their muscles with steroids can hit more than seven hundred home runs in a baseball career so long as one can see the ball, discern the pitch, connect with the sweet spot of the bat, and hit with precision that prevents a foul. Tiger Woods' success as a golfer is directly related to the timing of his swing—especially at times allowing for the amount of force necessary to sink difficult putts.

I recall, with chagrin, a band concert in Carson City, Nevada. I played euphonium for the Rio Linda Adventist Academy Wind Ensemble. We were performing Handel's "Hallelujah Chorus," and I glanced away from Mr. Lang, our director, right when he motioned with the baton to cut us off. Yours truly kept holding the note all by his lonesome—an unwanted solo. It would have been an otherwise perfect performance but for that one glaring mistake produced by inattentiveness to timing.

One of General Douglas MacArthur's greatest successes demanded perfect timing to achieve the element of surprise that resulted in overwhelming victory. Operation Chromite detailed the invasion plan of the Battle of Inchon. It noted every geographic handicap, manmade and natural, that greatly increased the risk of failure: the highest and lowest tides in the world, the small harbor for anchorage of a large invading fleet, the swiftness of the currents in the channels, the mudflats, the high seawalls, and enemy fortifications. The exploration for a suitable place to practice in these conditions concluded with the discovery of a similar site for the purpose of training the troops involved. These rehearsals helped refine the performance and precision of the landing craft, as well as the battle equipment. The successful amphibious invasion at Inchon is attributed to proper planning, diligent preparation, and the precise timing of maneuvers.

Satan viewed the first advent of Christ as an invasion. He boasted that Jesus would no better resist his temptations than others of Adam's race. "But when the fulness of the time was come,

God sent forth his Son, made of a woman, made under the law."[1] Christ was born as a human and was victorious over temptation as a child. When the time was right—in order to fulfill prophecy—Christ was baptized by John, and anointed by the Holy Spirit.

> Upon coming up out of the water, Jesus bowed in prayer on the river bank. A new and important era was opening before Him. He was now, upon a wider stage, entering on the conflict of His life. Though He was the Prince of Peace, His coming must be as the unsheathing of a sword. The kingdom He had come to establish was the opposite of that which the Jews desired. He who was the foundation of the ritual and economy of Israel would be looked upon as its enemy and destroyer. He who had proclaimed the law upon Sinai would be condemned as a transgressor. He who had come to break the power of Satan would be denounced as Beelzebub. No one upon earth had understood Him, and during His ministry He must still walk alone. Throughout His life His mother and His brothers did not comprehend His mission. Even His disciples did not understand Him. He had dwelt in eternal light, as one with God, but His life on earth must be spent in solitude.[2]

Led into the wilderness by the Holy Spirit, Jesus fasted and prayed for forty days and was tempted by Satan. Just as Adam was tempted by appetite in the Garden of Eden, Jesus was tempted by appetite in the wilderness. Where Adam failed, Jesus succeeded. Just as King Saul was tempted by presumption and rashness, Jesus was likewise tempted. Where King Saul failed, Jesus overcame. Just as the children of Israel were tempted into false worship at Mount Sinai during the forty days Moses was in the mount with God, so Jesus was tempted to false worship at the conclusion of His forty days of communion with God. But where they failed, Jesus succeeded.

With the victory so wondrously won, Jesus was revived by the ministration of holy angels, and shortly afterward returned to the Jordan River where John continued to preach and baptize. Upon seeing Jesus, John proclaimed, "Behold the Lamb of God, which taketh away the sin of the world."[3] The next day, two of John's disciples heard him pronounce again, "Behold the Lamb of God!" and they followed Jesus to learn more about Him.[4] After they heard Him preach, they shared what they had heard with their families and friends and brought together a small band of believers. Here "the first works of the church were seen when the believers sought out friends, relatives, and acquaintances, and with hearts overflowing with love, told the story of what Jesus was to them."[5] With this small gathering of disciples, Jesus began—by faith—to preach about the kingdom of God. Scripture says, "And Jesus returned in the power of the Spirit into Galilee:

---

1   Galatians 4:4
2   White, *The Desire of Ages*, p. 111.
3   John 1:29
4   John 1:35–37
5   White, "Return to the First Love," *Special Testimony to Our Ministers*, p. 17.

and there went out a fame of him through all the region round about. And he taught in their synagogues, being glorified of all."[6]

"Christ never flattered men. He never spoke that which would exalt their fancies and imaginations, nor did He praise them for their clever inventions; but deep, unprejudiced thinkers received His teaching, and found that it tested their wisdom. They marveled at the spiritual truth expressed in the simplest language. The most highly educated were charmed with His words, and the uneducated were always profited. He had a message for the illiterate; and He made even the heathen to understand that He had a message for them."[7]

A study of His burden, His methods, and His success will help us as we enter into the cycle of His discipline of preaching the gospel—by His faith. We can assuredly expect to achieve the same results if we will only obey the Gospel Commission according to Christ's example, for He promised that we would do greater works than those He demonstrated.[8] Furthermore, if we study the burden, methods, and successes of Christ's true disciples, we can glean additional insights for our successful proclamation of the three angels' messages, which is the "everlasting gospel."[9]

While Christ preached the kingdom of God is at hand, His "most favorite theme was the paternal character and abundant love of God."[10] We should ever remember that we could not be saved unless God, in His love for us, was willing to give us His Son as our atoning sacrifice. This gift is without estimation of value because the Father and the Son had never before been separated until Jesus hung on the cross for us, accepting the wrath of God on our behalf because of our sins! Throughout His earthly ministry:

> The burden of Christ's preaching was, "The time is fulfilled, and the kingdom of God is at hand; repent ye, and believe the gospel." *Thus the gospel message, as given by the Saviour Himself, was based on the prophecies*. The "time" which He declared to be fulfilled was the period made known by the angel Gabriel to Daniel. "Seventy weeks," said the angel, "are determined upon thy people and upon thy holy city, to finish the transgression, and to make an end of sins, and to make reconciliation for iniquity, and to bring in everlasting righteousness, and to seal up the vision and prophecy, and to anoint the most holy." Daniel 9:24. A day in prophecy stands for a year. See Numbers 14:34; Ezekiel 4:6. The seventy weeks, or four hundred and ninety days, represent four hundred and ninety years. A starting point for this period is given: "Know therefore and understand, that from the going forth of the commandment to restore and to build Jerusalem unto the Messiah the Prince shall be

6   Luke 4:14, 15
7   White, *The Desire of Ages*, p. 254.
8   John 14:12
9   Revelation 14:6
10 White, *Testimonies to Ministers and Gospel Workers*, p. 192.

seven weeks, and threescore and two weeks," sixty-nine weeks, or four hundred and eighty-three years. Daniel 9:25. The commandment to restore and build Jerusalem, as completed by the decree of Artaxerxes Longimanus (see Ezra 6:14; 7:1, 9, margin), went into effect in the autumn of B. C. 457. From this time four hundred and eighty-three years extend to the autumn of A. D. 27. According to the prophecy, this period was to reach to the Messiah, the Anointed One. In A. D. 27, Jesus at His baptism received the anointing of the Holy Spirit, and soon afterward began His ministry. Then the message was proclaimed. "The time is fulfilled."

Then, said the angel, "He shall confirm the covenant with many for one week [seven years]." For seven years after the Saviour entered on His ministry, the gospel was to be preached especially to the Jews; for three and a half years by Christ Himself; and afterward by the apostles. "In the midst of the week He shall cause the sacrifice and the oblation to cease." Daniel 9:27. In the spring of A. D. 31, Christ the true sacrifice was offered on Calvary. Then the veil of the temple was rent in twain, showing that the sacredness and significance of the sacrificial service had departed. The time had come for the earthly sacrifice and oblation to cease.

The one week—seven years—ended in A. D. 34. Then by the stoning of Stephen the Jews finally sealed their rejection of the gospel; the disciples who were scattered abroad by persecution "went everywhere preaching the word" (Acts 8:4); and shortly after, Saul the persecutor was converted, and became Paul, the apostle to the Gentiles.

The time of Christ's coming, His anointing by the Holy Spirit, His death, and the giving of the gospel to the Gentiles, were definitely pointed out. It was the privilege of the Jewish people to understand these prophecies, and to recognize their fulfillment in the mission of Jesus. Christ urged upon His disciples the importance of prophetic study. Referring to the prophecy given to Daniel in regard to their time, He said, "Whoso readeth, let him understand." Matthew 24:15. After His resurrection He explained to the disciples in "all the prophets" "the things concerning Himself." Luke 24:27. The Saviour had spoken through all the prophets. "The Spirit of Christ which was in them" "testified beforehand the sufferings of Christ, and the glory that should follow." 1 Peter 1:11.[11]

When Paul taught, his burden was to "preach Christ crucified, unto the Jews a stumblingblock, and unto the Greeks foolishness ... For I determined not to know anything among you, save Jesus Christ, and him crucified."[12]

When Luther preached, his burden was similar:

11   White, *The Desire of Ages*, pp. 233, 234.

12   1 Corinthians 1:23; 2:2

"Learn to know Christ and him crucified. Learn to despair of your own work and cry unto him, Lord Jesus thou art my righteousness and I am thy sin. Thou hast taken on thee what was mine, and given to me what was thine. What thou wast not, thou becamest, that I might become what I was not."

Thus fearlessly and firmly Luther presented those great truths which the apostles of Christ had proclaimed with such power. The voice of Paul, sounding down through the centuries, spoke through Luther, exposing superstitions, refuting error, and uprooting heresy.[13]

So we see Jesus' burden was the fulfillment of prophecy. Paul's and Luther's burden was the fulfillment of prophecy—Christ's faith and righteousness and Him crucified. When we go forth to preach the gospel, this should also be our burden as we diligently seek out souls for the kingdom. We must not only evangelize, we must evange-live. This means we must have the faith of Jesus, keep the commandments of God, and follow the methods of Christ in preaching the gospel.

In 2009 my home church enjoyed Jon Sweigart's eye-opening message titled "Jesus' IDEA for Evangelism."[14] As the ministerial director for the Kansas-Nebraska Conference, he had come to train us in a lay-driven evangelistic campaign using Share Him materials and other available resources. In sharing this concept of Jesus' IDEA for evangelism, we learned how Christ cultivated hearts and minds in preparation for the kingdom of God:

- **I** is for *instruction* about God's character, His purposes, His domain, and His power.
- **D** is for *demonstration* of God's power to overrule and overcome Satan's work in nature, in people's minds, and in human hearts. (We will dwell more on this topic in the next chapter.)
- **E** is for the *experience* of which God invites us to partake as we evange-live and evangelize.
- **A** is for the necessary *analysis* process of reviewing the instruction, demonstration, and experience we have just witnessed. What was accomplished? What went right? What went wrong? How can we do better next time? During this period of evangelism, we evaluate the *results*, *rejoice* in the success achieved, and obtain grace to go out and *repeat* the cycle of evange-living and evangelism. (I like to refer to these as the three "R's" of evangelism.)

Let's examine this model for winning souls to God's kingdom as it is revealed to us through Scripture and the writings of Ellen White. But be forewarned: "The curse of every church today is that men do not adopt Christ's methods. They think they can improve on the rules given in the gospel, and so are free to define them, hoping thus to reform the churches and the workmen. Let

---

13   White, "Luther at Wittenberg." *The Signs of the Times*, June 7, 1883.
14   Sweigart, "Jesus' IDEA for Evangelism," Sermon, February 21, 2009.

God be our one Master, our one Lord, full of goodness, compassion, and love."[15] Upon learning Christ's methods, we should be careful not to depart from them or else we will become unfit teachers, and be judged as reprobates, which would be a curse instead of a blessing.[16]

In Luke's record of Christ's ministry, we see that Jesus did not ignore His family and neighbors. He labored first for them as a child and youth. And early in His ministry, He returned to Nazareth for a visit.

> And, as his custom was, he went into the synagogue on the sabbath day, and stood up for to read. And there was delivered unto him the book of the prophet Esaias. And when he had opened the book, he found the place where it was written, The Spirit of the Lord is upon me, because he hath anointed me to preach the gospel to the poor; he hath sent me to heal the brokenhearted, to preach deliverance to the captives, and recovering of sight to the blind, to set at liberty them that are bruised, To preach the acceptable year of the Lord. And he closed the book, and he gave it again to the minister, and sat down. And the eyes of all them that were in the synagogue were fastened on him. And he began to say unto them, This day is this scripture fulfilled in your ears.[17]

We shouldn't be amazed at the idea that Christ invited the people of Nazareth to recognize His mission and join Him in His methods for reaching the lost. The Spirit of the Lord should be upon all who by faith cooperate with Christ in seeking and saving the lost. But the folk of Nazareth realized that in order to join with Christ they must first recognize their own need of a Savior! The idea that they were spiritually poor, captives, blind, bruised, lame, deaf, and leprous was more than their cultivated pride of position—children of Abraham—could tolerate. They rejected the faith of Jesus. They rejected Him as their only hope of salvation. Had not the angels of God interposed and protected Jesus, the people of Nazareth would have thrown Him from the cliff! Even though they rejected Him, Jesus called them to repentance before His death. "Toward the close of His ministry in Galilee, He again visited the home of His childhood."[18] After the fame of His success was echoed

We shouldn't be amazed at the idea that Christ invited the people of Nazareth to recognize His mission and join Him in His methods for reaching the lost.

---

15   White, *Testimonies to Ministers and Gospel Workers*, pp. 192, 193.
16   2 Corinthians 13:5, 6; 2 Timothy 3:8; Titus 1:16
17   Luke 4:16–21
18   White, *The Desire of Ages*, p. 241.

throughout the country, He once again invited them to partner with Him in His work, yet they continued in their rejection of Him.

So, if we are to follow the methods of Jesus, we should first minister to those close at hand. There is a spiritual application, in addition to the temporal one, mentioned by Paul to Timothy, "But if any provide not for his own, and specially for those of his own house, he hath denied the faith, and is worse than an infidel."[19] Many people talk about the need for missionaries to serve in distant fields, but we often neglect the mission work at home. "There are thousands in America perishing in ignorance and sin. And looking afar off to some distant field, those who know the truth are indifferently passing by the needy fields close to them. Christ says, 'Go work today in my vineyard.' 'Say not ye, There are yet four months, and then cometh harvest? behold, I say unto you, Lift up your eyes, and look on the fields; for they are white already to harvest.' Matthew 21:28; John 4:35."[20]

Jesus was being consistent in His methodology when He commanded His disciples to wait at Jerusalem for the outpouring of the Holy Spirit. Upon receiving the Comforter, they were to bear witness "in Jerusalem, and in all Judaea, and in Samaria, and unto the uttermost part of the earth."[21] The best way to cover the whole earth with the gospel is to spread it, not splatter it.

When rejected by Nazareth, Jesus moved to Capernaum. Making this the center of His ministry, it became known as "his own city."[22] Here Jesus taught the disciples how to do missionary work. But He did not stay in one place. After performing many miracles in Capernaum and preaching there, Jesus made plans to travel to another city, but the people begged Him to stay. He responded, "I must preach the kingdom of God to other cities also: for therefore am I sent. And he preached in the synagogues of Galilee."[23]

Jesus set the example for us to follow. "This was the way the Christian Church was established. Christ first selected a few persons, and bade them follow him. They then went in search of their relatives and acquaintances, and brought them to Christ. This is the way we are to labor. A few souls brought out and fully established on the truth, will, like the first disciples, be laborers for others."[24] "It is not preaching that is the most important; it is house-to-house work, reasoning from the Word, explaining the Word. It is those workers who follow the methods that Christ followed who will win souls for their hire."[25]

Why is house-to-house work of such value?

---

19 1 Timothy 5:8
20 White, "The Foreigners in America," *The Review and Herald*, October 29, 1914.
21 Acts 1:8
22 Matthew 9:1
23 Luke 4:43, 44
24 White, "To Our Missionary Workers," *The Review and Herald*, December 8, 1885.
25 White, *Gospel Workers*, p. 468.

Of equal importance with public effort is house-to-house work in the homes of the people….

Again, as the result of the presentation of truth in large congregations, a spirit of inquiry is awakened, and it is especially important that this interest be followed by personal labor. Those who desire to investigate the truth need to be taught to study diligently the word of God. Some one must help them to build on a sure foundation. At this critical time in their religious experience, how important it is that wisely directed Bible-workers come to their help, and open to their understanding the treasure-house of God's Word![26]

The personal labor extended to seekers of truth who have doubts and questions is more forcibly effective, having greater impact on the mind of the hearer because of the individual attention less apparent in public efforts.

While waiting in Jerusalem as commanded by Jesus, the disciples continued to labor after Christ's methods, "continuing daily with one accord in the temple, and breaking bread from house to house, did eat their meat with gladness and singleness of heart … and daily in the temple, and in every house, they ceased not to teach and preach Jesus Christ."[27] Paul labored the same way, reminding the elders of Ephesus when journeying to Jerusalem,

Ye know, from the first day that I came into Asia, after what manner I have been with you at all seasons, Serving the Lord with all humility of mind, and with many tears, and temptations, which befell me by the lying in wait of the Jews: And how I kept back nothing that was profitable unto you, but have shewed you, and have taught you publicly, and from house to house, Testifying both to the Jews, and also to the Greeks, repentance toward God, and faith toward our Lord Jesus Christ.[28]

"These words explain the secret of Paul's power and success. He kept back nothing that was profitable for the people. He preached Christ publicly, in the market-places and the synagogues. He taught from house to house, availing himself of the familiar intercourse of the home circle. He visited the sick and sorrowing, comforting the afflicted, and lifting up the oppressed. And in all that he said and did, he preached a crucified and risen Saviour."[29]

We have assurance with great promise that should we labor as Christ did we will have success. "The more closely the New Testament plan is followed in missionary labor, the more successful will be the efforts put forth."[30]

---

26 Ibid., p. 364.
27 Acts 2:46; 5:42
28 Acts 20:18–21
29 White, "From Persecutor to Disciple," *The Youth's Instructor*, November 22, 1900.
30 White, *Testimonies for the Church*, vol. 3, p. 210.

Jesus was not always able to labor in the cities as He desired because some published the news of His miracles when He forbade them to do so. The cured leper thought it because of Christ's modesty that Christ commanded him not to tell anyone of his cure. But the reality was that Christ foresaw lepers coming into the cities—something the Law of Moses prohibited—to be healed, thereby giving the priests and rulers an excuse to condemn Jesus before His time. Such conditions would prove a tremendous hindrance to the preaching of the gospel; therefore, Christ was forced to modify His methods to meet the crisis caused by this grateful but disobedient man.

"From Christ's methods of labor we may learn many valuable lessons. He did not follow merely one method; in various ways He sought to gain the attention of the multitude, and having succeeded in this, he proclaimed to them the truths of the gospel. His chief work lay in ministering to the poor, the needy, and the ignorant. In simplicity he opened before them the blessings they might receive, and thus he aroused their soul's hunger for the truth, the bread of life."[31]

Before Jesus could send the disciples as His representatives to do the work that He could no longer do except on a limited basis, He gave them more detailed instruction. The disciples were nearest to Christ when He did miracles and told His parables. But when the crowds were no longer pressing about Him, Jesus presented more plainly, more openly, the lessons clothed by illustrative stories. For the first few months of His constant labor, Jesus did not seek a total commitment from the disciples, but after some period of time, He invited them to follow Him, and He would make them "fishers of men."[32] After He ordained them to full-time discipleship, they traveled "throughout every city and village, preaching and shewing the glad tidings of the kingdom of God: and the twelve were with him, And certain women, which had been healed of evil spirits and infirmities, Mary called Magdalene, out of whom went seven devils, And Joanna the wife of Chuza Herod's steward, and Susanna, and many others, which ministered unto him of their substance."[33]

When questioned about the meaning of the parables, Jesus said, "Unto you it is given to know the mysteries of the kingdom of God: but to others in parables; that seeing they might not see, and hearing they might not understand.… No man, when he hath lighted a candle, covereth it with a vessel, or putteth it under a bed; but setteth it on a candlestick, that they which enter in may see the light. For nothing is secret, that shall not be made manifest; neither any thing hid, that shall not be known and come abroad. Take heed therefore how ye hear: for whosoever hath, to him shall be given; and whosoever hath not, from him shall be taken even that which he seemeth to have."[34] The disciples were prepared by personal instruction to teach others what Christ was teaching. Then Christ sent them out.

---

31   White, "Missionary Nurses," *The Review and Herald*, December 24, 1914.
32   Matthew 4:19
33   Luke 8:1–3
34   Luke 8:10, 16–18

Calling the twelve about Him, Jesus bade them go out two and two through the towns and villages. None were sent forth alone, but brother was associated with brother, friend with friend. Thus they could help and encourage each other, counseling and praying together, each one's strength supplementing the other's weakness. In the same manner He afterward sent forth the seventy. It was the Saviour's purpose that the messengers of the gospel should be associated in this way. In our own time evangelistic work would be far more successful if this example were more closely followed....

On this first tour the disciples were to go only where Jesus had been before them, and had made friends.... Nothing must be allowed to divert their minds from their great work or in any way excite opposition and close the door for further labor. They were not to adopt the dress of the religious teachers, nor use any guise in apparel to distinguish them from the humble peasants. They were not to enter into the synagogues and call the people together for public service; their efforts were to be put forth in house-to-house labor.... They were to enter the dwelling with the beautiful salutation, "Peace be to this house." Luke 10:5. That home would be blessed by their prayers, their songs of praise, and the opening of the Scriptures in the family circle.[35]

God blessed the disciples' efforts in the early days of their experience when Jesus first sent them to labor in preparation for His coming to all those cities and towns.

And they departed, and went through the towns, preaching the gospel, and healing every where. Now Herod the tetrarch heard of all that was done by him: and he was perplexed, because that it was said of some, that John was risen from the dead; And of some, that Elias had appeared; and of others, that one of the old prophets was risen again. And Herod said, John have I beheaded: but who is this, of whom I hear such things? And he desired to see him. And the apostles, when they were returned, told him all that they had done. And he took them, and went aside privately into a desert place belonging to the city called Bethsaida.[36]

King Herod must have been driven to the verge of insanity by the reports of the disciples' success! Not much time had passed since he had arrested and beheaded John the Baptist for rebuking his sin of marrying his brother's wife. And now there were twelve who were doing more than John had ever accomplished by preaching and healing the sick. Then Jesus sent out seventy

---

35   White, *The Desire of Ages*, pp. 350–352.
36   Luke 9:6–10

disciples to further expand the scope of the ministry.[37] Herod must have been sleep deprived from all the news of these miracles, given his guilty conscience.

We do not know the names of these seventy disciples. But an apparent indication is that they were family, friends, and acquaintances of those who benefitted from the ministry of Jesus and the twelve. The principle is that in the harvest we have the seed for the next harvest. From the labor of Christ and the twelve, we have seventy. And from the labor of the seventy, we know of about five hundred who met with Jesus in Galilee.

> The commission had been given to the twelve when Christ was with them in the upper chamber; but it was now to be given to a larger number. At the meeting on a mountain in Galilee, all the believers who could be called together were assembled. Of this meeting Christ Himself, before His death, had designated the time and place. The angel at the tomb reminded the disciples of His promise to meet them in Galilee. The promise was repeated to the believers who were gathered at Jerusalem during the Passover week, and through them it reached many lonely ones who were mourning the death of their Lord.[38]

But, of these, some doubted.[39] Yet there were one hundred and twenty who prayed for the outpouring of the Holy Spirit in Jerusalem. They continued there until God answered their prayers.[40]

When in the temple during Pentecost, the disciples followed Christ's example. Thousands repented and were baptized in a day. Why this success? For over three years, the disciples saw that "Christ's method alone will give true success in reaching the people. The Saviour mingled with men as one who desired their good. He showed His sympathy for them, ministered to their needs, and won their confidence. Then He bade them, 'Follow Me.'"[41] The disciples believed that "those who will study the manner of Christ's teaching, and educate themselves to follow His way, will attract and hold large numbers now, as Christ held the people in His day.... When the truth in its practical character is urged upon the people because you love them, souls will be convicted, because the Holy Spirit of God will impress their hearts."[42]

> *The principle is that in the harvest we have the seed for the next harvest.*

---

37   Luke 10:1
38   White, "Go Ye Therefore, and Teach All Nations," *The Signs of the Times*, August 5, 1903.
39   Matthew 28:16
40   Acts 1:15
41   White, *The Ministry of Healing*, p. 143.
42   White, *Evangelism*, p. 124.

We too should understand and believe that "the more closely the New Testament plan is followed in missionary labor, the more successful will be the efforts put forth. We should work as did our divine Teacher, sowing the seeds of truth with care, anxiety, and self-denial. We must have the mind of Christ if we would not become weary in well-doing. His was a life of continual sacrifice for others' good. We must follow His example."[43]

By the faith of Jesus we may obtain such success in being yoked to and following Him. But we must also note that we are only a part of the multitude following Jesus. And here we should be careful with what spirit we follow Christ. "And there went great multitudes with him…. Then drew near unto him all the publicans and sinners for to hear him. And the Pharisees and scribes murmured, saying, This man receiveth sinners, and eateth with them."[44] Not much earlier, Jesus had told of the cost of being a disciple. He had related how, on the great banquet day, those who had been invited were unworthy, for they placed temporal matters above the banquet feast. Though they considered themselves friends of the great Lord who furnished the festivity, they treated Him worse than an enemy by their improper prioritization. So they were passed over, and the poor, lame, blind, and beggars received invitations and filled the Lord's house. Yet, the Pharisees and scribes missed the point and tried to interpose themselves between God and the penitent sinner by their sharp criticism. Not able to find fault with Christ's character, they found fault with His actions because by them their own actions were rebuked. That not being enough, Christ related the importance of demonstrating His faith in preaching the gospel.

The parables of the lost sheep, the lost coin, and the lost son should remind us that we—when by faith seek the wandering sheep, the dirty coin, and the shabby son—will have greater cause for rejoicing upon finding them than do those who have never lost anything. Whether it is a loss of one one-hundreths, or one tenth, or one half of what God possesses, He chooses to rejoice upon making full recovery! But how many of us lack the faith of Jesus, as did the son who remained at home? We refuse to go to the party because we consider ourselves to be vastly superior to those who are received as guests of honor. Rather, we should contemplate the Scriptures: "Behold, his soul which is lifted up is not upright in him: but the just shall live by his faith."[45] Contempt for those who desire to follow Jesus, who have not yet met *our* standard of goodness, only places us under the very condemnation we would exercise against them.[46]

Jesus, by faith, preached that the kingdom of God is at hand and rejoiced over finding lost souls. The gratitude expressed by the truly repentant made them willing to serve God by demonstrating the faith of Jesus in their lives as they followed the example of Christ. Let us be certain that we have the faith of Jesus and are working with Him to gather together His saints.[47]

---

43   White, *Testimonies for the Church*, vol. 3, p. 210.
44   Luke 14:25; 15:1, 2
45   Habakkuk 2:4
46   Matthew 7:1, 2
47   Psalm 50:5

Chapter 8

By Faith Jesus Performed Miracles

Most folks will agree that miracles are our way of explaining the unexplainable. In the sports world, the 1980 USA hockey team experienced a "miracle on ice" when they defeated the USSR team and won the Olympic gold medal. Houdini's outrageous escape stunts were called miraculous. So, one might conclude that miracles are merely natural events inexplicable for lack of comprehension. Or perhaps, superstitiously we have called events miracles simply because human ignorance leaves us without a rationale for explaining what otherwise would be taken for granted, yet could not be the result of chance—the probability being far too great to withstand human reasoning.

In June of 2008, my wife, two sons, and I left for a family reunion at Lake Tahoe. Driving from Nebraska, we stopped long enough in Cheyenne, Wyoming, to connect with my sister and her older son so we could caravan the rest of the way. We had enough drivers between us that with careful planning and teamwork we could drive nonstop the rest of the way—except for fuel, food, conveniences, and an occasional driver change as needed. About thirty miles east of Rock Springs, Wyoming, with my sister in the lead, a trucker passed us and then slowed. In turn, we passed him. Then he passed us again and slowed down, so we passed him again. This process repeated itself for about ten miles. I couldn't understand what he was doing. He passed me once again, but then drifted to the right, looking like he was going to rear-end my sister. She sped up just as he pulled over to the right shoulder at about seventy miles per hour. I slowed in order to be of assistance because I thought he might need help. Suddenly he took a sharp right turn off the road into the wilderness.

He hit a shallow ditch that sent the truck completely airborne. I figured he would continue into the wilderness, so I passed a berm—a ledge about fifteen feet high—that separated us, and pulled over to go help him. I no sooner had the vehicle in park when my older son yelled, "Get moving! Get moving! He's coming right at us!" I tried to get the car back into gear, but performance anxiety took over—my body wanted to treat an automatic on the floor like a standard transmission. In my frustration, I glanced over my shoulder to see the Freightliner tractor bearing down upon us. I didn't even have time to pray when inexplicably the truck swerved again to the right—missing us by less than four inches—and continued its off-road excursion. It went another seventy yards or so before hitting a gully that stopped it cold. If we had been struck, we would have been pushed out into traffic. If not killed by the initial impact, then we certainly would have been by any other vehicles unable to avoid us.

You might ask, "What is so miraculous about that?" Well, the driver didn't have a seatbelt on, so when he hit the shallow ditch, he did a face-plant on his steering wheel, and then flopped out of his seat unconscious onto the floor, popping the gear stick into neutral. He had absolutely no control over that truck at the moment he should have struck us. Nor was there any natural rock formation to knock the steer tires onto a new course. The probability of chance dictating a change of direction defies reason. I believe it was a miracle.

As I started to study the earthly life and ministry of Christ with a perspective focusing on His faith, I wondered about the miracles Christ performed. Certainly Jesus demonstrated the power of God over the natural world and over Satan's control of men's minds and bodies. The more I studied, the more I learned that He performed His miracles by faith. That led me to ponder the questions, which takes more faith, receiving a miracle or performing one, and what makes one miracle more miraculous than another?

The strength of temptation when Satan asked for a stone to be turned into bread so that Jesus might relieve His own suffering is grounded in the fact that it was something that could be accomplished by God's power. Jesus was the Son of God, but He was also the Son of man. So, should Jesus misuse the power granted Him while He lived as a man upon the earth? "The power that rested upon him came directly from the Father, and he must not exercise it in his own behalf. With that long fast there was woven into his experience a strength and power that God alone could give. He met and resisted the enemy in the strength of a 'Thus saith the Lord.' 'Man shall not live by bread alone,' he said, 'but by every word that proceedeth out of the mouth of God.'"[1]

As we noted in an earlier chapter of this book, Jesus could do nothing but what He saw the Father doing. "The Son can do nothing of himself, but what he seeth the Father do: for what things soever he doeth, these also doeth the Son likewise.... I can of mine own self do nothing."[2] Yet Jesus had great power to perform miracles so that the singular cry of many hearts was, "if thou canst do anything, have compassion on us, and help us,"[3] and "Lord, if thou wilt, thou canst make me clean."[4]

---

1   White, "Tempted in All Points Like as We Are," *The Youth's Instructor*, December 21, 1899.
2   John 5:19, 30
3   Mark 9:22
4   Matthew 8:2

Jesus made the lowly paths of human life sacred by his example. For thirty years he was an inhabitant of Nazareth. His life was one of diligent industry. He, the Majesty of Heaven, walked the streets, clad in the simple garb of a common laborer. He toiled up and down the mountain steeps, going to and from His humble work. Angels were not sent to bear him on their pinions up the tiresome ascents, or to lend their strength in performing his lowly task. Yet when he went forth to contribute to the support of the family by his daily toil, he possessed the same power as when he wrought the miracle of feeding the five thousand hungry souls on the shore of Galilee.

But he did not employ his divine power to lessen his burdens or lighten his toil. He had taken upon himself the form of humanity with all its attendant ills, and he flinched not from its severest trials. He lived in a peasant's home, he was clothed in coarse garments, he mingled with the lowly, [and] he toiled daily with patient hands. His example shows us that it is man's duty to be industrious, that labor is honorable.

His life, written upon the pages of history, should encourage the poor and the lowly to perform contentedly the humble duties of their lot. Honorable work has received the sanction of Heaven, and men and women may hold the closest connection with God, yet occupy the humblest position in life. Jesus was as faithfully fulfilling his mission when hiding his divinity with the humble occupation of a carpenter, as when employed in healing the sick, or walking upon the white capped billows to the aid of his terrified disciples. Christ dignified the humble employments of life, by occupying a menial condition, that he might be able to reach the mass of mankind and exalt the race to become fit inmates for the Paradise of God....

It requires much more grace and stern discipline of character to work for God in the capacity of mechanic, merchant, lawyer, or farmer, carrying the precepts of Christianity into the ordinary business of life, than to labor as an acknowledged missionary in the open field, where one's position is understood, and half its difficulties obviated by that very fact. It requires strong spiritual nerve and muscle to carry religion into the work-shop and business office, sanctifying the details of every-day life, and ordering every worldly transaction according to the standard of a Bible Christian.[5]

All doubt regarding our ability to demonstrate the power of God, whatever our occupation, through possession of the faith of Jesus is removed in light of these statements. If we haven't come to a full comprehension of just what it was that Christ accomplished on our behalf, then we must take time to further expand our understanding. Jesus came to this earth as a man, to

---

5   White, "Missionary Work at Home," *The Health Reformer*, October 1, 1876.

experience our weaknesses, and to demonstrate how we might take hold of the strength of God in order to overcome the dominion of Satan in our lives so that He might have power to succor us as our High Priest. He lived by faith in God, never depending upon Himself alone. To better understand, let's consider the miracle Christ performed by which He demonstrated power over the forces of nature, which Satan used in an attempt to destroy Jesus and His followers.

> Now it came to pass on a certain day, that he went into a ship with his disciples: and he said unto them, Let us go over unto the other side of the lake. And they launched forth. But as they sailed he fell asleep: and there came down a storm of wind on the lake; and they were filled with water, and were in jeopardy. And they came to him, and awoke him, saying, Master, master, we perish. Then he arose, and rebuked the wind and the raging of the water: and they ceased, and there was a calm. And he said unto them, Where is your faith? And they being afraid wondered, saying one to another, What manner of man is this! for he commandeth even the winds and water, and they obey him.[6]

Let's take a closer look at this story from another perspective:

A hush fell upon the disciples. Even Peter did not attempt to express the awe that filled his heart. The boats that had set out to accompany Jesus had been in the same peril with that of the disciples. Terror and despair had seized their occupants; but the command of Jesus brought quiet to the scene of tumult. The fury of the storm had driven the boats into close proximity, and all on board beheld the miracle. In the calm that followed, fear was forgotten. The people whispered among themselves, "What manner of man is this, that even the winds and the sea obey Him?"

When Jesus was awakened to meet the storm, He was in perfect peace. There was no trace of fear in word or look, for no fear was in His heart. *But He rested not in the possession of almighty power. It was not as the "Master of earth and sea and sky" that He reposed in quiet. That power He had laid down, and He says, "I can of Mine own self do nothing." John 5:30. He trusted in the Father's might. It was in faith—faith in God's love and care—that Jesus rested, and the power of that word which stilled the storm was the power of God.*

> *"As Jesus rested by faith in the Father's care, so we are to rest in the care of our Saviour."*

As Jesus rested by faith in the Father's care, so we are to rest in the care of our Saviour. If the disciples had trusted in Him, they would have been kept in peace. Their fear in the time of danger revealed their unbelief. In their efforts to save themselves, they forgot Jesus; and it was only when, in despair of self-dependence, they turned to Him that He could give them help.[7]

In other words, the power came from the Father, in whom Christ rested by faith and trust. He rebuked the disciples for not having or maintaining that same kind of faith and trust. By this time they had witnessed many miracles. If we are to believe that Christ is God made manifest in the flesh, our flesh, so that we might see by His example how we are to live, then we must comprehend that Christ laid down His life of glory and power to take up our life of sin-weakened flesh that we might learn how to live the more abundant life God desires us to have.[8] Therefore, we must conclude that Jesus exerted no other power than that which we may obtain in order to live holy lives and to demonstrate God's supremacy over the realm Satan claims as his—the surrounding natural world, the minds and bodies of men, etc.—which territory he makes his dominion by the law of sin.

Jesus next demonstrated that the greatest miracle of all is not the controlling of nature's elements, or turning stones to bread as He was tempted by Satan to do, but the turning of stony hearts to hearts of flesh wherein abides the love of Christ for God and fellow man. For when they beached the boat on the far shore among the Gadarenes, or Gergesenes, naked madmen rushed out of the tombs to assault them.[9] All the disciples fled the beach for the safety of the boat and deeper waters when they noticed that Jesus was not with them.

In the storm they had not perceived that Jesus was with them as they tried to accomplish in their own power what they were helpless to perform, and already they had forgotten the lesson and were again trying to preserve their own lives in the face of a demonic onslaught. This time they noticed that Jesus was not with them but was still on the beach with the madmen—exhibiting the same calm demeanor as when He lay in quiet repose during the storm. They watched with amazement as the men regained their self-possession and two thousand pigs ran into the sea and drowned. They must have felt somewhat chagrined that they had done the same thing as the pigs, short of drowning, when they left Jesus alone! They still hadn't learned that the safest place to be was with Jesus! Oh that we would learn the same lesson and by faith maintain a relationship with Christ and always live in His presence!

When they recovered their composure and rejoined Jesus, they clothed the formerly devil-possessed men. And when the owners of the swine begged Jesus to leave them, the disciples—along with those who had followed in other boats—tried to tell them about the miracle on the

---

7   White, *The Desire of Ages*, pp. 335, 336, emphasis added.
8   1 Timothy 3:16; 1 Peter 2:21; John 10:10, 15, 17
9   Matthew 8:28; Luke 8:27; Mark 5:1

sea. Unable to change the people's minds, the believers sadly turned to leave. The healed demoniacs beseeched Jesus to let them come with Him, but Jesus sent them to do a work that He could not do in person. He sent—to those who refused to hear Him or His disciples—the very ones they had lived in proximity to for years. And when Jesus returned at a later date, the multitudes flocked to see and hear Him.

If we scrutinized any of Jesus' miracles, we would learn more about His life and faith. And one of the first things we would discover is the power of His word.

> The life of Christ that gives life to the world is in His word. It was by His word that Jesus healed disease and cast out demons; by His word He stilled the sea, and raised the dead; and the people bore witness that His word was with power. He spoke the word of God, as He had spoken through all the prophets and teachers of the Old Testament. The whole Bible is a manifestation of Christ, and the Saviour desired to fix the faith of His followers on the word. When His visible presence should be withdrawn, the word must be their source of power. Like their Master, they were to live "by every word that proceedeth out of the mouth of God." Matthew 4:4.[10]

Christ said, "It is the spirit that quickeneth; the flesh profiteth nothing: the words that I speak unto you, *they* are spirit, and *they* are life."[11] As we contemplate this thought, we should respond in gratitude that He has imbued His Word with power so that we might obtain that power—that faith—by the hearing of the Word. When acted upon in cooperative obedience by faith, we are strengthened, even quickened, by Scripture.

On the other hand, disobedience weakens faith. When we neglect God's Word, faith atrophies. Often times we shipwreck faith on the shoals of unbelief and doubt because we refuse to be guided by the navigational charts of God's Word.

> We are sometimes asked, Why does not God work miracles through the church today, as He did in the days of the apostles?—Because the church refuses to be guided and controlled by Him. Christ's love in the heart, revealing through the life its wondrous power,—this is the greatest miracle that can be performed before a fallen, quarreling world. Let us make it possible for God to work this miracle. Let us put on Christ, and the miracle-working power of His grace will be so plainly revealed, in the transformation of character, that the world will be convinced that God has sent His Son to make men as angels in life and character.[12]

---

10   White, *The Desire of Ages*, p. 390.
11   John 6:63
12   White, "Christ's Prayer for Unity," *The Signs of the Times*, November 26, 1902.

Christ's burden of ministry was to turn the hearts of men and women to God. His "most favorite theme was the paternal character and abundant love of God."[13] Every miracle He performed was consistent with this theme. It was consistent with God's righteous character of unselfish love. So why should it surprise us that the power used to perform these miracles was the Father's power displayed through the Son's life? Could it be that we so believe the lies of Satan about God that we stubbornly cherish the idea that the Father must be reconciled to us when indeed it was God reconciling the world to Himself through His Son? We cannot overlook the evil of sin, which God positively hates. But Paul assures us, writing plainly, that "all things are of God, who hath reconciled us to himself by Jesus Christ, and hath given to us the ministry of reconciliation; To wit, that God was in Christ, reconciling the world unto himself, not imputing their trespasses unto them; and hath committed unto us the word of reconciliation. Now then we are ambassadors for Christ, as though God did beseech you by us: we pray you in Christ's stead, be ye reconciled to God. For he hath made him to be sin for us, who knew no sin; that we might be made the righteousness of God in him."[14] Truly Christ, though the Son of God and having power to give life to whomsoever He wills, was the conduit of the Father's power exercised on our behalf.

Certainly Christ desires the very best for us. Take, for example, the demonstration of His wonderful love at the wedding feast in Cana. This miracle provides us with plentiful lessons. Invited to the marriage feast, Jesus and His disciples arrive and freely mingle among the guests. The wedding feasts of those days didn't last a few hours as they do now. They lasted days. Over the course of time, the supply of wine was used up until none remained. As was the custom, the best wine was served first and then the quality of the wine diminished as they went from fresh squeezed grape juice to the variety made from crushed raisins mixed with water. Mary, the mother of Jesus, noting that the wine was used up, exercised her faith in Him by notifying Him of the embarrassing situation. She believed He would remedy the shortfall, but the motivation of her plea was misplaced.

Mary believed in the temporal reign of the Messiah as taught by the leading rabbis of the period. Jesus, ever so gently and respectfully, reminded her that His time was not yet come. He had not yet announced His public ministry. And certainly He well understood that before the throne must come the crown of thorns and the cross.

> Jesus loved his mother tenderly; for thirty years he had been subject to parental control; but the time had now come when he was to go about his Father's business. In rebuking his mother, Jesus also rebukes a large class who have an idolatrous love for their family, and allow the ties of relationship to draw them from the service of

---

13   White, *Testimonies to Ministers and Gospel Workers*, p. 192.
14   2 Corinthians 5:18–21

God. Human love is a sacred attribute; but should not be allowed to mar our religious experience, or draw our hearts from God.

The future life of Christ was mapped out before him. His divine power had been hidden, and he had waited in obscurity and humiliation for thirty years, and was in no haste to act until the proper time should arrive. But Mary, in the pride of her heart, longed to see him prove to the company that he was really the honored of God. It seemed to her a favorable opportunity to convince the people present of his divine power, by working a miracle before their eyes, that would place him in the position he should occupy before the Jews. But he answered that his hour had not yet come. His time to be honored and glorified as King was not yet come; it was his lot to be a Man of sorrows and acquainted with grief.[15]

In Jesus' words to His mother, "Woman, what have I to do with thee?"[16] we see a change in their relationship. With the words of His Father still ringing in His ears from His baptism, He clearly points out to her that He is now answering to His heavenly Father and working for the salvation of all humanity, including Mary.

The earthly relation of Christ to his mother was ended. He who had been her submissive son was now her divine Lord. Her only hope, in common with the rest of mankind, was to believe him to be the Redeemer of the world, and yield him implicit obedience. The fearful delusion of the Roman church exalts the mother of Christ equal with the Son of the Infinite God; but he, the Saviour, places the matter in a vastly different light, and in a pointed manner indicates that the tie of relationship between them in no way raises her to his level, or insures her future. Human sympathies must no longer affect the One whose mission is to the world.

The mother of Christ understood the character of her Son, and bowed in submission to his will. She knew that he would comply with her request if it was best to do so. Her manner evidenced her perfect faith in his wisdom and power, and it was this faith to which Jesus responded in the miracle that followed. Mary believed that Jesus was able to do that which she had desired of him, and she was exceedingly anxious that everything in regard to the feast should be properly ordered, and pass off with due honor. She said to those serving at table, "Whatsoever he sayeth unto you, do it." Thus she did what she could to prepare the way.[17]

---

15   White, *The Spirit of Prophecy*, vol. 2, pp. 101, 102.

16   John 2:4

17   White, *The Spirit of Prophecy*, vol. 2, pp. 102, 103.

Mary's submission did not change her faith, but it changed her motive, which we see revealed in her persistence as she turned to the servants and told them to do whatever Jesus should command them to do. And Jesus responded to that faith with its corrected motive. We should understand that we cannot command God to do even what He is willing to do. We are not to use Him, but He is willing that we might be used by Him as He completes a work that He is already willing to do. When we submit unconditionally to and obey unreservedly His authority, we will be blessed in the cooperative union that shall do the works of Christ—and even greater.

"Some may say, 'If we believe the Bible, why does not the Lord work miracles for us?' He will, if we will let Him. When a human mind is allowed to come under the control of God, that mind will reveal the miracle-working power of God; the power of that mind in action is like the miracle-working power of God."[18]

Such was the lesson Christ taught to the nobleman from Capernaum. News of the temple cleansing, and other miracles like the one performed in Cana, had reached the nobleman. So when his son was on the verge of death, he acted upon an imperfect faith that rested upon the condition of receiving a miracle for his son as the basis for his future support of Christ's mission. When Jesus opened to the nobleman's mind that He knew the very thoughts and conditions in the man's heart, he was alarmed that his unbelief would prevent his son's recovery, and in that moment, true faith was born.

> This courtier represented many of his nation. They were interested in Jesus from selfish motives. They hoped to receive some special benefit through His power, and they staked their faith on the granting of this temporal favor; but they were ignorant as to their spiritual disease, and saw not their need of divine grace.
>
> Like a flash of light, the Saviour's words to the nobleman laid bare his heart. He saw that his motives in seeking Jesus were selfish. His vacillating faith appeared to him in its true character. In deep distress he realized that his doubt might cost the life of his son. He knew that he was in the presence of One who could read the thoughts, and to whom all things were possible. In an agony of supplication he cried, "Sir, come down ere my child die." His faith took hold upon Christ as did Jacob, when, wrestling with the Angel, he cried, "I will not let Thee go, except Thou bless me." Genesis 32:26.
>
> Like Jacob he prevailed. The Saviour cannot withdraw from the soul that clings to Him, pleading its great need. "Go thy way," He said; "thy son liveth." The nobleman left the Saviour's presence with a peace and joy he had never known before. Not only did he believe that his son would be restored, but with strong confidence he trusted in Christ as the Redeemer.[19]

---

18 White, *Notebook Leaflets From The Elmshaven Library*, vol. 1, p. 77.
19 White, *The Desire of Ages*, pp. 198, 199.

The nobleman and his household were ardent followers of Christ because imperfect faith was changed by a realization of personal need for spiritual healing. No small wonder that the centurion, also from Capernaum, would recognize the authority in Christ's word by which healing could take place from a distance. The centurion knew of the power and authority of Rome, and the investment of that power in himself, according to his rank, as he ordered soldiers to go and do in the name of the emperor. He recognized in Christ a submission to a greater Power by his acknowledgment: "For I am a man under authority."[20]

We must realize that if we are to perform miracles in our day and age, amidst prevailing post-modernism and all, we must be a people who are completely and unreservedly under the authority of God—keeping His commandments in letter and spirit and having the faith of Jesus.

What kept Jesus from healing everyone He saw suffering in torment? The ones who suffered most were those who, by diagnosis of their malady, were considered cut off from God and His people. If one was beyond the help of a physician, or pronounced leprous by a priest, then one had to endure the emotional pain of separation and spiritual torment in addition to the physical suffering. Anyone who heard a pronouncement by a ruler of the synagogue, or by a rabbi, that their physical suffering—palsy, blindness, unceasing bleeding, etc.—was the result of judgment from God received all the comfort provided by Job's three friends. Their suffering increased exponentially as mental and spiritual anguish was heaped upon them in addition to the physical malady.

How quick, then, was He to heal the leper who by faith came to Jesus notwithstanding his wretched, putrid condition. To the plea, "Lord, if thou wilt, thou canst make me clean,"[21] Jesus responded with a touch! According to Moses' law, anyone who touched anything or anyone who was unclean, they themselves must wash with water and be unclean until sunset, or up to seven days, before being clean again.[22] Yet Jesus was not defiled by this touch. Those who believe that Jesus was defiled by sin because He partook of our fallen flesh, thereby placing Christ in a position where He Himself would need a savior, ought to consider the ramifications of this wonderful miracle.

The disciples sought to prevent their Master from touching him; for he who touched a leper became himself unclean. But in laying His hand upon the leper, Jesus received no defilement. His touch imparted life-giving power. The leprosy was cleansed. Thus it is with the leprosy of sin,—deep-rooted, deadly, and impossible to be cleansed by human power.... *But Jesus, coming to dwell in humanity, receives no pollution. His presence has healing virtue for the sinner.* Whoever will fall at

---

20   Matthew 8:9
21   Matthew 8:2
22   Leviticus 13–15

His feet, saying in faith, "Lord, if Thou wilt, Thou canst make me clean," shall hear the answer, "I will; be thou made clean."[23]

In other words, although sin was imputed to Him via sinful flesh as our Sin-bearer, He remained morally undefiled in character. He was affected by sin in His flesh to the extent that He felt the strength of our temptations, but His character was not infected by the propensity to sin as our characters are inclined to do.[24] And as long as He obeyed God, rather than Satan, He would remain undefiled by sin.

Upon healing the leper, Jesus strictly charged him to tell no one but to go directly to the priests for certification of restoration to family and friends according to the ceremonial demands of the Law of Moses. One must understand the tremendous difference between moral and ceremonial defilement as represented by leprosy. Yet the importance of Christ's command to obey quickly and quietly were twofold:

Had the priests known the facts concerning the healing of the leper, their hatred of Christ might have led them to render a dishonest sentence. Jesus desired the man to present himself at the temple before any rumors concerning the miracle had reached them. Thus an impartial decision could be secured, and the restored leper would be permitted to unite once more with his family and friends.

There were other objects which Christ had in view in enjoining silence on the man. The Saviour knew that His enemies were ever seeking to limit His work, and to turn the people from Him. He knew that if the healing of the leper were noised abroad, other sufferers from this terrible disease would crowd about Him, and the cry would be raised that the people would be contaminated by contact with them. Many of the lepers would not so use the gift of health as to make it a blessing to themselves or to others. And by drawing the lepers about Him, He would give occasion for the charge that He was breaking down the restrictions of the ritual law. Thus His work in preaching the gospel would be hindered....

Every act of Christ's ministry was far-reaching in its purpose. It comprehended more than appeared in the act itself. So in the case of the leper. While Jesus ministered to all who came unto Him, He yearned to bless those who came not. While He drew the publicans, the heathen, and the Samaritans, He longed to reach the priests and teachers who were shut in by prejudice and tradition. He left untried no means

---

23 White, *The Desire of Ages*, p. 266, emphasis added.

24 Dr. Woodrow W. Whidden, II, shared with me in an interview this concept of making a difference between being affected by sin and being infected with sin. He attributes the idea to Dr. Edward Heppenstall (1901–1994), which I dealt with in an earlier chapter.

by which they might be reached. In sending the healed leper to the priests, He gave them a testimony calculated to disarm their prejudices.[25]

By disobeying Christ's charge to keep silent, the healed leper hindered His ministry to others in the most effectual and efficient manner. Jesus had to cease His labor for a while, and then modify His methods so that the work might continue in the countryside round about the cities and towns so as to avoid the accusation that lepers were unlawfully coming into contact with others.

Jesus never performed a miracle that would unnecessarily provoke the religious leaders. For example, while in Jerusalem one Sabbath day early in His ministry, He saw all those suffering from disease huddled around the pools of Bethesda, thinking that the rippling waters, supposedly caused by an angel, were their only hope for healing, and He longed to heal them. But it was the Sabbath day, and He knew that such an act of mercy would cut short His ministry—for it was not yet His time to die.

> *To those who realized their spiritual poverty, Christ never hesitated to demonstrate the Father's love and mercy.*

But the Saviour saw one case of supreme wretchedness. It was that of a man who had been a helpless cripple for thirty-eight years. His disease was in a great degree the result of his own sin, and was looked upon as a judgment from God. Alone and friendless, feeling that he was shut out from God's mercy, the sufferer had passed long years of misery. At the time when it was expected that the waters would be troubled, those who pitied his helplessness would bear him to the porches. But at the favored moment he had no one to help him in. He had seen the rippling of the water, but had never been able to get farther than the edge of the pool. Others stronger than he would plunge in before him. He could not contend successfully with the selfish, scrambling crowd. His persistent efforts toward the one object, and his anxiety and continual disappointment, were fast wearing away the remnant of his strength.[26]

To those who realized their spiritual poverty, Christ never hesitated to demonstrate the Father's love and mercy. The priests and rabbis were offended by this miracle, but not to the degree that His work was completely cut short. Jesus left Jerusalem, not to return until the year of His death because of the hatred of the rulers. Still, the priests and rabbis sent spies to track Him as He labored in Galilee. The blessing Jesus could have been to those in and around Jerusalem

---

25   White, *The Desire of Ages*, pp. 264, 265.
26   Ibid., pp. 201, 202.

was lost by reason of the hardness of the leaders' hearts. That is the reason why, after His resurrection and ascension, the priests were so alarmed when multitudes showed up at the temple asking for Jesus, the compassionate Savior who spoke healing words to soul and body.

> Never had Christ attracted the attention of the multitude as now that He was laid in the tomb. According to their practice, the people brought their sick and suffering ones to the temple courts, inquiring, Who can tell us of Jesus of Nazareth? Many had come from far to find Him who had healed the sick and raised the dead. On every side was heard the cry, We want Christ the Healer! Upon this occasion those who were thought to show indications of the leprosy were examined by the priests. Many were forced to hear their husbands, wives, or children pronounced leprous, and doomed to go forth from the shelter of their homes and the care of their friends, to warn off the stranger with the mournful cry, "Unclean, unclean!" The friendly hands of Jesus of Nazareth, that never refused to touch with healing the loathsome leper, were folded on His breast. The lips that had answered his petition with the comforting words, "I will; be thou clean" (Matthew 8:3), were now silent. Many appealed to the chief priests and rulers for sympathy and relief, but in vain. Apparently they were determined to have the living Christ among them again. With persistent earnestness they asked for Him. They would not be turned away. But they were driven from the temple courts, and soldiers were stationed at the gates to keep back the multitude that came with their sick and dying, demanding entrance.
>
> The sufferers who had come to be healed by the Saviour sank under their disappointment. The streets were filled with mourning. The sick were dying for want of the healing touch of Jesus. Physicians were consulted in vain; there was no skill like that of Him who lay in Joseph's tomb.[27]

Although Christ was no longer on the earth, His disciples continued to work miracles through the power of God. One day Peter and John met a crippled man at the Gate Beautiful. Begging for alms because he had no other hope of being made well, he looked to the two apostles for financial support, but he was healed instead because the faith of Jesus infused His converted disciples.

Peter and John well remembered the day when five thousand men had gathered around Jesus. All that day He had instructed and healed those in the crowd. They had tried to persuade Him to desist and send the crowd home for much needed food and rest. But Christ's thoughts were for the needs of the people. He said, "Give ye them to eat."[28] He already knew what He

27 Ibid., p. 776.
28 Mark 6:37

would do, but He tested their faith and reliance upon God by His imperative. The disciples did not have any more means at their disposal than Jesus appeared to have at His command. They had no food or money to provide every soul present according to their wants. But they learned an important lesson that day about God's providence.

The providence of God had placed Jesus where He was; and He depended on His heavenly Father for the means to relieve the necessity.

And when we are brought into strait places, we are to depend on God. We are to exercise wisdom and judgment in every action of life, that we may not, by reckless movements, place ourselves in trial. We are not to plunge into difficulties, neglecting the means God has provided, and misusing the faculties He has given us. Christ's workers are to obey His instructions implicitly. The work is God's, and if we would bless others His plans must be followed. Self cannot be made a center; self can receive no honor. If we plan according to our own ideas, the Lord will leave us to our own mistakes. But when, after following His directions, we are brought into strait places, He will deliver us. We are not to give up in discouragement, but in every emergency we are to seek help from Him who has infinite resources at His command. Often we shall be surrounded with trying circumstances, and then, in the fullest confidence, we must depend upon God. He will keep every soul that is brought into perplexity through trying to keep the way of the Lord....

In Christ's act of supplying the temporal necessities of a hungry multitude is wrapped up a deep spiritual lesson for all His workers. Christ received from the Father; He imparted to the disciples; they imparted to the multitude; and the people to one another. So all who are united to Christ will receive from Him the bread of life, the heavenly food, and impart it to others.

In full reliance upon God, Jesus took the small store of loaves; and although there was but a small portion for His own family of disciples, He did not invite them to eat, but began to distribute to them, bidding them serve the people. The food multiplied in His hands; and the hands of the disciples, reaching out to Christ Himself the Bread of Life, were never empty. The little store was sufficient for all. After the wants of the people had been supplied, the fragments were gathered up, and Christ and His disciples ate together of the precious, Heaven-supplied food.

The disciples were the channel of communication between Christ and the people. This should be a great encouragement to His disciples today. Christ is the great center, the source of all strength. His disciples are to receive their supplies from Him. The most intelligent, the most spiritually minded, can bestow only as they receive. Of themselves they can supply nothing for the needs of the soul. We can impart only that which we receive from Christ; and we can receive only as we impart to others. As we continue imparting, we continue to receive; and the more we impart, the more we shall receive. Thus we may be constantly believing, trusting, receiving, and imparting.

The work of building up the kingdom of Christ will go forward, though to all appearance it moves slowly and impossibilities seem to testify against advance. The work is of God, and He will furnish means, and will send helpers, true, earnest disciples, whose hands also will be filled with food for the starving multitude. God is not unmindful of those who labor in love to give the word of life to perishing souls, who in their turn reach forth their hands for food for other hungry souls.[29]

Later, Peter and John and the other disciples were to learn of God's power to perform even greater miracles, such as changing one's heart, as they witnessed the transformation of Saul of Tarsus, who went from persecutor of the church to leader of the cause. God used Saul, renamed Paul, to bring the gospel to the Gentiles. Oh the multitude of stories we have of the faith of Jesus demonstrated in the lives of God's true people. Let us not be found as the Pharisees and scribes who chose to hinder Christ's work by unbelief and disobedience. Instead, let us be found striving to obtain the faith of Jesus once delivered to the saints and, with complete submission to God's will, be found demonstrating that faith to those around us!

---

29 White, *The Desire of Ages*, pp. 368–370.

Chapter 9

By Faith Jesus Discipled

When I think of discipleship today, there are four areas that come to mind—military, business, athletics, and religion. In each of these areas, there are thousands of people who "follow" a person(s), a team, an organization, or a specific denomination, many being willing to die for the "cause" they subscribe to.

For example, if one desires to master the art and science of war, one might consider studying *The Art of War* by Sun Tzu. This same person may then proceed to improving their tactical understanding of war by pondering the maneuvering abilities of various generals throughout history, carefully critiquing successes and failures by reason of strengths and weaknesses in order to learn how to become superior to the heroes of the past and the peers of the present. All one needs is submersion in the discipline necessary to accomplish the masterful applications of those principles involving deception, speed, and attacking the enemy's weaknesses. Amazing enough, Sun Tzu's philosophy on war has been implemented in the workplace by corporate executives who wish to crush the competition and strengthen their financial positions. Doubtless it is also being practiced by the best of coaches in competitive athletics.

Now let's turn our attention to sports. Everybody loves a winner, and none will tolerate consistent losers for long. As a result, tremendous amounts of money are invested in those who are perceived as being successful. The Detroit Lions football team may eventually go bankrupt for lack of devoted fans if the right combination of coach and players is not soon achieved. One of the highest paid coaches ever, Phil Jackson, led the Chicago Bulls to six national championships, and the Los Angeles Lakers to five for a total of eleven championships as a coach, surpassing another great basketball coach, Arnold "Red" Auerbach, who had nine.

Great coaches attract and retain great players, thereby creating dynasties. Jackson became known as the "Zen Master" because his holistic approach to coaching is so heavily influenced by

Eastern mystical philosophies associated with Lao Tsu and Taoism—an interesting development, since both of his parents were Assemblies of God ministers.

History provides us with an endless list of those who would have had greater success if they hadn't been overly ambitious in seeking their own fame and glory. Consider, then, how Christ discipled by faith.

One must contextually understand that the success of great leaders is greatly influenced by how they themselves were discipled in their formative years. While Jesus was growing up, He was discipled by His mother and Joseph, angels, and ultimately God the Father through the study of Scripture and nature.[1] The cognitive development through rigorous discipline was foundational for Jesus' understanding of His mission when He saw the temple for the first time at the age of twelve. "He saw the white-robed priests performing their solemn ministry. He beheld the bleeding victim upon the altar of sacrifice. With the worshipers He bowed in prayer, while the cloud of incense ascended before God. He witnessed the impressive rites of the paschal service. Day by day He saw their meaning more clearly. Every act seemed to be bound up with His own life. New impulses were awakening within Him. Silent and absorbed, He seemed to be studying out a great problem. The mystery of His mission was opening to the Saviour."[2]

> *Three days passed before His presence produced the fruit of two disciples.*

Jesus began His work by sharing with the rabbis at the temple the wonderful things He now understood. He showed them that their "expectation in regard to the Messiah was not sustained by prophecy; but they would not renounce the theories that had flattered their ambition. They would not admit that they had misapprehended the Scriptures they claimed to teach."[3]

So we should not wonder, when eighteen years later, Jesus—by faith—did not seek out the un-teachable to be His disciples. Instead, following His baptism and His victory over temptation of our three most besetting sins, Jesus returned to the Jordan where John was still baptizing. He longed to draw to Himself those who would receive John's proclamation, "Behold the Lamb of God!"[4] Three days passed before His presence produced the fruit of two disciples. How symbolic of the three years of labor, or even the three days in the grave!

Two days earlier, the representatives of the Sanhedrin questioned John's authority to baptize. "John had not recognized the authority of the Sanhedrin by seeking their sanction for his work; and he had reproved rulers and people, Pharisees and Sadducees alike."[5] When John admitted that he was neither the Christ nor Elijah or Moses, they pressed him for an answer as to why he baptized.

---

1   White, *The Desire of Ages*, pp. 69, 70.
2   Ibid., p. 78.
3   Ibid., p. 80.
4   John 1:36
5   White, *The Desire of Ages*, pp. 132, 133.

The deputies from Jerusalem had demanded of John, "Why baptizest thou?" and they were awaiting his answer. Suddenly, as his glance swept over the throng, his eye kindled, his face was lighted up, his whole being was stirred with deep emotion. With outstretched hands he cried, "I baptize in water: in the midst of you standeth One whom ye know not, even He that cometh after me, the latchet of whose shoe I am not worthy to unloose." John 1:26, 27, R. V., margin.

The message was distinct and unequivocal, to be carried back to the Sanhedrin. The words of John could apply to no other than the long-promised One. The Messiah was among them! In amazement priests and rulers gazed about them, hoping to discover Him of whom John had spoken. But He was not distinguishable among the throng.[6]

They did not recognize the Messiah because their preconceived ideas as to how Christ would come and what He would look like didn't coincide with the reality of Jesus' ministry or mission. They had already rejected Him when He first taught them in the temple at the age of twelve.

He passed by the wise men of His time, because they were so self-confident that they could not sympathize with suffering humanity, and become colaborers with the Man of Nazareth. In their bigotry they scorned to be taught by Christ. The Lord Jesus seeks the co-operation of those who will become unobstructed channels for the communication of His grace. The first thing to be learned by all who would become workers together with God is the lesson of self-distrust; then they are prepared to have imparted to them the character of Christ.[7]

The next day, John the Baptist again pointed to Jesus, and declared, "Behold the Lamb of God, which taketh away the sin of the world!"[8] The crowd looked around to identify the One to whom John referred. Upon spotting Jesus, they saw His poverty and humility, not the pompous majesty they desired.

To the multitude, however, it seemed impossible that the One designated by John should be associated with their lofty anticipations. Thus many were disappointed, and greatly perplexed.

The words which the priests and rabbis so much desired to hear, that Jesus would now restore the kingdom to Israel, had not been spoken. For such a king they had been waiting and watching; such a king they were ready to receive. But

---

6   Ibid., p. 136.
7   Ibid., pp. 249, 250.
8   John 1:29

one who sought to establish in their hearts a kingdom of righteousness and peace, they would not accept.[9]

So the people began to reject Jesus. Yet His faith was strong and persevering. I am certain that during the night seasons of this time period Jesus was praying for the providence of God to work in the hearts of those men the Father would draw to Him.[10]

When on the third day the two disciples of John the Baptist heard him speak about the Lamb of God, they followed Jesus to learn more about Him. Jesus knew these two were following Him, and joy filled His heart as these first fruits of His labors and prayers responded to the call of grace. Jesus tested their curiosity, giving them opportunity to follow Him or return home. They followed. And after spending time with Jesus, one of the two—Andrew—went to his brother Peter and brought him to Christ. Then Jesus departed to Galilee where He found and bade Philip to follow Him.[11] Philip then found Nathanael, leading him to Christ. When Jesus saw Nathanael, He said, "Behold an Israelite indeed, in whom is no guile!"[12] Notice the repeated theme of Jesus calling one, and that one calling another? When we learn of Christ, we desire for others to learn of Him too.

Notice also the attitude of Jesus' first followers.

> If John and Andrew had possessed the unbelieving spirit of the priests and rulers, they would not have been found as learners at the feet of Jesus. They would have come to Him as critics, to judge His words. Many thus close the door to the most precious opportunities. But not so did these first disciples. They had responded to the Holy Spirit's call in the preaching of John the Baptist. Now they recognized the voice of the heavenly Teacher. To them the words of Jesus were full of freshness and truth and beauty. A divine illumination was shed upon the teaching of the Old Testament Scriptures. The many-sided themes of truth stood out in new light....
>
> If Nathanael had trusted to the rabbis for guidance, he would never have found Jesus. It was by seeing and judging for himself that he became a disciple. So is the case of many today whom prejudice withholds from good. How different would be the result if they would "come and see"!
>
> While they trust to the guidance of human authority, none will come to a saving knowledge of the truth. Like Nathanael, we need to study God's word for ourselves, and pray for the enlightenment of the Holy Spirit. He who saw Nathanael under the

---

9   White, *The Desire of Ages*, p. 138.
10   "No man can come to me, except the Father which hath sent me draw him" (John 6:44).
11   John 1:43
12   John 1:47

fig tree will see us in the secret place of prayer. Angels from the world of light are near to those who in humility seek for divine guidance.[13]

It is not enough to hear what we might consider as good preaching. We must compare it to the Scriptures, as did the Bereans in Paul's time, to find out for ourselves if what we heard is truth. Not as an exercise of skepticism should this work be undertaken, but as a matter of ownership, of personal investment in the truth. We must, under the guidance of the Holy Spirit, be led to a personal knowledge of the truth as it is in Jesus and receive it as a gift intended personally for us. Keep in mind that "Satan is constantly endeavoring to attract attention to man in the place of God. He leads the people to look to bishops, to pastors, to professors of theology, as their guides, instead of searching the Scriptures to learn their duty for themselves. Then, by controlling the minds of these leaders, he can influence the multitudes according to his will."[14] The ensuing danger of such a deception is that we can live by presumption instead of living by faith.

At first the disciples thought that Jesus was going to set up a temporal kingdom. They did not comprehend His mission. During their early ministry with Christ, they did not follow Him full time. They still had employment responsibilities, and Jesus allowed them to return to family at times so they might be refreshed and enjoy the company of those closest to them.[15] But when they were home they would search Him out to receive His instruction as well as observe His demonstrated faith.

On one occasion they journeyed from Jerusalem to Galilee via Samaria. Jesus stopped at Jacob's well in Sychar, while the disciples entered town to get food. They did not think of Jesus' need for water. But the Father was already drawing a needy soul to Christ for the purpose of giving Jesus cause for great joy—giving Him water and food the disciples had yet to understand. Finishing her questions of Jesus, the woman who had come to draw water forgot her own task and ran to tell others what she had learned. The disciples returned in time to observe her hasty departure. Although they thought it strange, they didn't question Jesus about her; instead they encouraged Him to eat. They thought His refusal bizarre and questioned in their hearts who had given Jesus food and drink. Jesus then instructed them further regarding His faith:

Christ longed to help and save the perishing, and he expressed his longing in the words, "Say not ye, There are yet four months, and then cometh harvest? Behold, I say unto you, Lift up your eyes, and look on the fields; for they are white already to harvest. And he that reapeth receiveth wages, and gathereth fruit unto life eternal; that both he that soweth and he that reapeth may rejoice together. And herein is

---

13 White, *The Desire of Ages*, pp. 139–141.
14 White, "The Scriptures a Safeguard," *The Review and Herald*, June 7, 1906.
15 White, *The Desire of Ages*, pp. 248, 249.

that saying true, One soweth, and another reapeth. I sent you to reap that whereon ye bestowed no labor: other men labored, and ye are entered into their labors."

The labor for which Christ saw there was so much need was harvesting. Harvesters are few. The work of gathering in the grain takes tact and skill, that none be lost. Winnowers of souls are needed in every place where the standard of truth, on which is inscribed the commandments of God and the faith of Jesus, has been uplifted.

> *"The work of gathering in the grain takes tact and skill, that none be lost."*

"The harvest truly is great, but the laborers are few." When Christ made this statement, there were scribes and Pharisees, priests and rulers, in every city and town in the land. But the Saviour saw that these teachers were wholly unfitted to minister to the spiritual needs of the people. "Ye know not the Scriptures, neither the power of God," he said to them. Ye teach for doctrine the commandments of men.

To every one God has committed a work. Each one is invited to take Christ's yoke and learn of him. Intensity is needed in the work of seeking to save those who are perishing out of Christ. Satan is intense in his efforts to deceive souls and gather them under his banner of apostasy and rebellion, and his helpers are without number.[16]

Within short order the disciples witnessed a multitude of Samaritans coming to Jesus, not as an angry mob to toss Him off a cliff, but as those hungering and thirsty after righteousness. For two days the disciples watched Him bless them with His presence through His teaching and healing. And they came to realize of Jesus that to "minister to a soul hungering and thirsting for the truth was more grateful to Him than eating or drinking. It was a comfort, a refreshment, to Him."[17]

When my wife and I were expecting our first child, she decided that she didn't want to know the gender of the baby until its birth. I determined to be an intimate part of the development of our child, so throughout the pregnancy I read to my unborn child. I can't remember when or where I had learned it, yet I had heard that a newborn could immediately recognize the mother's voice but not the father's, because throughout the pregnancy the mother's voice is constantly heard. However, fathers generally aren't around the developing fetus as much. I wanted my voice to be recognized from day one, so we purchased a set of Uncle Arthur's Bedtime Stories, as well as the Bible Story books. Every morning and evening I would put my head close to my wife's abdomen and read to our child from those books. As soon as our son was born, I exclaimed to my

---

16   White, "A Call to Service," *The Southern Watchman*, June 18, 1907.
17   White, *The Desire of Ages*, p. 191.

wife, "Honey, it's a boy!" As I spoke, he turned his face toward me in recognition. I know it to be true because I was not the only one talking. He knew my voice! It was a thrill that was repeated with the birth of our second son.

The same is true with Jesus. "Our Redeemer thirsts for recognition. He hungers for the sympathy and love of those whom He has purchased with His own blood. He longs with inexpressible desire that they should come to Him and have life. As the mother watches for the smile of recognition from her little child, which tells of the dawning of intelligence, so does Christ watch for the expression of grateful love, which shows that spiritual life is begun in the soul."[18] As with the Teacher, so with the disciple—we should have the same love and faith refreshed by a hungering and thirsting soul's recognition of Christ's claim upon one's person.

Not all who acknowledged Jesus as Messiah and Saviour became disciples in the same sense at the twelve who followed Him everywhere He went. There were the seventy who Jesus sent out. There were those who stayed home, fulfilling their duties in the workplace, in the community. Theirs was a life of discipline through the agencies of the Scriptures, the testimonies of friends, family, and hovering angels, and the abiding presence of the Holy Spirit in the heart—all tools of the Father's providential instruction—rather than the personal presence and instruction of Christ. While these carried out a witness to those about them, the twelve were being especially fitted for representing Christ after His ascension and the commencement of His mediatory work in the heavenly sanctuary.

In any case, we may rest assured that "God takes men as they are, with the human elements in their character, and trains them for His service, if they will be disciplined and learn of Him. They are not chosen because they are perfect, but notwithstanding their imperfections, that through the knowledge and practice of the truth, through the grace of Christ, they may become transformed into His image."[19]

> Jesus chose unlearned fishermen because they had not been schooled in the traditions and erroneous customs of their time. They were men of native ability, and they were humble and teachable,—men whom He could educate for His work. In the common walks of life there is many a man patiently treading the round of daily toil, unconscious that he possesses powers which, if called into action, would raise him to an equality with the world's most honored men. The touch of a skillful hand is needed to arouse those dormant faculties. It was such men that Jesus called to be His colaborers; and He gave them the advantage of association with Himself. Never had the world's great men such a teacher. When the disciples came forth from the Saviour's training, they were no longer ignorant and uncultured. They had become

---

18   Ibid., p. 191.
19   Ibid., p. 294.

like Him in mind and character, and men took knowledge of them that they had been with Jesus.[20]

"In these first disciples was presented marked diversity. They were to be the world's teachers, and they represented widely varied types of character. In order successfully to carry forward the work to which they had been called, these men, differing in natural characteristics and in habits of life, needed to come into unity of feeling, thought, and action. This unity it was Christ's object to secure. To this end He sought to bring them into unity with Himself."[21] As with the twelve, so with the seventy, and even so with us, for a righteous God searches the hearts and tries the reins, determining who is willing to be used of Him to further God's glory and accomplish His purposes.[22]

What kind of persons will God use? God will use those who seek first the kingdom of God and His righteousness.[23] Those who will not entangle themselves with the affairs of this life and will strive for masteries lawfully, such are not enemies of the cross.[24] Those who hide God's Word in their hearts that they might not sin against Him, such will receive His Word and hide His commandments with them.[25] Those who are converted, and become as little children, such can God use as servants of all and master of none but oneself.[26] Yet they do not have an independent spirit that interposes self between Christ and those we are to seek to save. They "worship God in the spirit, and rejoice in Christ Jesus, and have no confidence in the flesh."[27] Having said all this, one must conclude that none of these traits originate with humanity. Christ said to Peter, "for flesh and blood hath not revealed it unto thee, but my Father which is in heaven."[28] And that brings us right back to the faith of God as He exercises faith in calling us while, to all outward appearances, His righteousness is not yet manifested in us.[29]

All the disciples had serious faults when Jesus called them to His service. Even John, who came into closest association with the meek and lowly One, was not himself naturally meek and yielding. He and his brother were called "the sons of thunder." While they were with Jesus, any slight shown to Him aroused their indignation and combativeness. Evil temper, revenge, the spirit of criticism, were all in the beloved disciple. He was proud, and ambitious to be first in the kingdom of

20   Ibid., p. 250.
21   White, *The Acts of the Apostles*, p. 20.
22   Psalm 7:9
23   Matthew 6:33
24   2 Timothy 2:4, 5; Philippians 3:18
25   Psalm 119:11; Proverbs 2:1
26   Matthew 18:3; 20:27, 28
27   Philippians 3:3
28   Matthew 16:17
29   Romans 4:17

God. But day by day, in contrast with his own violent spirit, he beheld the tenderness and forbearance of Jesus, and heard His lessons of humility and patience. He opened his heart to the divine influence, and became not only a hearer but a doer of the Saviour's words. Self was hid in Christ. He learned to wear the yoke of Christ and to bear His burden.

Jesus reproved His disciples, He warned and cautioned them; but John and his brethren did not leave Him; they chose Jesus, notwithstanding the reproofs. The Saviour did not withdraw from them because of their weakness and errors. They continued to the end to share His trials and to learn the lessons of His life. By beholding Christ, they became transformed in character....

These were brought together, with their different faults, all with inherited and cultivated tendencies to evil; but in and through Christ they were to dwell in the family of God, learning to become one in faith, in doctrine, in spirit. They would have their tests, their grievances, their differences of opinion; but while Christ was abiding in the heart, there could be no dissension. His love would lead to love for one another; the lessons of the Master would lead to the harmonizing of all differences, bringing the disciples into unity, till they would be of one mind and one judgment. Christ is the great center, and they would approach one another just in proportion as they approached the center.[30]

As Jesus taught His disciples the principles and nature of His kingdom, the most receptive and responsive of them ventured to humble self and learn from potential mistakes. James and John had witnessed another man casting out demons in Christ's name. Definitely not one of the twelve, and apparently not one of the seventy, John said, "Master, we saw one casting out devils in thy name, and he followeth not us: and we forbad him, because he followeth not us." Jesus gently rebuked them, for never were Christ's disciples to forbid anyone expressing faith in Christ from laboring for Him in His name.[31]

None who showed themselves in any way friendly to Christ were to be repulsed. There were many who had been deeply moved by the character and the work of Christ, and whose hearts were opening to Him in faith; and the disciples, who could not read motives, must be careful not to discourage these souls. When Jesus was no longer personally among them, and the work was left in their hands, they must not indulge a narrow, exclusive spirit, but manifest the same far-reaching sympathy which they had seen in their Master.

---

30   White, *The Desire of Ages*, pp. 295, 296.
31   Mark 9:38

The fact that one does not in all things conform to our personal ideas or opinions will not justify us in forbidding him to labor for God. Christ is the Great Teacher; we are not to judge or to command, but in humility each is to sit at the feet of Jesus, and learn of Him. Every soul whom God has made willing is a channel through which Christ will reveal His pardoning love. How careful we should be lest we discourage one of God's light bearers, and thus intercept the rays that He would have shine to the world![32]

Those who forbid others from joining in the work are clearly jealous and not concerned about the glory of God. Again, it comes down to the right understanding of the principles of God's kingdom. Self-exaltation has no place in heaven, nor should it have any place in the hearts of Christ's disciples. So Jesus, in the most solemn manner, taught:

> *Self-exaltation has no place in heaven, nor should it have any place in the hearts of Christ's disciples.*

"If any man desire to be first, the same shall be last of all, and servant of all." There was in these words a solemnity and impressiveness which the disciples were far from comprehending. That which Christ discerned they could not see. They did not understand the nature of Christ's kingdom, and this ignorance was the apparent cause of their contention. But the real cause lay deeper. By explaining the nature of the kingdom, Christ might for the time have quelled their strife; but this would not have touched the underlying cause. Even after they had received the fullest knowledge, any question of precedence might have renewed the trouble. Thus disaster would have been brought to the church after Christ's departure. The strife for the highest place was the outworking of that same spirit which was the beginning of the great controversy in the worlds above, and which had brought Christ from heaven to die. There rose up before Him a vision of Lucifer, the "son of the morning," in glory surpassing all the angels that surround the throne, and united in closest ties to the Son of God. Lucifer had said, "I will be like the Most High" (Isaiah 14:12, 14); and the desire for self-exaltation had brought strife into the heavenly courts, and had banished a multitude of the hosts of God. Had Lucifer really desired to be like the Most High, he would never have deserted his appointed place in heaven; for the spirit of the Most High is manifested in unselfish ministry. Lucifer desired God's power, but not His character. He sought for himself the highest place, and every

---

32   White, *The Desire of Ages*, pp. 437, 438.

being who is actuated by his spirit will do the same. Thus alienation, discord, and strife will be inevitable. Dominion becomes the prize of the strongest. The kingdom of Satan is a kingdom of force; every individual regards every other as an obstacle in the way of his own advancement, or a steppingstone on which he himself may climb to a higher place.[33]

We have received clear warning consistent with the rebuke Jesus gave James and John. If they had continued to forbid those who exercised faith in Jesus, they would have done injury to their own characters, and quite possibly caused the forbidden one to stumble. It is so important for us not to exalt self or self-esteem but rather to discipline ourselves and exhort others to join in the work of righteous self-abasement that characterizes the genuine disciple of Christ.

Ministers would be more successful in their labor, if they would talk less of self and more of Christ. Of ourselves, we have no power to reach hearts; it is only by divine aid that we can find access to them. Brethren, teach the people to rely upon Jesus; lead them to feel that they are not dependent on the minister, but must have an experience for themselves. The minister is not infallible. He may err; ambition and unhallowed passion may burn in his heart; the vampire of envy may mar his work; he may defraud God of the glory due to his name by so laboring that the credit will be given to the poor, erring, finite instrument. The true laborer will take care that his hearers understand the leading points of our faith, and that they keep distinctly in mind the old landmarks, the way by which the Lord has led his people. He will teach them to look to God for themselves, expecting the outpouring of his Spirit. If those who profess to be teachers of the truth teach their own ideas independent of the opinions of their brethren, they should be labored with as unfaithful in their work. One who feels at liberty to advance what he chooses and keep back what he chooses, should not be encouraged to labor in the ministry; for he is failing to prepare a people to stand in the day of the Lord….

Some fail to educate the people to do their whole duty. They preach that part of our faith which will not create opposition and displease their hearers; but they do not declare the whole truth. The people enjoy their preaching; but there is a lack of spirituality, because the claims of God are not met. His people do not give him in tithes and offerings that which is his own. This robbery of God, which is practiced by both rich and poor, brings darkness into the churches; and the minister who labors with them, and who does not show them the plainly revealed will of God, is brought under condemnation with the people, because he neglects his duty.[34]

33   Ibid., pp. 435, 436.
34   White, "Humility and Faithfulness in Laborers," *The Review and Herald*, April 8, 1884.

Converts are born again. But disciples are not born—they are made by daily being born again and practicing obedience to all the commandments of God by faith. We are deficient in our labor if we are not striving to make disciples of converts. We need to realize, in the act of yoking with Christ, we are to be co-laborers in discipling others. When Jesus gave the great commission before ascending to the Father, He clearly said, "[Teach] them to observe all things whatsoever I have commanded you."[35] Let us always remember: "He who called the fisherman of Galilee is still calling men to His service. And He is just as willing to manifest His power through us as through the first disciples. However imperfect and sinful we may be, the Lord holds out to us the offer of partnership with Himself, of apprenticeship to Christ. He invites us to come under the divine instruction, that, uniting with Christ, we may work the works of God."[36]

As we conclude this study about discipleship, we cannot overlook the importance of three statements about the harvest that Jesus made to His disciples. The first occasion was at Jacob's well. "Say not ye, There are yet four months, and *then* cometh harvest? behold, I say unto you, Lift up your eyes, and look on the fields; for they are white already to harvest."[37] Here Jesus desired to break down the prejudice of His disciples regarding His mission. It was early in His ministry, and the disciples were just beginning to witness Christ's faith and power—not only in His teaching but in His miracles.

It seems strange, but John did not include the same phrase as Matthew and Luke in the other two sayings of similar importance. Notice the key phrase: "The harvest truly *is* plenteous, but the labourers *are* few; *Pray ye therefore the Lord of the harvest*, that he will send forth labourers into his harvest"[38]; "The harvest truly *is* great, but the labourers *are* few: *pray ye therefore the Lord of the harvest*, that he would send forth labourers into his harvest. Go your ways: behold, I send you forth as lambs among wolves."[39]

Jesus did not declare a shortage of laborers while in Samaria, nor did He entreat His disciples. But after they had been with Jesus for quite some time, after they had witnessed the greatness of God's power demonstrated in His life of faith, Jesus entreated them.

In a way so as to impress upon them their dependence upon God, He reminded them that He was the Lord of the harvest. Just as when God revealed Himself to Isaiah, Jesus impressed upon the disciples their unworthiness and complete dependence upon God. And just as God asked of Isaiah, Christ asked His disciples, "Whom shall I send, and who will go for us?"[40] By extending His faith as a gift to His disciples, Jesus empowered them to go as His representatives to do a work of preparation before Him. In Matthew, we see Jesus sending out the twelve. In Luke, He sends out the seventy. Each disciple was brought to the place where they acknowledged Jesus

---

35   Matthew 28:20
36   White, *The Desire of Ages*, p. 297.
37   John 4:35
38   Matthew 9:37, 38
39   Luke 10:2, 3
40   Isaiah 6:8

as the Son of God and, grasping the power of Omnipotence by faith, were enabled to do the works of Christ in preparing hearts for the kingdom.

We need to have the same experience as Isaiah, the twelve, and the seventy. We need to acknowledge Jesus Christ as the Son of God sent to purchase our redemption. We need to accept the faith of Jesus as a gift we can call our own. We should be disciples at the feet of Jesus every day. Then we ought to be found discipling others by faith, just as Jesus did. Only then can we be a part of an ever-increasing army under the banner of God, finishing the work set before us so that Jesus may come to gather His loved ones home.

Chapter 10

By Faith Jesus Died

A young man functioning as a co-leader for the youth in the church where he had attended from the time of his childhood found himself in the pastor's office facing a disciplinary committee. His accuser, a young married woman, was present to attack his character. The disciplinary committee asked questions, mostly to the accuser, while the young man patiently and quietly sat. Most of the accusations were so outlandish that sometimes the young man struggled to stifle even a slight smile of humor. Prayer concluded the proceeding without any discipline for the young man, but the woman was censored for a couple of months. She left the office very disgruntled. Turning to the young man, the pastor commented, "I noticed that you had nothing to say in your defense. How could you sit so quietly through the storm of accusation?" The young man didn't even hesitate with his response. "I knew that those on the committee have known me from the time I was small. I was confident you all would see the truth of the matter and find me innocent."

Perhaps it is not so great a test of faith to be silent in trial when you believe those judges to be fair and just in their assessment of your character and actions. But what about those times when justice turns a blind eye to the truth? What about those times when the judges have already determined to sacrifice innocence to maintain their own prestige?

I recall the story of a church elder in Africa who suffered great embarrassment one Sabbath morning when a woman, a known prostitute in the village, walked up to the front of the church with her newborn child and said to him in everybody's hearing, "This baby is yours. You take care of him." Then she placed the baby on the floor, turned around, and walked out. Silently the church elder stood up to gather the baby in his arms. For two weeks he cared for the baby without saying a word in his defense. The church board met and determined that what the woman had said must have been truth. So they chose to disfellowship the elder. For the next twenty-three years he continued going to church, while uncomplainingly caring for the son who wasn't his. While the boy was attending medical school and was soon to graduate, the truth came out. All these years of saying nothing in his defense culminated one Sabbath morning when the mother walked into church once again. Tears streamed down her cheeks as she sobbed uncontrollably. Through stammering lips, she confessed, "This man is innocent. He is not my son's father.

I knew it when I accused him. I hoped he would take care of my son and raise him as I never could. I lived in fear that he would denounce me all these years. But now, how can I keep silent any longer?"

A closer look at how Jesus faced persecution, false accusation, and death will reveal to us His demonstration of faith. When we rightly understand His faith under these trying circumstances, we too, by faith, can bear insult, pain, suffering, and, if need be, death.

Following the events of the transfiguration and Jesus casting out the devil from the boy, He said to His disciples, "Let these sayings sink down into your ears: for the Son of man shall be delivered into the hands of men. But they understood not this saying, and it was hid from them, that they perceived it not: and they feared to ask him of that saying."[1] This was not the first time the disciples had heard Jesus say this. After the feeding of the five thousand men, besides women and children, Jesus had said, "The Son of man must suffer many things, and be rejected of the elders and chief priests and scribes, and be slain, and be raised the third day."[2] From Matthew's account, Jesus kept telling the disciples the immediate future He faced, "From that time forth began Jesus to shew unto his disciples, how that he must go unto Jerusalem, and suffer many things of the elders and chief priests and scribes, and be killed, and be raised again the third day."[3]

Peter loved Jesus, and he attempted to shield Him from what he considered to be unnecessary suffering. But Jesus reproved that sentimentalism—or blind love—for it showed Christ that Peter was not willing to deny himself. "Peter did not desire to see the cross in the work of Christ. The impression which his words would make was directly opposed to that which Christ desired to make on the minds of His followers, and the Saviour was moved to utter one of the sternest rebukes that ever fell from His lips…. Jesus now explained to His disciples that His own life of self-abnegation was an example of what theirs should be."[4]

"Then said Jesus unto his disciples, If any man will come after me, let him deny himself, and take up his cross, and follow me. For whosoever will save his life shall lose it: and whosoever will lose his life for my sake shall find it. For what is a man profited, if he shall gain the whole world, and lose his own soul? or what shall a man give in exchange for his soul?"[5]

The fact that by faith Jesus died for us and that all the suffering was worth the travail of His soul should awaken in us an understanding regarding the cost of discipleship. When Jesus made this statement to His followers, it was possible for the disciples to change their minds and leave Him to take up their former employment. Yet they refused to believe what Jesus foretold of His sufferings because they clung to the belief that He would set up an earthly kingdom and throw off the yoke of Rome. Talk of willingly taking up a cross—Rome's choice of execution as a demonstration of her power—galled them, so they journeyed forth with sorrow in their hearts.

---

1   Luke 9:44, 45
2   Luke 9:22
3   Matthew 16:21
4   White, *The Desire of Ages*, pp. 415, 416.
5   Matthew 16:24–26

When Jesus told them that He was to be put to death and to rise again, He was trying to draw them into conversation in regard to the great test of their faith. Had they been ready to receive what He desired to make known to them, they would have been saved bitter anguish and despair. His words would have brought consolation in the hour of bereavement and disappointment. But although He had spoken so plainly of what awaited Him, His mention of the fact that He was soon to go to Jerusalem again kindled their hope that the kingdom was about to be set up.[6]

Before his crucifixion, the Saviour explained to his disciples that he was to be put to death, and to rise again from the tomb; and angels were present to impress his words on minds and hearts. But the disciples were looking for temporal deliverance from the Roman yoke, and they could not tolerate the thought that he in whom all their hopes centered should suffer an ignominious death. The words which they needed to remember were banished from their minds; and when the time of trial came, it found them unprepared.[7]

To the heart of Christ it was a bitter task to press His way against the fears, disappointment, and unbelief of His beloved disciples. It was hard to lead them forward to the anguish and despair that awaited them at Jerusalem. And Satan was at hand to press his temptations upon the Son of man. Why should He now go to Jerusalem, to certain death? All around Him were souls hungering for the bread of life. On every hand were suffering ones waiting for His word of healing. The work to be wrought

> *The foe who in the wilderness had confronted Christ assailed Him now with fierce and subtle temptations.*

by the gospel of His grace was but just begun. And He was full of the vigor of manhood's prime. Why not go forward to the vast fields of the world with the words of His grace, the touch of His healing power? Why not take to Himself the joy of giving light and gladness to those darkened and sorrowing millions? Why leave the harvest gathering to His disciples, so weak in faith, so dull of understanding, so slow to act? Why face death now, and leave the work in its infancy? The foe who in the wilderness had confronted Christ assailed Him now with fierce and subtle temptations. Had Jesus yielded for a moment, had He changed His course in the least

6   White, *The Desire of Ages*, p. 435.
7   White, "The Scriptures a Safeguard," *The Review and Herald*, June 7, 1906.

particular to save Himself, Satan's agencies would have triumphed, and the world would have been lost.[8]

As the time approached for Jesus to yield up His life for us, "He stedfastly set his face to go to Jerusalem, And sent messengers before his face: and they went, and entered into a village of the Samaritans, to make ready for him. And they did not receive him, because his face was as though he would go to Jerusalem."[9] It appears that the Samaritans who had spent two days with Jesus at the beginning of His ministry had lessons of their own to learn about the Messiah's mission and ministry. Despite what Jesus taught them, saying, "Ye worship ye know not what: we know what we worship: for salvation is of the Jews. But the hour cometh, and now is, when the true worshippers shall worship the Father in spirit and in truth: for the Father seeketh such to worship him. God is a Spirit: and they that worship him must worship him in spirit and in truth,"[10] they were determined to look for the restoration of their temple. "Had He come to restore the temple and worship upon Mount Gerizim, they would gladly have received Him; but He was going to Jerusalem, and they would show Him no hospitality."[11]

Incensed at the apparent lack of respect for One who had treated them so kindly, James and John determined to use the power Christ had given them to cast out devils and to heal the afflicted with all the vengeance of Elijah in destroying those Samaritan captains and their companies of fifty who didn't show the proper respect to their Master.

> Seeing Mount Carmel in the distance, where Elijah had slain the false prophets, they said, "Wilt Thou that we command fire to come down from heaven, and consume them, even as Elias did?" They were surprised to see that Jesus was pained by their words, and still more surprised as His rebuke fell upon their ears....
>
> Under a pretense of zeal for righteousness, men who are confederate with evil angels bring suffering upon their fellow men, in order to convert them to their ideas of religion; but Christ is ever showing mercy, ever seeking to win by the revealing of His love. He can admit no rival in the soul, nor accept of partial service; but He desires only voluntary service, the willing surrender of the heart under the constraint of love. There can be no more conclusive evidence that we possess the spirit of Satan than the disposition to hurt and destroy those who do not appreciate our work, or who act contrary to our ideas.[12]

Instead of punishing the Samaritans, they moved on to another village.

---

8   White, *The Desire of Ages*, p. 486.
9   Luke 9:51–53
10   John 4:22–24
11   White, *The Desire of Ages*, p. 487.
12   White, *The Desire of Ages*, p. 487.

About this time, Jesus received word that His friend Lazarus was sick. He did not hasten to heal Lazarus. Instead, He remained where He was for two more days. This must have surprised the disciples, for they knew of the close bond of affection Jesus had for Lazarus, Martha, and Mary. They wondered at the delay. Then, to learn that Lazarus was dead must have puzzled them in view of the words of comfort Jesus had earlier declared, saying, "This sickness is not unto death, but for the glory of God, that the Son of God might be glorified thereby."[13]

Could the Pharisees be correct in saying that Jesus was a false prophet? What did Jesus mean by these words? And why go to Judea now when He had told them what would happen upon arriving there? So they said to Jesus, "Master, the Jews of late sought to stone thee; and goest thou thither again?" Upon hearing Christ's steadfast response, Thomas said to his fellow disciples, "Let us also go, that we may die with him."[14]

Days earlier, the Pharisees and Sadducees had come to Jesus asking for a sign from heaven to affirm His authority and mission. Despite the varied witnesses from heaven at His birth and to the present—the angels declaring the manner of it, the witness of the prophets Simeon and Anna, the star guiding the journey of the wise men from the east, the Father's voice from heaven at His baptism—they tempted Christ to produce a further sign. But He refused to yield to their temptation. Instead, He prophesied of His death as all the sign they should need—as if the wonderful miracles and teachings were not enough testimony for His authority and work—, saying, "An evil and adulterous generation seeketh after a sign; and there shall no sign be given to it, but the sign of the prophet Jonas: For as Jonas was three days and three nights in the whale's belly; so shall the Son of man be three days and three nights in the heart of the earth."[15]

What the disciples didn't know is that Jesus was going to Bethany to perform a great miracle, not to satisfy the curiosity of the religious leaders, but to strengthen the faith of His disciples as He yielded Himself up to death on the cross.

By raising Lazarus from the dead, Christ provided ample evidence that He was the resurrection and the life. By giving a man—dead for four days and stinking of corruption—life again, Jesus attempted to strengthen the faith of His disciples that He would conquer death by fulfilling prophecy: "Therefore my heart is glad, and my glory rejoiceth: my flesh also shall rest in hope. For thou wilt not leave my soul in hell; neither wilt thou suffer thine Holy One to see corruption. Thou wilt shew me the path of life: in thy presence is fulness of joy; at thy right hand there are pleasures for evermore."[16]

> In delaying to come to Lazarus, Christ had a purpose of mercy toward those who
> had not received Him. He tarried, that by raising Lazarus from the dead He might

---

13   John 11:4, 11–14
14   John 11:8, 16
15   Matthew 12:39, 40
16   Psalm 16:9–11

give to His stubborn, unbelieving people another evidence that He was indeed "the resurrection, and the life." He was loath to give up all hope of the people, the poor, wandering sheep of the house of Israel. His heart was breaking because of their impenitence. In His mercy He purposed to give them one more evidence that He was the Restorer, the One who alone could bring life and immortality to light. This was to be an evidence that the priests could not misinterpret. This was the reason of His delay in going to Bethany. This crowning miracle, the raising of Lazarus, was to set the seal of God on His work and on His claim to divinity.[17]

If the disciples had rightly understood the prophecies, they would have been greatly encouraged for the coming crisis. They would have rejoiced in Christ's steadfastness instead of sorrowing for their dashed misguided dreams of temporal glory.

We are no better than they. In fact, we are worse off than they. As Laodiceans we try to serve both God and mammon just as the disciples did. Yet we have their example before us. Therefore, we should know and do better. Instead, we try to work in such a way as to make the gospel more acceptable to the world as a means of avoiding persecution and death. Compromising the purity of the truth, we yield to the temptations that Satan urged upon Christ so as to avoid premature demise, somehow thinking that extended life through yielding to temptation will bring glory to God. But what does Paul say? "Yea, and all that will live godly in Christ Jesus shall suffer persecution."[18]

A retired religion professor once told me about two missionaries in Central America who got lost in the jungle. The duration of their lost condition was great enough that both became very famished. One chose to remain true to his beliefs regarding diet while the other killed and ate whatever moved—rats, snakes, etc. The point of this story is that the one who ate unclean meats remained healthy and appeared to do a great work for God while the other who refused to compromise his beliefs became an invalid and could do no further great work for God. But oh how we need to see things as God does!

Those who endeavor to obey all the commandments of God will be opposed and derided. They can stand only in God. In order to endure the trial before them, they must understand the will of God as revealed in his Word; they can honor him only as they have a right conception of his character, government, and purposes, and act in accordance with them. None but those who have fortified the mind with the truths of the Bible will stand through the last great conflict. To every soul will come the searching test, Shall I obey God rather than men? The decisive hour is even now at hand. Are our feet planted on the rock of God's immutable Word? Are we

---

17   White, *The Desire of Ages*, p. 529.
18   2 Timothy 3:12

prepared to stand firm in defense of the commandments of God and the faith of Jesus?[19]

Half-hearted Christians obscure the glory of God, misinterpret piety, and cause men to receive false ideas as to what constitutes vital godliness. Others think that they, also, can be Christians and yet consult their own tastes and make provision for the flesh, if these false-hearted professors can do so. On many a professed Christian's banner the motto is written, 'You can serve God and please self,—you can serve God and mammon.' They profess to be wise virgins, but not having the oil grace in their vessels with their lamps, they shed forth no light to the glory of God and for the salvation of men. They seek to do what the world's Redeemer said was impossible to do; he has declared, 'Ye cannot serve God and mammon.' Those who profess to be Christians, but do not follow in the footsteps of Christ, make of none effect his words, and obscure the plan of salvation. By their spirit and deportment they virtually say, 'Jesus, in your day you did not understand as well as we do in our day, that man can serve God and mammon.' These professors of religion claim to keep the law of God, but they do not keep it. O, what would the standard of true manhood have become had it been left in the hands of man! God has lifted his own standard,—the commandments of God and the faith of Jesus; and the experience that follows complete surrender to God, is righteousness, peace, and joy in the Holy Ghost. Everything that man touches with unholy hands and unsanctified intellect, even the gospel of truth, becomes, by the contact, contaminated. Man puts confidence in man, and makes flesh his arm, but all the work of man is of the earth, earthy.[20]

"Those who profess to be Christians, but do not follow in the footsteps of Christ, make of none effect his words, and obscure the plan of salvation."

We are encouraged by the pen of inspiration: "If you would work as Christ worked, if you would overcome as he overcame, go straight to him for help needed to subdue the inclinations of the carnal mind and the passions of the natural heart. Resist every sinful indulgence, every inclination to gratify wrong desires, remembering that Christ is all and in all, and that he is able

19   White, "The Scriptures a Safeguard," *The Review and Herald*, June 7, 1906.
20   White, "The Righteousness of Christ," *The Review and Herald*, August 19, 1890.

to do 'exceeding abundantly, above all that we ask or think.' "[21] This is consistent with Paul's exhortation:

> Looking unto Jesus the author and finisher of our faith; who for the joy that was set before him endured the cross, despising the shame, and is set down at the right hand of the throne of God. For consider him that endured such contradiction of sinners against himself, lest ye be wearied and faint in your minds. Ye have not yet resisted unto blood, striving against sin. And ye have forgotten the exhortation which speaketh unto you as unto children, My son, despise not thou the chastening of the Lord, nor faint when thou art rebuked of him: For whom the Lord loveth he chasteneth, and scourgeth every son whom he receiveth. If ye endure chastening, God dealeth with you as with sons; for what son is he whom the father chasteneth not? But if ye be without chastisement, whereof all are partakers, then are ye bastards, and not sons.[22]

And so the disciples, though warned, were to be deeply disappointed. And the same will happen to us unless we awake to our spiritual condition and zealously repent of it.

> The death of Jesus as fully destroyed their hopes as if he had not forewarned them. So in the prophecies the future is opened before us as plainly as it was opened to the disciples by the words of Christ. The events connected with the close of probation and the work of preparation for the time of trouble, are clearly presented. But multitudes have no more understanding of these important truths than if they had never been revealed. Satan watches to catch away every impression that would make them wise unto salvation, and the time of trouble will find them unready.[23]

From the triumph over Lazarus' tomb, we move to the feast at Simon's house, where Jesus once more made reference to His impending death. Mary had come, uninvited to the feast, for the purpose of expressing her gratitude to Jesus for forgiveness of her sins and for the restoration of her beloved brother. Breaking a jar of perfume, she anointed Christ's feet with a most expensive ointment mingled with her tears of thanksgiving. The harsh words of condemnation from Judas combined with the doubting thoughts of repulsion from Simon wounded Mary. But Jesus soothed her embarrassment and shame with tones of balm for her distraught soul: "Why trouble ye the woman? for she hath wrought a good work upon me. For ye have the poor always with you; but me ye have not always. For in that she hath poured this ointment on my body, she

21 White, "Go Work Today in My Vineyard," *The Signs of the Times*, April 1, 1897.
22 Hebrews 12:2–8
23 White, "The Scriptures a Safeguard," *The Review and Herald*, June 7, 1906.

did it for my burial. Verily I say unto you, Wheresoever this gospel shall be preached in the whole world, there shall also this, that this woman hath done, be told for a memorial of her."[24]

From the feast at Simon's house to the last supper, we contemplate where Jesus again spoke of His death. Leading up to that moment, we learn of the ordinance of humiliation:

> His ministry was nearly completed; He had only a few more lessons to impart. And that they might never forget the humility of the pure and spotless Lamb of God, the great and efficacious Sacrifice for man humbled Himself to wash the feet of His disciples. It will do you good, and our ministers generally, to frequently review the closing scenes in the life of our Redeemer. Here, beset with temptations as He was, we may all learn lessons of the utmost importance to us. It would be well to spend a thoughtful hour each day reviewing the life of Christ from the manger to Calvary. We should take it point by point and let the imagination vividly grasp each scene, especially the closing ones of His earthly life. By thus contemplating His teachings and sufferings, and the infinite sacrifice made by Him for the redemption of the race, we may strengthen our faith, quicken our love, and become more deeply imbued with the spirit which sustained our Saviour. If we would be saved at last we must all learn the lesson of penitence and faith at the foot of the cross. Christ suffered humiliation to save us from everlasting disgrace. He consented to have scorn, mockery, and abuse fall upon Him in order to shield us. It was our transgression that gathered the veil of darkness about His divine soul and extorted the cry from Him, as of one smitten and forsaken of God. He bore our sorrows; He was put to grief for our sins. He made Himself an offering for sin, that we might be justified before God through Him. Everything noble and generous in man will respond to the contemplation of Christ upon the cross.[25]

Then, after breaking the bread and serving the communion cup, Jesus said, "Verily I say unto you, that one of you shall betray me."[26] The disciples were dumbfounded at first. They should not have been, because Jesus had told them earlier, "Behold, we go up to Jerusalem; and the Son of man shall be betrayed unto the chief priests and unto the scribes, and they shall condemn him to death, And shall deliver him to the Gentiles to mock, and to scourge, and to crucify him: and the third day he shall rise again."[27] But now they sat stunned, until having searched their hearts for such an act of treachery, determining to what cause would one betray Christ, they asked one by one, "Lord, is it I?"[28] The last one to do so, Judas Iscariot, was the guilty party. And yet Christ's

---

24   Matthew 26:10–13
25   White, *Testimonies for the Church*, vol. 4., p. 374.
26   Matthew 26:21
27   Matthew 20:18, 19
28   Matthew 26:22

revelation of this act was to further increase the faith of the disciples once they were acquainted with the prophecies of Scripture: "Yea, mine own familiar friend, in whom I trusted, which did eat of my bread, hath lifted up his heel against me."[29]

Later the disciples would understand that this treachery was not a surprise to Jesus. The faith of Jesus would sustain them during their own sufferings for His sake. Jesus' words spoken before His death would sustain them during their own trials and temptations. "Remember the word that I said unto you, The servant is not greater than his lord. If they have persecuted me, they will also persecute you; if they have kept my saying, they will keep yours also. But all these things will they do unto you for my name's sake, because they know not him that sent me."[30]

Afterward they would yield their own lives up for Christ's cause: James (brother to John) to Herod Agrippa's sword in AD 44; Philip, to the scourge, imprisonment, and crucifixion in AD 54; Matthew, to the halberd (an axe and spike on a wooden shaft) in AD 60; Matthias (Judas Iscariot's replacement), stoned in Jerusalem, then beheaded; Andrew and Peter, by crucifixion; Thaddeus (Jude), by crucifixion in AD 72; Bartholemew, in India by crucifixion; Thomas Didymus, in India by a spear thrust of a Brahman in AD 72; and Simon the zealot by crucifixion in AD 74. Of all the disciples, John the Revelator is supposed to be the only one who didn't die a violent death—having miraculously escaped death in a cauldron of boiling oil.[31]

By beholding Jesus, as He submitted by faith to death by crucifixion, the disciples lived, suffered persecution, and died as He did. They beheld Jesus, the Son of God manifested in the flesh, dwelling amongst them, and testified, "And the Word was made flesh, and dwelt among us, (and we beheld his glory, the glory as of the only begotten of the Father,) full of grace and truth."[32] They came to recognize that Jesus had left infinite glory to come to this earth, placing infinite value upon the souls of lost individuals. And they accepted, finally, His call to take up the cross and follow Him.

> But Jesus bade His followers take up the cross and bear it after Him. To the disciples His words, though [at first] dimly comprehended, pointed to their submission to the most bitter humiliation,—submission even unto death for the sake of Christ. No more complete self-surrender could the Saviour's words have pictured. But all this He had accepted for them. Jesus did not count heaven a place to be desired while we were lost. He left the heavenly courts for a life of reproach and insult, and a death of shame. He who was rich in heaven's priceless treasure, became poor, that through His poverty we might be rich. We are to follow in the path He trod.[33]

---

29   Psalm 41:9; see also John 13:18
30   John 15:20, 21
31   Foxe, *Book of Martyrs*, pp. 28–32; Wilkinson, *Truth Triumphant*, p. 293.
32   John 1:14
33   White, *The Desire of Ages*, p. 417.

As He approached Gethsemane with His disciples, His conversation with them ceased. They were surprised by His facial expressions of sorrow and sadness. They recognized that He was under great stress, but they didn't understand the cause for His distress.

> But now He seemed to be shut out from the light of God's sustaining presence. Now He was numbered with the transgressors. The guilt of fallen humanity He must bear. Upon Him who knew no sin must be laid the iniquity of us all. So dreadful does sin appear to Him, so great is the weight of guilt which He must bear, that He is tempted to fear it will shut Him out forever from His Father's love....
>
> As the substitute and surety for sinful man, Christ was suffering under divine justice. He saw what justice meant. Hitherto He had been as an intercessor for others; now He longed to have an intercessor for Himself.[34]

Three times He prayed, His fallen humanity striving with His divine will. Each time He yielded to the Father. "Could mortals have viewed the amazement of the angelic host as in silent grief they watched the Father separating His beams of light, love, and glory from His beloved Son, they would better understand how offensive in His sight is sin."[35] Finally, after falling to the ground as though dead, an angel of light appeared to strengthen Him. Unlike the deceiver who had appeared as an angel of light in the wilderness, this mighty angel did not inform Christ that He had suffered enough. No, instead he encouraged Jesus with a message of the Father's love even as Christ was feeling separated from that love.

> The angel came not to take the cup from Christ's hand, but to strengthen Him to drink it, with the assurance of the Father's love. He came to give power to the divine-human suppliant. He pointed Him to the open heavens, telling Him of the souls that would be saved as the result of His sufferings. He assured Him that His Father is greater and more powerful than Satan, that His death would result in the utter discomfiture of Satan, and that the kingdom of this world would be given to the saints of the Most High. He told Him that He would see of the travail of His soul, and be satisfied, for He would see a multitude of the human race saved, eternally saved.[36]

Have we fully comprehended what it means to have the faith of Jesus as it was demonstrated in His trial and death? He maintained silence except to honor His Father by the truth. He did not defend Himself through the travesty of seven trials in quick succession—one before Annas,

---

34   Ibid., pp. 685, 686.
35   Ibid., p. 693.
36   Ibid., pp. 693, 694.

another before Caiaphas, an illegal gathering of the Sanhedrin, then another at dawn for legal formality, the judgment before Pilate, then before Herod, and finally at Pilate's judgment hall. Throughout the whole unjust process, Jesus, the Lamb of God, was led to the slaughter.

The Lord hath laid on him the iniquity of us all. He was oppressed, and he was afflicted, yet he opened not his mouth: he is brought as a lamb to the slaughter, and as a sheep before her shearers is dumb, so he openeth not his mouth. He was taken from prison and from judgment: and who shall declare his generation? for he was cut off out of the land of the living: for the transgression of my people was he stricken.[37]

And the Lord hath given me knowledge of it, and I know it: then thou shewedst me their doings. But I was like a lamb or an ox that is brought to the slaughter; and I knew not that they had devised devices against me, saying, Let us destroy the tree with the fruit thereof, and let us cut him off from the land of the living, that his name may be no more remembered.[38]

Christ suffered keenly under abuse and insult. At the hands of the beings whom He had created, and for whom He was making an infinite sacrifice, He received every indignity. And He suffered in proportion to the perfection of His holiness and His hatred of sin. His trial by men who acted as fiends was to Him a perpetual sacrifice. To be surrounded by human beings under the control of Satan was revolting to Him. And He knew that in a moment, by the flashing forth of His divine power, He could lay His cruel tormentors in the dust. This made the trial the harder to bear.

The Jews were looking for a Messiah to be revealed in outward show. They expected Him, by one flash of overmastering will, to change the current of men's thoughts, and force from them an acknowledgment of His supremacy. Thus, they believed, He was to secure His own exaltation, and gratify their ambitious hopes. Thus when Christ was treated with contempt, there came to Him a strong temptation to manifest His divine character. By a word, by a look, He could compel His persecutors to confess that He was Lord above kings and rulers, priests and temple. But it was His difficult task to keep to the position He had chosen as one with humanity.[39]

37 Isaiah 53:6–8
38 Jeremiah 11:18, 19
39 White, *The Desire of Ages*, p. 700.

Those seven trials embraced four scenes of the cruel abuse and mockery committed by the rabble hired by the priests and rulers to arrest Jesus—people of His own nation—and by King Herod, as well as two scourgings ordered by Pilate.

> Priests and rulers forgot the dignity of their office, and abused the Son of God with foul epithets. They taunted Him with His parentage. They declared that His presumption in proclaiming Himself the Messiah made Him deserving of the most ignominious death. The most dissolute men engaged in infamous abuse of the Saviour….
>
> The Roman soldiers joined in this abuse. All that these wicked, corrupt soldiers, helped on by Herod and the Jewish dignitaries, could instigate was heaped upon the Saviour. Yet His divine patience failed not….
>
> Jesus was taken, faint with weariness and covered with wounds, and scourged in the sight of the multitude….
>
> And when he had again scourged Jesus, he delivered Him to be crucified.[40]

With what divine patience Christ suffered on our behalf! With what great faith He yielded Himself up to die for our rebellion, for our sins!

The agony Jesus suffered on the cross surpassed the physical pain He endured, for He was separated from His heavenly Father for the first time in His life. As the weight of the sins of the world crushed His spirit, He held on to His faith. I don't think we can ever fully understand how sorely tried His faith was.

> Even doubts assailed the dying Son of God. He could not see through the portals of the tomb. Bright hope did not present to him his coming forth from the tomb a conqueror, and his Father's acceptance of his sacrifice. The sin of the world with all its terribleness was felt to the utmost by the Son of God. The displeasure of the Father for sin, and its penalty, which was death, were all that he could realize through this amazing darkness. He was tempted to fear that sin was so offensive in the sight of his Father that he could not be reconciled to his Son. The fierce temptation that his own Father had forever left him, caused that piercing cry from the cross "My God, my God, why hast thou forsaken me?"[41]

With what great faith He yielded Himself up to die for our rebellion, for our sins!

---

40   Ibid., pp. 715, 731, 734, 738.
41   White, "The Love of Christ," *The Signs of the Times*, February 15, 1883.

Yet in His suffering His obedience was made perfect. "Let integrity and uprightness preserve me; for I wait on thee."[42]

What a wonderful example Christ offers us in the gift of His faith. Let us fall on our knees, pleading forgiveness for our lukewarm state, and obtain the faith of Jesus for ourselves, which He offers to us so freely, in order that, when He appears, we might be found blameless in His sight.

42   Psalm 25:21

Chapter 11

By Faith Jesus Resurrected

A person is usually not pronounced dead until blood circulation and breathing cease. Clinical death is considered by most professionals as a process occurring just before death—consciousness is lost within a few seconds, measurable brainwave activity flat-lines within twenty to forty seconds, and ischemic injury (due to lack of oxygen and nutrients necessary to sustain vital organ viability because the heart has ceased to pump blood) begins to occur, resulting in dysfunctional or permanent damage depending upon the ability of medical professionals to resuscitate the patient before toxic metabolic wastes build beyond the point of no return.[1] The build-up of wastes causes necrosis, which, if not reversed at body temperature within three to four hours, is terminal (and that timeframe is only if cessation of blood circulation is not complete). Otherwise one faces irreversible necrosis within twenty minutes. So, if a patient is pronounced clinically dead and is resuscitated, then such a person can claim a near-death experience (NDE).

Some years ago James Mauro wrote in an *Psychology Today* article titled "Bright Lights, Big Mystery" that there are as many as "eight million other Americans who, according to a recent poll by George Gallup, Jr., claim to have had a near-death experience (NDE). They have all had visions of lights, tunnels, and dead relatives greeting them and taking them to a place of beauty, warmth, and peace. And they all say they have been profoundly changed by the experience."[2] The article continues with information about the various ramifications or influence the experience has upon people of diverse cultures and whether or not what one sees or hears is impacted by cultural or social influences. If eight million Americans had NDEs prior to 1992, doesn't it make you wonder how many claim such experiences today?

The Lazarus syndrome, or Lazarus phenomenon, is the condition experienced by a very few who were pronounced dead after resuscitation efforts were unsuccessful, and yet, after

---

1   "Clinical Death," Wikipedia, http://1ref.us/3
2   Mauro, "Bright Lights, Big Mystery," *Psychology Today*, http://1ref.us/1.

resuscitation ceased, the blood circulation and breathing "spontaneously" restarted. The phenomenon is named after Lazarus because he was raised from the dead after being in the grave for four days; however, the phenomenon that occurs in some patients today is a misnomer since there are no known patients who have survived clinical death beyond a few minutes or hours.

Medical records show that at least twenty-five such cases have been reported since 1985. One patient that experienced the so-called Lazarus syndrome was Judith Johnson. In May of 2007 she was admitted to the hospital while suffering a heart attack. Within forty-five minutes of admittance, she was declared clinically dead from cardiac arrest. Medical records showed that she never regained a pulse when efforts to resuscitate her were ended. After informing her husband of her demise, her body was wheeled to the morgue. Sometime later someone, walking by the morgue, heard screaming. It turned out that Mrs. Johnson was very much alive, although she still suffers from brain and liver damage, chronic chest pains, memory loss, speech problems, and personality changes, among other ailments allegedly brought on by the medical treatment she received, or the lack thereof.[3]

Throughout history a fear of being buried alive has existed. Some cemeteries hooked up a rope and bell system in the casket so if one should regain awareness while in the coffin the living soul could communicate with the world above and be disinterred. Sailors who died at sea would be sown into body bags and wrapped with chains and weights in preparation for burial, with the last stitch of the heavy gauged needle passing through the nasal septum—a painful piercing that was designed to arouse to consciousness someone who might possibly not be dead—before the body was committed to the sea.

Skeptics reading about resurrection accounts in the Bible may attribute successful resuscitations to a primitive practice of cardiopulmonary resuscitation (CPR) in the cases of Elijah and Elisha.[4] They may even say the same of Jesus in the raising of Jairus' daughter or the widow's son from the village of Nain.[5] The objection they try to sustain is that Jesus Himself said that the little girl was sleeping. But the Bible is quite clear about death so that no mistake ought to be made regarding the matter:

> And when he came into the house, he suffered no man to go in, save Peter, and James, and John, and the father and the mother of the maiden. And all wept, and bewailed her: but he said, Weep not; she is not dead, but sleepeth. *And they laughed him to scorn, knowing that she was dead*. And he put them all out, and took her by the hand, and called, saying, Maid, arise. And her spirit came again, and she arose

3   "Woman Declared Dead, Still Breathing in Morgue," Fox News, http://1ref.us/7.
4   1 Kings 17:17–22; 2 Kings 4:32–35; 2 Kings 13:20, 21
5   Mark 5:35–43; Luke 7:11–17

straightway: and he commanded to give her meat. And her parents were aston-
ished: but he charged them that they should tell no man what was done.[6]

The little girl was dead. When Jairus had finally made the decision to even come to Jesus for help, she lay dying. Shortly after reaching Jesus, a messenger arrived with the sad news that she had died. When they arrived at the house, they were greeted by professional mourners who knew death when they saw it. The reason for Jesus' expression of sleep, as it pertains to the first death, is because of a tremendous teaching in the Scriptures upon which He rested His faith. The Law of Moses stated that anyone who touched a dead body was considered unclean for seven days.[7] Yet Jesus suffered no defilement when He touched the body of the dead girl because, by His touch, He imparted life.

In order to best deal with our ignorance regarding Jesus' faith in the resurrection, we need to go back to the genesis of history. From the time of creation, the living soul, which makes up a man, consists of two parts: dust and the breath of God. "And the Lord God formed man of the dust of the ground, and breathed into his nostrils the breath of life; and man became a living soul."[8]

God required obedience from Adam and Eve, testing them by virtue of a pledge in the form of the tree of knowledge of good and evil. If they ate of the tree of life, they would live. But the day they ate of the forbidden fruit, they would forfeit their very lives and begin to die. "The path of obedience is possible, and it leads to the tree of life. This is the path that leads to the paradise of God. The requirement of God to obey and live was given to Adam. The only way to life is found through obedience to the commandments."[9] To disobey results in death since "the wages of sin is death."[10] So, upon the entrance of sin with Adam's and Eve's fall, God pronounced the death sentence against the whole of Adam's race when He said, "In the sweat of thy face shalt thou eat bread, till thou return unto the ground; for out of it wast thou taken: for dust thou art, and unto dust shalt thou return."[11] This is why Paul parenthetically wrote, "Nevertheless death reigned from Adam to Moses, even over them that had not sinned after the similitude of Adam's transgression, who is the figure of him that was to come."[12] Therefore, we see death as the opposite of the creation of life. The breath of God returns to Him, and the living soul becomes nothing as the body returns to the dust from which Adam was made.

Job well knew the teaching of God regarding death when he said to his miserable comforters, "And why dost thou not pardon my transgression, and take away mine iniquity? for now shall

---

6   Luke 8:51–56
7   Numbers 19:11
8   Genesis 2:7
9   White, "Obedience the Path to Life," *The Review and Herald*, March 28, 1893.
10   Romans 6:23
11   Genesis 3:19
12   Romans 5:14

I sleep in the dust; and thou shalt seek me in the morning, but I *shall* not *be*.... Remember, I beseech thee, that thou hast made me as the clay; and wilt thou bring me into dust again?... And where *is* now my hope? As for my hope, who shall see it? They shall go down to the bars of the pit, when *our* rest together *is* in the dust."[13] Elihu confirmed Job's words regarding death when he spoke these words: "All flesh shall perish together, and man shall turn again unto dust."[14] Still, Job had this one hope left—the resurrection—as he intoned, "And though after my skin worms destroy this body, yet in my flesh shall I see God."[15]

The psalmist clearly tells us that death is not "soul sleep" as some have come to call it. He stated, under the inspiration of the Holy Spirit, "Thou hidest thy face, they are troubled: thou takest away their breath, they die, and return to their dust."[16]

Isaiah spoke of the resurrection as an awakening from sleep, writing, "Thy dead men shall live, together with my dead body shall they arise. Awake and sing, ye that dwell in dust: for thy dew is as the dew of herbs, and the earth shall cast out the dead."[17]

When writing about the time of the end, Daniel wrote about a special resurrection, "And many of them that sleep in the dust of the earth shall awake, some to everlasting life, and some to shame and everlasting contempt."[18]

I recall a conversation between a Jewish physician and a Christian nurse touching upon the terrible things done in the concentration camps of the Third Reich. The doctor voiced concern over those victims who were incinerated in the huge crematorium ovens as to how they could possibly be resurrected since their bones were now ashes. The nurse replied, "Is it easier for God to make man from dust, or from water?" The lesson embedded in the mind of the physician was that if God could create humans from the liquid composed of sperm and ova, if God could form Adam from the dust, then why not trust God to recreate those dear to His heart from ashes?

> *The nurse replied, "Is it easier for God to make man from dust, or from water?"*

Ezekiel, by the hand of the Lord, flew through the air to a valley filled with bones. God asked him, "Son of man, can these bones live?" Ezekiel replied, "O Lord God, thou knowest."[19] Then the Lord commanded Ezekiel to prophesy unto the bones.

---

13   Job 7:21; 10:9; 17:15, 16
14   Job 34:15
15   Job 19:26
16   Psalm 104:29
17   Isaiah 26:19
18   Daniel 12:2
19   Ezekiel 37:3

O ye dry bones, hear the word of the Lord…. Behold, I will cause breath to enter into you, and ye shall live: And I will lay sinews upon you, and will bring up flesh upon you, and cover you with skin, and put breath in you, and ye shall live; and ye shall know that I am the Lord….

Prophesy unto the wind, prophesy, son of man, and say to the wind, Thus saith the Lord God; Come from the four winds, O breath, and breathe upon these slain, that they may live….

Son of man, these bones are the whole house of Israel: behold, they say, Our bones are dried, and our hope is lost: we are cut off for our parts. Therefore prophesy and say unto them, Thus saith the Lord God; Behold, O my people, I will open your graves, and cause you to come up out of your graves, and bring you into the land of Israel. And ye shall know that I am the Lord, when I have opened your graves, O my people, and brought you up out of your graves, And shall put my spirit in you, and ye shall live, and I shall place you in your own land: then shall ye know that I the Lord have spoken it, and performed it, saith the Lord.[20]

These testimonies of the prophets were the basis for the faith of Jesus concerning the doctrine of the resurrection. So then, it should be no wonder to us that Jesus responded to the Sadducees as He did when they posed their entrapping question. They thought they might stump the Savior with the same arguments they used against the Pharisees. "Master, Moses said, If a man die, having no children, his brother shall marry his wife, and raise up seed unto his brother. Now there were with us seven brethren: and the first, when he had married a wife, deceased, and, having no issue, left his wife unto his brother: Likewise the second also, and the third, unto the seventh. And last of all, the woman died also. Therefore in the resurrection whose wife shall she be of the seven? for they all had her."[21]

Jesus well understood their purpose. The psalmist had prophesied concerning these very events, writing, "Mine enemies speak evil of me, When shall he die, and his name perish? And if he come to see me, he speaketh vanity: his heart gathereth iniquity to itself; when he goeth abroad, he telleth it. All that hate me whisper together against me: against me do they devise my hurt."[22] He knew that they rejected His teachings and discounted His miracles.

By His words and His works, Christ testified to a divine power that produces supernatural results, to a future life beyond the present, to God as a Father of the children of men, ever watchful of their true interests. He revealed the working of divine power in benevolence and compassion that rebuked the selfish exclusiveness

20   Ezekiel 37:4–6, 9, 11–14
21   Matthew 22:24–28
22   Psalm 41:5–7

of the Sadducees. He taught that both for man's temporal and for his eternal good, God moves upon the heart by the Holy Spirit. He showed the error of trusting to human power for that transformation of character which can be wrought only by the Spirit of God.

This teaching the Sadducees were determined to discredit. In seeking a controversy with Jesus, they felt confident of bringing Him into disrepute, even if they could not secure His condemnation. The resurrection was the subject on which they chose to question Him. Should He agree with them, He would give still further offense to the Pharisees. Should He differ with them, they designed to hold His teaching up to ridicule.[23]

But having memorized Scripture from His youth, Jesus understood that the Sadducees were not acquainted with the power of God as so beautifully illustrated in Ezekiel's account of the resurrection. They might think themselves the true expositors of the Scriptures, but they didn't even know the Scriptures, or the power of God.

They professed to believe the greater portion of the Scriptures, and to regard them as the rule of action; but practically they were skeptics and materialists....

They denied that the Spirit of God works through human efforts or natural means. Yet they still held that, through the proper employment of his natural powers, man could become elevated and enlightened; that by rigorous and austere exactions his life could be purified....

[Jesus] taught that both for man's temporal and for his eternal good, God moves upon the heart by the Holy Spirit. He showed the error of trusting to human power for that transformation of character which can be wrought only by the Spirit of God.

This teaching the Sadducees were determined to discredit.[24]

"Jesus answered and said unto them, Ye do err, not knowing the scriptures, nor the power of God. For in the resurrection they neither marry, nor are given in marriage, but are as the angels of God in heaven. But as touching the resurrection of the dead, have ye not read that which was spoken unto you by God, saying, I am the God of Abraham, and the God of Isaac, and the God of Jacob? God is not the God of the dead, but of the living."[25] Mark wrote, "He is not the God of

---

23   White, *The Desire of Ages*, p. 605.
24   Ibid., pp. 603, 604, 605.
25   Matthew 22:29–32

the dead, but the God of the living: ye therefore do greatly err."[26] And Luke gives further insight: "For he is not a God of the dead, but of the living: *for all live unto him*."[27]

In other words, those who obey God through faith in Jesus will live again. Some may have seen Jesus—through faith—as a sacrificial lamb. Some may have witnessed His life upon this earth. We may see Jesus today—by faith—interceding for us by the presentation of His shed blood. We may acknowledge that faith in the token of unleavened bread and fresh grape juice. But the faith in Him is unchanged. He who hung upon a tree, accounted as cursed of God because of our disobedience, is our tree of life—our resurrection because of His obedience. He claims our obedience by exhorting us to overcome as He overcame. And the promise given to the obedient is that we will take part in the first resurrection, with the unrepentant wicked reserved for the second resurrection to take place after a thousand years.[28]

Jesus gave Martha a gentle reminder of the resurrection when she voiced her faith in Him, acknowledging, "But I know, that even now, whatsoever thou wilt ask of God, God will give it thee. Jesus saith unto her, Thy brother shall rise again."[29]

> His answer was not intended to inspire hope of an immediate change. He carried Martha's thoughts beyond the present restoration of her brother, and fixed them upon the resurrection of the just. This He did that she might see in the resurrection of Lazarus a pledge of the resurrection of all the righteous dead, and an assurance that it would be accomplished by the Saviour's power....
>
> The miracle which Christ was about to perform, in raising Lazarus from the dead, would represent the resurrection of all the righteous dead. By His word and His works He declared Himself the Author of the resurrection. He who Himself was soon to die upon the cross stood with the keys of death, a conqueror of the grave, and asserted His right and power to give eternal life.[30]

Martha then went to retrieve Mary, and together they accompanied Jesus to Lazarus' tomb. At the graveside Jesus joined His tears to theirs, though it was not for Lazarus that He wept. "It was not only because of His human sympathy with Mary and Martha that Jesus wept. In His tears there was a sorrow as high above human sorrow as the heavens are higher than the earth. Christ did not weep for Lazarus; for He was about to call him from the grave. He wept because many of those now mourning for Lazarus would soon plan the death of Him who was the resurrection and the life. But how unable were the unbelieving Jews rightly to interpret His tears!"[31] He wept

26   Mark 12:27
27   Luke 20:38
28   John 5:29; Revelation 20:5, 6
29   John 11:22, 23
30   White, *The Desire of Ages*, p. 530.
31   Ibid., p. 533.

for the unbelief that would later result in their being resurrected to their own damnation. How He desired to impart to them His faith in exchange for their unbelief, which was destroying their faith!

> With prophetic eye Christ saw the enmity of the Pharisees and the Sadducees. He knew that they were premeditating His death. He knew that some of those now apparently so sympathetic would soon close against themselves the door of hope and the gates of the city of God. A scene was about to take place, in His humiliation and crucifixion, that would result in the destruction of Jerusalem, and at that time none would make lamentation for the dead. The retribution that was coming upon Jerusalem was plainly portrayed before Him. He saw Jerusalem compassed by the Roman legions. He knew that many now weeping for Lazarus would die in the siege of the city, and in their death there would be no hope.[32]

When Jesus commanded the stone rolled away, Martha objected. She did not fully comprehend what Christ was about to do, and she did not want the decaying body of her brother brought to view. As such, she displayed a degree of unbelief that comes with misapprehension due to a lack of comprehension. So often we are like Martha, desiring a miracle and expressing faith in the divinity of Christ, yet slow to cooperate with Christ in fulfilling the answer to our prayers. Upon His reassurance all would be done to the glory of God, the stone was rolled away. All gathered about the entrance of the tomb could see Lazarus' dead body. None could later scandalize the miracle on account of any treachery or fraud on Christ's part as He brought Lazarus back to life. Still, Jesus took time to pray.

> In all that He did, Christ was co-operating with His Father. Ever He had been careful to make it evident that He did not work independently; it was by faith and prayer that He wrought His miracles. Christ desired all to know His relationship with His Father…. Here the disciples and the people were to be given the most convincing evidence in regard to the relationship existing between Christ and God. They were to be shown that Christ's claim was not a deception.[33]

And by this miracle we have been shown how Christ demonstrated His faith, which He desires to impart to us. Today, we have counsel given for the purpose of expanding our ministry of healing. Especially to physicians are these words written:

---

32   Ibid., p. 534.
33   Ibid., p. 536.

The Scriptures are to be received as God's word to us, not written merely, but spoken. When the afflicted ones came to Christ, He beheld not only those who asked for help, but all who throughout the ages should come to Him in like need and with like faith. When He said to the paralytic, "Son, be of good cheer; thy sins be forgiven thee;" when He said to the woman of Capernaum, "Daughter, be of good comfort: thy faith hath made thee whole; go in peace," He spoke to other afflicted, sin-burdened ones who should seek His help. Matthew 9:2; Luke 8:48.

"So with all the promises of God's word. In them He is speaking to us individually, speaking as directly as if we could listen to His voice. It is in these promises that Christ communicates to us His grace and power. They are leaves from that tree which is "for the healing of the nations." Revelation 22:2. Received, assimilated, they are to be the strength of the character, the inspiration and sustenance of the life. Nothing else can have such healing power. Nothing besides can impart the courage and faith which give vital energy to the whole being.

To one who stands trembling with fear on the brink of the grave, to the soul weary of the burden of suffering and sin, let the physician as he has opportunity repeat the words of the Saviour—for all the words of Holy Writ are His.[34]

Jesus finished His prayer, and then said, "Lazarus, come forth…. Loose him, and let him go."[35]

"Lazarus is set free, and stands before the company, not as one emaciated from disease, and with feeble, tottering limbs, but as a man in the prime of life, and in the vigor of a noble manhood. His eyes beam with intelligence and with love for his Saviour. He casts himself in adoration at the feet of Jesus.

The beholders are at first speechless with amazement. Then there follows an inexpressible scene of rejoicing and thanksgiving. The sisters receive their brother back to life as the gift of God, and with joyful tears they brokenly express their thanks to the Saviour. But while brother, sisters, and friends are rejoicing in this reunion, Jesus withdraws from the scene. When they look for the Life-giver, He is not to be found.[36]

By the time Jesus reached Gethsemane on the night He was betrayed, His soul was exceedingly sorrowful because He already felt the weight of the sins of the world upon Him. His faith didn't obtain any more evidence that He and the Father were one. His prayer that His disciples

---

34   White, *The Ministry of Healing*, p. 122.
35   John 11:43, 44
36   White, *The Desire of Ages*, p. 536.

might be one with Them was a prayer of faith. Even with the encouragement from the great angel, He had to proceed by a faith that could not see beyond the portal of the grave. Sin was so exceedingly hateful to God that Jesus—our Substitute—feared He would be cut off from the Father forever. As He hung upon the cross for us, His faith had to rest upon the past evidences in the Father's providential leading.

In accordance with that faith, Jesus always had taught:

> I am the living bread which came down from heaven: if any man eat of this bread, he shall live for ever: and the bread that I will give is my flesh, which I will give for the life of the world....
>
> As the Father knoweth me, even so know I the Father: and I lay down my life for the sheep.... Therefore doth my Father love me, because I lay down my life, that I might take it again. No man taketh it from me, but I lay it down of myself. I have power to lay it down, and I have power to take it again. *This commandment have I received of my Father.*[37]

Jesus believed the commandment of His Father, and that was the basis for His obedience—even to death upon the cross!

Now that He was dead, the priests and rulers remembered His words regarding being raised up in three days. They feared the words to be true, given the power of His word to raise Lazarus to life. And they remembered His first words spoken three and a half years earlier: "Destroy this temple, and in three days I will raise it up."[38] They thought to pervert these words as a means of garnering Roman support for His execution. So they went back to Pilate—even upon the Sabbath day—and secured additional support for Christ's burial.

> Sir, we remember that that deceiver said, while he was yet alive, After three days I will rise again. Command therefore that the sepulchre be made sure until the third day, lest his disciples come by night, and steal him away, and say unto the people, He is risen from the dead: so the last error shall be worse than the first. Pilate said unto them, Ye have a watch: go your way, make it as sure as ye can. So they went, and made the sepulchre sure, sealing the stone, and setting a watch.[39]

While the disciples' faith had died with Jesus, the unbelieving religious leaders believed and trembled. By their own advice the soldiers broke the legs of the two thieves so that they would die more quickly and could be taken off the crosses. Coming to Jesus, they could see He

---

37   John 6:51; 10:15–18
38   John 2:19
39   Matthew 27:62–66

was already dead, but because death was difficult to determine, and not wanting to risk that He had merely fainted, the priests and rulers suggested the well aimed spear thrust—to which the Roman soldiers complied. This was done before the witness of the disciples, crushing their faint hopes. Then, because the religious leaders feared Jesus more in resurrection than they did in death, they obtained a watch, which ultimately glorified God with additional witnesses to the veracity of Christ's resurrection.

None of this would have occurred if they hadn't been so ignorant of the Scriptures and the power of God, for they would have attempted to accomplish their plans in a manner so as to avoid fulfilling Scripture—if it were possible—because of their intense, jealous hatred of Jesus. By their counsel to the soldiers, the law of the Passover—which pointed to Jesus Christ the Son of God—was fulfilled:

> They shall leave none of it unto the morning, nor break any bone of it: according to all the ordinances of the passover they shall keep it.[40]

> He keepeth all his bones: not one of them is broken.[41]

> And I will pour upon the house of David, and upon the inhabitants of Jerusalem, the spirit of grace and of supplications: and they shall look upon me whom they have pierced, and they shall mourn for him, as one mourneth for his only son, and shall be in bitterness for him, as one that is in bitterness for his firstborn.[42]

> Why do the heathen rage, and the people imagine a vain thing? The kings of the earth set themselves, and the rulers take counsel together, against the Lord, and against his anointed, saying, Let us break their bands asunder, and cast away their cords from us. He that sitteth in the heavens shall laugh: the Lord shall have them in derision.[43]

If only the priests and rulers had been at the tomb that night and into the morning. They had asked for a sign from heaven, but they assuredly missed it because they entrusted the care of the tomb to Roman soldiers. Suddenly there was another great earthquake. Perhaps in fleeing from their homes in the earthquake, they saw the flash of light in the vicinity of the garden tomb. Certainly they were aroused at the thought that an earthquake marked the death of Christ, and this one also marked His resurrection.

---

40   Numbers 9:12
41   Psalm 34:20
42   Zechariah 12:10
43   Psalm 2:1–4

How sweet it must have been to the ears of Jesus to hear the words, "Son of God, come forth; Thy Father calls Thee."[44] The Firstborn of the first fruits of the resurrection arose, folded the grave clothes that had been wrapped about Him, and appeared to the very soldiers who had witnessed His unjust trial, His unmerciful judgment, His cruel death, and now His glorious resurrection. It was more than they could bear. These soldiers, who constantly trained in

If only the priests and rulers had been at the tomb that night and into the morning.

warfare so as to establish unshakeable confidence at the sight of any human foe, fainted like dead men before the risen Savior. When they regained their composure, Jesus was gone and the tomb was empty. Again they feared for their lives and thought to tell Pilate straight away so that they would not lose their lives by reason of alleged dereliction of duty—for the act of fainting could not be any more justified than sleeping while on duty. But they were intercepted by the wily priests and persuaded for huge amounts of money to perjure themselves to Pilate and the people.

This act of false witness did not confound God. For at the resurrection, "the graves were opened; and many bodies of the saints which slept arose, And came out of the graves after his resurrection, and went into the holy city, and appeared unto many."[45]

When Christ cried out while upon the cross, "It is finished," there was a mighty earthquake, that rent open the graves of many who had been faithful and loyal, bearing their testimony against every evil work, and magnifying the Lord of hosts. As the Life-giver came forth from the sepulcher, proclaiming. "I am the resurrection, and the life," he summoned these saints from the grave. When alive, they had borne their testimony unflinchingly for the truth; now, they were to be witnesses to him who had raised them from the dead. These, said Christ, are no longer the captives of Satan. I have redeemed them; I have brought them from the grave as the first-fruits of my power, to be with me where I am, nevermore to see death or experience sorrow.

During his ministry, Jesus raised the dead to life. He raised the son of the widow of Nain, the daughter of Jairus, and Lazarus; but these were not clothed with immortality. After they were raised, they continued to be subject to death. But those who came forth from the grave at Christ's resurrection were raised to everlasting life. They were the multitude of captives that ascended with him as trophies of his victory over death and the grave.

---

44   White, *The Desire of Ages*, p. 780.
45   Matthew 27:52, 53

After his resurrection, Christ did not show himself to any save his followers; but testimony in regard to his resurrection was not wanting. Those who were raised with Christ "appeared unto many," declaring, Christ has risen from the dead, and we are risen with him. They bore testimony in the city to the fulfillment of the scripture, "Thy dead men shall live, together with my dead body shall they arise. Awake and sing, ye that dwell in dust: for thy dew is as the dew of herbs, and the earth shall cast out the dead." These saints contradicted the lie which the Roman guard had been hired to circulate,—that the disciples had come by night and stolen him away. This testimony could not be silenced.[46]

Even Josephus knew from these evidences that Jesus was the Messiah. "Now, there was about this time Jesus, a wise man, if it be lawful to call him a man, for he was a doer of wonderful works—a teacher of such men [that] receive the truth with pleasure. He drew over to him both many of the Jews, and many of the Gentiles. He was [the] Christ; and when Pilate, at the suggestion of the principal men amongst us, had condemned him to the cross, those that loved him at the first did not forsake him, for he appeared to them alive again the third day, as the divine prophets had foretold these and ten thousand other wonderful things concerning him; and the tribe of Christians, so named from him, are not extinct at this day."[47]

As Jesus kept the commandments of God, and had faith in God, so we are called to patiently endure hardship, persecution, and death with the glorious hope of the resurrection, as is clearly promised in Scripture.

Yea, and all that will live godly in Christ Jesus shall suffer persecution.[48]

And they overcame him by the blood of the Lamb, and by the word of their testimony; and they loved not their lives unto the death.... And the dragon was wroth with the woman, and went to make war with the remnant of her seed, which keep the commandments of God, and have the testimony of Jesus Christ.[49]

Here is the patience of the saints: here are they that keep the commandments of God, and the faith of Jesus. And I heard a voice from heaven saying unto me, Write, Blessed are the dead which die in the Lord from henceforth: Yea, saith the Spirit, that they may rest from their labours; and their works do follow them.[50]

46   White, "The Risen Saviour," *The Youth's Instructor*, August 11, 1898.
47   Josephus, *The Genuine Works of Flavius Josephus*, p. 67.
48   2 Timothy 3:12
49   Revelation 12:11, 17
50   Revelation 14:12, 13

Wherefore seeing we also are compassed about with so great a cloud of witnesses, let us lay aside every weight, and the sin which doth so easily beset us, and let us run with patience the race that is set before us, Looking unto Jesus the author and finisher of our faith; who for the joy that was set before him endured the cross, despising the shame, and is set down at the right hand of the throne of God. For consider him that endured such contradiction of sinners against himself, lest ye be wearied and faint in your minds. Ye have not yet resisted unto blood, striving against sin.[51]

Let us be found as saints, keeping the commandments of God and having the faith of Jesus, being true to principle and faithful in obedience though the earth tremble and the heavens fall. Let us face whatever Satan hurls at us, as God allows, with undaunted courage, looking unto Jesus so that our faith may be perfected to the glory of God.

---

51 Hebrews 12:1–4

Chapter 12

By Faith Jesus Promised Another Comforter

In the heartland of the Great Plains, the weather sometimes changes rapidly—even drastically. We often joke about experiencing all four seasons within a twenty-four hour period. If you happen to live in this region, or are merely visiting, and don't like the weather, stick around; it will change. Because geographical obstacles are lacking, the differences between the temperatures of land and air masses can generate winds with great velocity because of the extreme changes in air density—with the flow of air moving from the higher to lower pressure. Denizens experience property damage from two kinds of wind: whirlwinds (tornados) and straight-line winds (derechos).

The town where we once resided has never experienced damage directly from a tornado, although we occasionally have had some close calls. In the spring of 2007, I was on the road and decided to call my wife. She informed me that she was hiding in a closet with our sons, surrounded with mattresses and wearing bike or hockey helmets, because a tornado was heading in their direction. I later learned that when the tornado reached just south of town, it lifted off the ground and didn't drop back down until it was north of the town limits. Another smaller town ended up with some damage to their public school and a few other buildings, but our town was untouched.

However, derechos are another story. They don't have the velocity of the whirlwind, but they can do damage comparable to that of a category one hurricane because they sweep across a large swath of country with some gusts in excess of one hundred miles per hour.

It is interesting to note that the story of Job begins with a straight-line wind and ends with a whirlwind. With the one, Job loses all his children. With the other, Job learned of his need for self-abasement and God's exaltation.[1]

---

1   Job 1:19; 40:1–11

The plagues of Egypt included a horde of devouring locusts brought in by an east wind and removed by a west wind.[2] And the escape through the Red Sea involved a miraculous wind, preparing dry land for the Israelites to walk over to the opposite shore, and providing a trap by which all the Egyptian hosts were drowned.[3] And it was by a wind that God brought quail to the Israelites that they might have food to eat.[4]

When the time came for Elijah's ministry to close, God determined to gather him up with a chariot of fire in a whirlwind. Elisha beheld the departure and was granted a double portion of God's spirit with the symbol of Elijah casting to him the mantle used to part the Jordan River.[5]

The combination of wind and fire can create a catastrophic condition appropriately named firestorm. As a natural phenomenon associated with brushfires, forest fires, or more generically known as wildfires, great winds are created by the thermal draft produced in the flames that are then drawn into the fire—fueling it. The turbulence produces "fire-whirls"—small dust-devil like tornados of sparks and flames that move erratically, spreading the fire amongst vegetation and isolated buildings dried by the radiated heat of the advancing fire. Firestorms are capable, as are volcanoes, of producing pyrocumulus clouds that emit lightning—the strikes of which create other fires in advance of the firestorm itself. Once such a conflagration is started, there is very little that firefighters can do to contain it—except pray for lower temperatures, higher humidity, or rain to slow it down.

Manmade firestorms, such as the ones that resulted from the bombings of Hamburg, Dresden, Tokyo, and Hiroshima, show us the extreme danger of fire and high winds to human life by the casualties incurred with each of these disasters. These events give us pause to consider a couple of very important thoughts: "For the Lord thy God is a consuming fire, even a jealous God,"[6] and "fear him which is able to destroy both soul and body in hell."[7]

After Jesus' ascension to heaven, the remaining eleven disciples, in addition to more than one hundred other followers of Christ, waited in Jerusalem "for the promise of the Father,"[8] the outpouring of the Holy Spirit. The time was well spent in prayer, meditation upon the teachings of Jesus, and daily going to the temple to praise God.[9] With ever increasing faith and love, they claimed God's blessing through Christ's merits: "It is Christ that died, yea rather, that is risen again, who is even at the right hand of God, who also maketh intercession for us."[10] "These days of preparation were days of deep heart searching. The disciples felt their spiritual need and cried to the Lord for the holy unction that was to fit them for the work of soul saving. They did not

---

2   Exodus 10:13, 19
3   Exodus 14:21–30
4   Numbers 11:31
5   2 Kings 2:1, 8–14
6   Deuteronomy 4:24; see also Hebrews 12:29
7   Matthew 10:28
8   Acts 1:4
9   Luke 24:53
10   Romans 8:34

ask for a blessing for themselves merely. They were weighted with the burden of the salvation of souls. They realized that the gospel was to be carried to the world, and they claimed the power that Christ had promised."[11]

Then it happened. The promised gift arrived on Pentecost like a mighty rushing wind accompanied by tongues of fire filling the whole room. The Holy Spirit manifested His presence like a mighty firestorm. But, just as in the story of Moses and the bush burning yet unconsumed, those within the room were not physically harmed. Instead, they were empowered to preach salvation to all who would listen because self was dead and their lives were hid in Christ.[12] Jesus' prayers of faith for unity in thought, feeling, purpose, and action had been answered.

Christ's teaching regarding the Holy Spirit, so radically different from that of the Pharisees and Sadducees, needed time to take root and overcome the misconceptions and lack of experiential knowledge of God's workings throughout history. The confusion and misunderstanding is reflected in Christ's question to Nicodemus on that quiet night outside Jerusalem, "Art thou a master of Israel, and knowest not these things?"[13] Everything that Jesus taught by faith is found in the Scripture, and every one of the children of Israel could have and should have known it.

> ### *The promised gift arrived on Pentecost like a mighty rushing wind accompanied by tongues of fire filling the whole room.*

The problem is that the unregenerate heart cannot receive the things of God, being at enmity with God.[14]

So often the natural, unregenerate heart will deceive the soul into creating a fantasy—a fatal error—which is then passed down from one generation to another until tradition is taught as doctrine in place of the commandments of God because they "became vain in their imaginations, and their foolish heart was darkened."[15] Such was the historical background for the disciples of Jesus, who were slow to comprehend the lessons Jesus presented to them.

The Sadducees taught that "having created man, God had left him to himself, independent of a higher influence. They held that man was free to control his own life and to shape the events of the world; that his destiny was in his own hands. They denied that the Spirit of God works through human efforts or natural means. Yet they still held that, through the proper employment of his natural powers, man could become elevated and enlightened; that by rigorous and austere exactions his life could be purified."[16] We see a similar position to this held by proponents of deism and modern deism.

---

11   White, *The Acts of the Apostles*, p. 37.
12   Colossians 3:3
13   John 3:10
14   1 Corinthians 2:14; Romans 8:7
15   Romans 1:21
16   White, *The Desire of Ages*, p. 604.

On the other hand, the Pharisees taught the tradition handed down to them for years:

> Several centuries prior to the advent of the Savior, the rabbis instituted this spuri-
> ous substitution for the Spirit of God, known as "Bath-kol," the daughter of a voice.
> This fraud, however, could not be discerned but by the rabbis; and the poor people
> were left in entire ignorance of this precious gift. This, no doubt, partially explains
> the reason why the disciples were so perplexed when Jesus told them of the com-
> ing of the Spirit to *them*, which they should receive, while the world and even the
> learned rabbis would reject it. To think *they* could have the real gift, which Jesus told
> them was so precious, and the rabbis and other learned men would not receive, was
> to them inexplicable. However, all *could* receive this blessed gift, if they would only
> open their hearts to it.[17]

Such teaching ignored that Pharaoh perceived the Holy Spirit working in Joseph's life before he was promoted from slave and prisoner to second from the throne.[18] Or that Eli perceived
his being bypassed by the Lord for a child who up to that time had not known "the Lord, neither
was the word of the Lord yet revealed unto him."[19] Nor should we exclude the working of the
Holy Spirit in the lives of shepherds like David, or herdsmen and wild fig gatherers like Amos.[20]

In modern times we see this teaching repeated in the doctrine of the nominal clergy who
dupe their church members into thinking that God speaks only through the chief theologians.
Unfortunately, too many professed Christians are content to defer to the doctrines of ministers and priests rather than take ownership of the truth for themselves by diligent study of the
Scripture to see if these things are so—as did the believers in Berea.[21] We are given the following
counsel regarding studying the Word of God for ourselves.

> There is today the same disposition to substitute the theories and traditions of men
> for the word of God as in the days of Christ, of Paul or of Luther. Ministers advance
> doctrines which have no foundation in the Scriptures of truth, and in place of Bible
> proof, they present their own assertions as authority. The people accept the minis-
> ter's interpretation of the word, without earnest prayer that they may know what is
> truth. There is no safety in depending upon human wisdom and judgment.[22]

---

17 Gilbert, *Practical Lessons From the Experience of Israel for the Church of To-day*, pp. 118, 119.
18 Genesis 41:38
19 1 Samuel 3:7; see also verses 1–15
20 2 Samuel 7:8; Amos 7:14
21 Acts 17:11
22 White, "Luther's Source of Strength," *The Signs of the Times*, June 21, 1883.

There are many who have a merely nominal faith, but this faith will not save you. Many believe in Christ because somebody else does, because the minister has told them this or that; but if you rest your faith only on the minister's word, you will be lost.[23]

It is extremely important, then, to see how the Scriptures influenced the faith of Jesus in His teachings regarding the Holy Spirit's work in our lives—the role the Spirit has in the plan of salvation.

From the beginning of Creation, God made men and women to be filled with the Holy Spirit. It is by sin that the Holy Spirit is grieved away, and it is by God's forgiveness through the righteousness of Christ that He is restored.[24] Isaiah had this to say:

> *Clearly God intended that all might receive the Holy Spirit to safeguard us from the deceptions of Satan.*

But your iniquities have separated between you and your God, and your sins have hid his face from you, that he will not hear.... And he saw that there was no man, and wondered that there was no intercessor: therefore his arm brought salvation unto him; and his righteousness, it sustained him.... And the Redeemer shall come to Zion, and unto them that turn from transgression in Jacob, saith the Lord. As for me, this is my covenant with them, saith the Lord; My spirit that is upon thee, and my words which I have put in thy mouth, shall not depart out of thy mouth, nor out of the mouth of thy seed, nor out of the mouth of thy seed's seed, saith the Lord, from henceforth and for ever.[25]

Clearly God intended that all might receive the Holy Spirit to safeguard us from the deceptions of Satan.

Isaiah was not the only prophet to reveal God's intent in bestowing the Holy Spirit. Moses reproved Joshua's protectiveness with words of desire and hope: "Enviest thou for my sake? would God that all the Lord's people were prophets, and that the Lord would put his spirit upon them!"[26] Samuel told Saul, upon his being anointed king, that the spirit of the Lord would enter him—making him a new man.[27]

The psalmist wrote in his plea for forgiveness, "Cast me not away from thy presence; and take not thy holy spirit from me. Restore unto me the joy of thy salvation; and uphold me with

23 White, "Christ May Dwell in Your Hearts by Faith," *The Review and Herald*, October 1, 1889.
24 Ephesians 4:29–31
25 Isaiah 59:2, 16, 20, 21
26 Numbers 11:29
27 1 Samuel 10:6

thy free spirit."[28] David also wrote, "Whither shall I go from thy spirit? or whither shall I flee from thy presence?"[29] and "Teach me to do thy will; for thou art my God: thy spirit is good; lead me into the land of uprightness."[30] Solomon recorded these words of wisdom, "Turn you at my reproof: behold, I will pour out my spirit unto you, I will make known my words unto you."[31]

Joel prophesied, "And it shall come to pass afterward, that I will pour out my spirit upon all flesh; and your sons and your daughters shall prophesy, your old men shall dream dreams, your young men shall see visions: And also upon the servants and upon the handmaids in those days will I pour out my spirit."[32] Nehemiah regaled, "Thou gavest also thy good spirit to instruct them, and withheldest not thy manna from their mouth, and gavest them water for their thirst. Yea, forty years didst thou sustain them in the wilderness, so that they lacked nothing; their clothes waxed not old, and their feet swelled not…. Yet many years didst thou forbear them, and testifiedst against them by thy spirit in thy prophets: yet would they not give ear: therefore gavest thou them into the hand of the people of the lands."[33] So the only obstacle to meeting the conditions for receiving the Holy Spirit is the unregenerate, selfish heart.

Even as God's professed people were in Babylon, He tried to instruct them as to the purpose He had for them through Jeremiah and Ezekiel. Both prophets emphasized the need for a new heart and a new spirit. "I will put my law in their inward parts, and write it in their hearts … And I will give them one heart, and one way, that they may fear me for ever, for the good of them, and of their children after them … I will put my fear in their hearts, that they shall not depart from me."[34] "And I will give them one heart, and I will put a new spirit within you; and I will take the stony heart out of their flesh, and will give them an heart of flesh…. A new heart also will I give you, and a new spirit will I put within you: and I will take away the stony heart out of your flesh, and I will give you an heart of flesh…. Cast away from you all your transgressions, whereby ye have transgressed; and make you a new heart and a new spirit: for why will ye die, O house of Israel?"[35]

Accompanying the new heart of flesh—with God's law written upon it—is the Holy Spirit of God, teaching us: "This is the way, walk ye in it, when ye turn to the right hand, and when ye turn to the left,"[36] "Obey my voice, and I will be your God, and ye shall be my people: and walk ye in all the ways that I have commanded you, that it may be well unto you,"[37] "And they shall teach no

---

28 Psalm 51:11, 12
29 Psalm 139:7
30 Psalm 143:10
31 Proverbs 1:23
32 Joel 2:28, 29
33 Nehemiah 9:20, 21, 30
34 Jeremiah 31:33; 32:39, 40
35 Ezekiel 11:19; 36:26; 18:31
36 Isaiah 30:21
37 Jeremiah 7:23

more every man his neighbour, and every man his brother, saying, Know the Lord: for they shall all know me, from the least of them unto the greatest of them."[38]

Because Jesus was with His disciples visibly on a day-to-day basis for almost three and a half years, they did not feel their need for the Holy Spirit, nor did they recognize that the power of the Holy Spirit was behind the miracles they did in Christ's name. "Before this the Spirit had been in the world; from the very beginning of the work of redemption He had been moving upon men's hearts. But while Christ was on earth, the disciples had desired no other helper. Not until they were deprived of His presence would they feel their need of the Spirit, and then He would come."[39]

Still working and teaching by faith, Jesus tried to prepare the disciples to acknowledge their need of, and to receive, the Holy Spirit. Concerning upcoming trials and persecutions, Jesus taught, "But when they shall lead you, and deliver you up, take no thought beforehand what ye shall speak, neither do ye premeditate: but whatsoever shall be given you in that hour, that speak ye: for it is not ye that speak, but the Holy Ghost."[40] "For the Holy Ghost shall teach you in the same hour what ye ought to say."[41] "For it is not ye that speak, but the Spirit of your Father which speaketh in you."[42]

On another occasion, Jesus taught the willingness of the Father to give of the Spirit to those who asked. "If a son shall ask bread of any of you that is a father, will he give him a stone? or if he ask a fish, will he for a fish give him a serpent? Or if he shall ask an egg, will he offer him a scorpion? If ye then, being evil, know how to give good gifts unto your children: how much more shall your heavenly Father give the Holy Spirit to them that ask him?"[43] "The Lord is more willing to give His Holy Spirit to those who earnestly desire it than earthly parents are to give good gifts to their children. Christ has promised the Holy Spirit to guide us into all truth and righteousness and holiness. The Spirit of God is not given by measure to those who earnestly seek for it, who by faith stand upon the promises of God."[44]

Again Jesus preached, "If any man thirst, let him come unto me, and drink. He that believeth on me, as the scripture hath said, out of his belly shall flow rivers of living water. (But this spake he of the Spirit, which they that believe on him should receive: for the Holy Ghost was not yet given; because that Jesus was not yet glorified.)"[45] The problem is we do not recognize our need. Because we do not sense our need or, worse still, desire to unconditionally surrender our lives and lifestyles to God, we are less willing to receive what God is more than willing to bestow!

---

38 Jeremiah 31:34
39 White, *The Desire of Ages*, p. 669.
40 Mark 13:11
41 Luke 12:12
42 Matthew 10:20
43 Luke 11:11–13
44 White, "Christ's Example in Prayer," *The Signs of the Times*, July 15, 1908.
45 John 7:37–39

But that wasn't so much the case for the disciples. They loved Jesus and desired to be in His presence. As long as He was with them, they would not desire what they needed. Because Jesus limited His presence by taking upon Himself the form and flesh of humanity, He interceded on our behalf for the outpouring of the Holy Spirit. Then, by faith, He prepared His disciples to receive this tremendous gift—another Comforter. "Even the Spirit of truth; whom the world cannot receive, because it seeth him not, neither knoweth him: but ye know him; for he dwelleth with you, and shall be in you…. But the Comforter, which is the Holy Ghost, whom the Father will send in my name, he shall teach you all things, and bring all things to your remembrance, whatsoever I have said unto you…. But when the Comforter is come, whom I will send unto you from the Father, even the Spirit of truth, which proceedeth from the Father, he shall testify of me… Howbeit when he, the Spirit of truth, is come, he will guide you into all truth: for he shall not speak of himself; but whatsoever he shall hear, that shall he speak: and he will shew you things to come."[46] Having said these things, He recognized that the disciples were unprepared to receive more of what He desired to tell them in order to establish their faith: "I have yet many things to say unto you, but ye cannot bear them now."[47]

With their hopes dashed upon Christ's death, and their immense relief and joy at His resurrection, the disciples were again in danger of not appreciating their need of the Holy Spirit. Even so, Jesus once more—by faith—reminded them that they should receive this most precious gift that the Father wanted to bestow on them. While with the ten—Thomas being absent for one reason or another—Jesus said, "Peace be unto you: as my Father hath sent me, even so send I you. And when he had said this, he breathed on them, and saith unto them, Receive ye the Holy Ghost: Whose soever sins ye remit, they are remitted unto them; and whose soever sins ye retain, they are retained."[48]

In all this, they remembered His words to them concerning His departing and His promise of another Comforter who was not limited by a body of flesh as to where His presence must be. "The Holy Spirit is Christ's representative, but divested of the personality of humanity, and independent thereof. Cumbered with humanity, Christ could not be in every place personally. Therefore it was for their interest that He should go to the Father, and send the Spirit to be His successor on earth. No one could then have any advantage because of his location or his personal contact with Christ. By the Spirit the Saviour would be accessible to all. In this sense He would be nearer to them than if He had not ascended on high."[49]

The promise of another Comforter, which Jesus made by faith, was one that the disciples did not immediately comprehend. They struggled with the idea that Christ should be invisible and yet made manifest. Just as Nicodemus had failed to comprehend the spiritual lessons Jesus

46   John 14:17, 26; 15:26; 16:13
47   John 16:12
48   John 20:21–23
49   White, *The Desire of Ages*, p. 669.

taught him, so the disciples failed to grasp the significance of the spiritual manifestation Christ spoke of. But He assured them that very soon they would understand. They failed to learn that Jesus was about to be glorified as our atonement—the Lamb of God slain from the foundation of the world—by being lifted up in the most humiliating manner. But upon understanding His role as the sacrifice for sinners, they would soon comprehend His glorified role as High Priest, pleading before the Father in the heavenly sanctuary for those who love and believe on Him. "The promise of the Comforter presented a rich truth to the disciples. It assured them that they should not lose their faith under the most trying circumstances. The Holy Spirit, sent in the name of Christ, was to be their Guide, teaching them all things, and bringing all things to their remembrance. This comforter was to be the representative of Christ their Advocate, who is constantly pleading in behalf of the fallen race."[50]

And what lessons the apostles learned! We are blessed to have, in what remains of their letters to fellow believers, the lessons they were inspired by the Comforter to pass on to us for our times. To the Jews, Peter preached, "Repent, and be baptized every one of you in the name of Jesus Christ for the remission of sins, and ye shall receive the gift of the Holy Ghost."[51] But when the Holy Spirit perceived the prejudice of the Jews against the Gentiles, and the Comforter was poured out upon the Gentiles prior to baptism, Peter remarked, "Can any man forbid water, that these should not be baptized, which have received the Holy Ghost as well as we?"[52] With this revelation we see the consistency of Paul's words, "For by one Spirit are we all baptized into one body, whether we be Jews or Gentiles, whether we be bond or free; and have been all made to drink into one Spirit."[53] "There is neither Jew nor Greek, there is neither bond nor free, there is neither male nor female: for ye are all one in Christ Jesus."[54]

When Ananias and Sapphira conspired in covetousness to withhold part of their donation and lie so as to maintain their prestige among the new believers, Peter reminded them that they were not lying to men but to God: "Why hath Satan filled thine heart to lie to the Holy Ghost, and to keep back part of the price of the land? Whiles it remained, was it not thine own? and after it was sold, was it not in thine own power? why hast thou conceived this thing in thine heart? thou hast not lied unto men, but unto God."[55]

We begin to see that the Comforter, whom Jesus had promised by faith, was as fully a member of the Godhead as the Father and the Son.

> The Comforter that Christ promised to send after He ascended to heaven, is the
> Spirit in all the fullness of the Godhead, making manifest the power of divine grace

---

50 White, "Farewell Words—Words of Comfort," *The Signs of the Times,* November 18, 1897.
51 Acts 2:38
52 Acts 10:47
53 1 Corinthians 12:13
54 Galatians 3:28
55 Acts 5:3, 4

to all who receive and believe in Christ as a personal Saviour. There are three living persons of the heavenly trio. In the name of these three powers,—the Father, the Son, and the Holy Ghost, those who receive Christ by living faith are baptized, and these powers will cooperate with the obedient subjects of heaven in their efforts to live the new life in Christ.[56]

In all of these thoughts, we are empowered to obtain and exercise the faith of Jesus as we yield our lives to the Holy Spirit who is sent to abide in us forever—so long as we do not grieve Him away by persistent disobedience made manifest by bitterness, anger or wrath, evil speaking, and malice.[57] Clearly Jesus won for us a title in heaven by His righteousness—justification by faith. And through the sanctifying work of the Holy Spirit, we are made fit for heaven—a work without which our title is meaningless.[58]

By the words of the apostles, we learn just how Jesus intended for us to be connected to Him like grafted branches to the vine.[59] "And he that keepeth his commandments dwelleth in him, and he in him. And hereby we know that he abideth in us, by the Spirit which he hath given us."[60] "What? know ye not that your body is the temple of the Holy Ghost which is in you, which ye have of God, and ye are not your own?"[61]

> *"The Holy Spirit first dwells in the heart as the truth, and this He does through the truth."*

By their testimony we perceive the inner workings of the spiritual battle we are called to undertake, and we receive hope because those who walk in the Spirit are not under condemnation.[62]

But ye are not in the flesh, but in the Spirit, if so be that the Spirit of God dwell in you. Now if any man have not the Spirit of Christ, he is none of his. And if Christ be in you, the body is dead because of sin; but the Spirit is life because of righteousness. But if the Spirit of him that raised up Jesus from the dead dwell in you, he that raised up Christ from the dead shall also quicken your mortal bodies by his Spirit that dwelleth in you…. For if ye live after the flesh, ye shall die: but if ye through the Spirit do mortify the deeds of the body, ye shall live. For as many as are led by the Spirit of God, they are the sons of God.[63]

---

56 White, "The Father, Son, and Holy Ghost," *Bible Training School*, March 1, 1906.
57 Ephesians 4:30, 31
58 Titus 3:5; 2 Thessalonians 2:13; 1 Peter 1:2; Hebrews 10:29
59 John 15:1–7
60 1 John 3:24
61 1 Corinthians 6:19
62 Romans 8:1
63 Romans 8:9–14

We also have evidence from the apostles as to those to whom the Comforter is sent. "And we are his witnesses of these things; and so is also the Holy Ghost, whom God hath given to them that obey him."[64] So, we should ever keep in mind that "the Comforter is promised only as the Spirit of truth. There is no comfort in a lie. The work of the Comforter is to define and maintain the truth; and there should be no worry lest the comfort will not follow. The Holy Spirit first dwells in the heart *as* the truth, and this He does *through* the truth."[65] "The Comforter is called the Spirit of truth because there is comfort and hope and peace in the truth. Falsehood cannot give genuine peace; this can be received only through the truth. We need heavenly culture and refinement. Under all circumstances we should manifest Christian sympathy and politeness. Daily we should send our supplications to heaven for divine grace and power. We must put away selfishness, and seek the heavenly adornment of a meek and quiet spirit, in the sight of God of great price."[66]

At Pentecost, Peter recognized the partial fulfillment of the prophecy of Joel chapter two concerning the outpouring of the Holy Spirit.[67] But in that same chapter, we read the promise, "Be glad then, ye children of Zion, and rejoice in the Lord your God: for he hath given you the former rain moderately, and he will cause to come down for you the rain, the former rain, and the latter rain in the first month."[68] Since the Holy Spirit is to dwell in us "*as* the truth," "*through* the truth," then we can see the connection between the outpouring of the Holy Spirit and the former and latter rains. "My doctrine shall drop as the rain, my speech shall distil as the dew, as the small rain upon the tender herb, and as the showers upon the grass."[69]

"The heart must be emptied of every defilement, and cleansed for the indwelling of the Spirit."

The truth is that while many are looking for the outpouring of the Holy Spirit they are in darkness as to the reasons why they have not received Him.

Many have in a great measure failed to receive the former rain. They have not obtained all the benefits that God has thus provided for them. They expect that the lack will be supplied by the latter rain. When the richest abundance of grace shall be bestowed, they intend to open their hearts to receive it. They are making a terrible mistake. The work that God has begun in the human heart in giving his light and knowledge, must be continually going forward. Every individual must realize

64   Acts 5:32
65   White, "Faith and Good Works," *The Signs of the Times*, May 19, 1898.
66   White, "Sanctification Through the Truth," *The Review and Herald*, April 12, 1892.
67   Joel 2:28; Acts 2:17
68   Joel 2:23
69   Deuteronomy 32:2

his own necessity. The heart must be emptied of every defilement, and cleansed for the indwelling of the Spirit. It was by the confession and forsaking of sin, by earnest prayer and consecration of themselves to God, that the early disciples prepared for the outpouring of the Holy Spirit on the day of Pentecost. The same work, only in greater degree, must be done now. Then the human agent had only to ask for the blessing, and wait for the Lord to perfect the work concerning him. It is God who began the work, and he will finish his work, making man complete in Jesus Christ. But there must be no neglect of the grace represented by the former rain. Only those who are living up to the light they have, will receive greater light. Unless we are daily advancing in the exemplification of the active Christian virtues, we shall not recognize the manifestations of the Holy Spirit in the latter rain. It may be falling on hearts all around us, but we shall not discern or receive it.[70]

How important it is then, that we understand just how great our need for the promised Comforter in the times we now live! As a fellow Laodicean, there remains only two choices to us: continue on unrepentant in our self-deception regarding our true condition or realize our wretchedness—our spiritual poverty, nakedness, and blindness—and repent by obtaining the gold purified in the fire depicting Christ's faith and love, the white raiment depicting Christ's unblemished righteousness, and the eye-salve symbolizing the Holy Spirit's discernment exercised in our hearts as our eyes are opened to our condition and our duty. If repenting, then we must trust the faith of Jesus in promising and sending us another Comforter. He knows what is best for us.

He who knows the end from the beginning had provided for the attack of Satanic agencies; and he will fulfill his Word to the faithful in every age. That Word is sure and steadfast; not one jot or tittle of it can fail. The Holy Spirit is constantly at work, teaching, reminding, testifying, coming to the soul as a divine comforter, and convincing of sin as an appointed judge and guide. If men will keep under the protection of God, he will be to them as an impregnable fortress. He will give evidence that his Word can never fail. He will prove a light that shineth in a dark place until the day dawn; as the Sun of Righteousness he will arise with healing in his beams.[71]

May we then move forward by God's grace to overcome as Jesus did—by faith—through the Spirit.

---

70   White, "Pray for the Latter Rain," *The Review and Herald*, March 2, 1897.
71   White, "Farewell Words—Words of Comfort," *The Signs of the Times*, November 18, 1897.

Chapter 13

By Faith Jesus Prophesied

Many years ago I remember packing our camping gear and heading to Philo, California, to spend the weekend at camp meeting. The campground was located in Anderson Valley, about one hundred miles north of San Francisco, on the north bank of Indian Creek. Much to the delight of the children, the campground had a small earthen dam on the west side of the grounds that formed a shallow swimming hole where a thick hemp rope hung from a stout tree branch.

I recall one instance after the youth meeting on a warm Friday night when one of my schoolmates tried to get the rope so he could swing on it even though he was still in his Sabbath best. He managed to snag the rope with a branch, keeping his freshly polished dress shoes dry. At this point, I asked him what he was doing. He told me he was going to swing out over the creek. I said he shouldn't do it, and if he did, he would only get his Sabbath clothes all wet. He declared that he would stay dry because he had no intent on letting go of the rope. Having said this, he paced as far up the bank as the rope allowed, then ran as fast as he could go—jumping at the water's edge. It was a magnificent effort. He sailed as far as the pendulum arch would allow, and then, for reasons I could not perceive in the darkness, he let go of the rope. After making a huge splash, he waded back to shore, glaring at me as though I was the reason for his misery—the psychological self-fulfilling prophecy being the cause for the end result—before making his way back to his folks.

Nowadays, hardly anyone would think twice about this incident. Parents allow their children to play and swim on Sabbath as though there was nothing wrong with it. But at that time, most parents were more careful about Sabbath preparation on Fridays, and observing the Sabbath more carefully than we do now. I knew what trouble was going to come from the careless attitude lurking behind the adventurous spirit!

When one looks at the prophetic predictions of the Bible and sees how they have been fulfilled throughout history, one must conclude that all has been directly connected in some manner or another to the faith of Jesus—from the time He first offered Himself on our behalf to the time sin and death will be destroyed with all those who cling to wickedness. The multitude of Bible prophecies directly pointing to Christ's birth, His ministry, His death and resurrection, all of which He fulfilled, staggers the mind with the statistical probability that one person could fulfill all these prophecies concerning the Messiah—and yet be rejected as such by so many who claim to believe in God.

Ponder the fantastic statement made by Jesus to Nathanael upon their first encounter. "Because I said unto thee, I saw thee under the fig tree, believest thou? thou shalt see greater things than these. And he saith unto him, Verily, verily, I say unto you, Hereafter ye shall see heaven open, and the angels of God ascending and descending upon the Son of man."[1] This was a declaration to these few disciples confirming John the Baptist's proclamation concerning Him. And they did see greater things. They saw miracles of water changed to the best unfermented wine, blindness and deafness cured, demons cast out, lepers healed, all manner of disease removed so that health was restored, and even the dead raised to life. Greater still, they saw some who underwent a change of heart, like Jairus the synagogue ruler and Simon the Pharisee.

They didn't fully comprehend Christ's predictions concerning the crucifixion, but they knew from past experiences that Jesus had an uncanny manner of foretelling events. Peter was hardly back from bragging to the temple tax collector that of course Jesus paid temple tax, when Jesus took up that very subject with him without Peter even saying anything about it. Having gently corrected Peter's perspective, Jesus then sent him on the errand to catch a single fish in order to obtain enough money to

Everything He related to the disciples was based upon Scripture prophecy.

pay the temple tax for both.[2] The prediction that Peter would deny Jesus three times in a short period of time should have awakened in Peter a persistent urge to pray for deliverance from such an eventuality.

In any case, Jesus told His disciples of such things so that when they happened, they would know that Jesus was prepared because He foreknew it. Whether it was persecution, separation from physical presence, or false prophets and Christs, Jesus foreknew it and was prepared for it. "And now I have told you before it come to pass, that, when it is come to pass, ye might believe,"[3] "for there shall arise false Christs, and false prophets, and shall shew great signs and wonders; insomuch that, if it were possible, they shall deceive the very elect. Behold, I have told you before."[4] So, we should not be surprised by the deceiver's attempted ambuscades.

1   John 1:50, 51
2   Matthew 17:24–27
3   John 14:29
4   Matthew 24:24, 25

Still, there can be no doubt that Jesus prophesied by faith. Everything He related to the disciples was based upon Scripture prophecy. Because of their dysfunctional understanding of the prophecies, He did not overwhelm them with a sharp delineation of events. He would leave it to the Holy Spirit to guide them into all truth.

The disciples had wondered in amazement at Christ's tears over Jerusalem during what otherwise was a triumphal entry. They had expected Him to be crowned king at that time, but He was not. Then He had cursed a fruitless fig tree, which withered within twenty-four hours. Next, He cleansed the temple again, and on the following day was questioned about His authority to accomplish the purging. Instead of answering the inquisition, He asked them a question, which they refused to answer.

Shortly after that, He departed from the temple, speaking words of terrible import to the priests and rulers seeking to kill him, "Behold, your house is left unto you desolate: and verily I say unto you, Ye shall not see me, until the time come when ye shall say, Blessed is he that cometh in the name of the Lord."[5] The religious leaders had withheld their praise and had tried to stop the triumphal procession. Now they felt as though an unseen danger lurked around them. These words troubled the disciples as well. "Christ's words had been spoken in the hearing of a large number of people; but when He was alone, Peter, John, James, and Andrew came to Him as He sat upon the Mount of Olives. 'Tell us,' they said, 'when shall these things be? and what shall be the sign of Thy coming, and of the end of the world?'"[6]

> Christ knew that the disciples could not comprehend the instruction he had given them in answer to their question, "When shall these things be? and what shall be the sign of thy coming, and of the end of the world?" He knew the terrible future of the once-chosen people of God; but he knew, also, that his disciples could not then fully understand his description of the fearful scenes to be enacted at the destruction of Jerusalem. In his answer, the two events—the destruction of Jerusalem, and the end of the world—were merged into one. It was in mercy to his disciples that Christ blended these events, leaving them to study out the meaning for themselves.[7]

He referenced the prophet Daniel in this discourse as a means to prompt them to study for themselves the future.[8] Near the close of His discourse, Jesus repeated something that He had spoken in the temple just before making His terrifying statement about its desolation. "All these things shall come upon this generation…. This generation shall not pass, till all these things be fulfilled. Heaven and earth shall pass away, but my words shall not pass away."[9]

---

5   Luke 13:35
6   White, *The Desire of Ages*, p. 628. See also Mark 13:3, 4.
7   White, "Words of Warning—No. 3," *The Review and Herald*, December 27, 1898.
8   Matthew 24:13–15; Mark 13:13, 14; Luke 21:32, 33
9   Matthew 23:36; 24:34, 35

Some skeptics doubt these gospel accounts of Christ's prophecies because they do not understand what Jesus meant by the words "this generation." But to serious Bible students who plead for the Holy Spirit to guide them into all truth, the answer is found in the time prophecies of Scripture. One such Bible student, a former deist—William Miller—who as a young man scoffed at apparent contradictions in the Bible, not only found the answer but shared what he learned in one of the most thrilling periods of history.

> With intense interest he studied the books of Daniel and the Revelation, employing the same principles of interpretation as in the other scriptures, and found, to his great joy, that the prophetic symbols could be understood. He saw that the prophecies, so far as they had been fulfilled, had been fulfilled literally; that all the various figures, metaphors, parables, similitudes, etc., were either explained in their immediate connection, or the terms in which they were expressed were defined in other scriptures, and when thus explained, were to be literally understood…. Link after link of the chain of truth rewarded his efforts, as step by step he traced down the great lines of prophecy. Angels of heaven were guiding his mind and opening the Scriptures to his understanding.[10]

So, what did Jesus mean by "this generation," and what did William Miller conclude from his study on the matter? Miller said,

> The wicked generation was not there, Christ was not addressing them, and there could not have been any propriety in saying "this generation." If he had been talking about them, they not being present, he would have said, that generation. In every place where Christ has used the words "this generation," some of the class whom he meant by this designation were present. Therefore, I am led to believe he had particular reference to his children, the generation of the righteous.[11]

Then he proceeded to quote from Scriptures, "There were they in great fear: for God is in the generation of the righteous."[12] "A seed shall serve him; it shall be accounted to the Lord for a generation."[13] "This is the generation of them that seek him, that seek thy face, O Jacob."[14] "If I say, I will speak thus; behold, I should offend against the generation of thy children."[15] "But

10   White, *The Great Controversy*, pp. 320, 321.
11   Miller, *Miller's Works Exposition of the Twenty-fourth of Matthew*, vol. 1, p. 34.
12   Psalm 14:5
13   Psalm 22:30
14   Psalm 24:6
15   Psalm 73:15

ye are a chosen generation, a royal priesthood, an holy nation, a peculiar people; that ye should shew forth the praises of him who hath called you out of darkness into his marvellous light."[16]

The whole of Miller's premise is based upon Christ—at the time He spoke these words—referring to a people present (Peter, James, John, and Andrew) to hear the words, as representatives of the generation. "Therefore the language of the text is like this: 'Verily, I say unto you, these my children shall not pass till all these things be fulfilled.'"[17] Miller's conclusions are based upon Scripture and are uncannily accurate considering his mistaken conclusion that Jesus would come the second time in 1843, or 1844. But a more careful examination may bring us closer to a potential conclusion that was overlooked.

On another occasion, Jesus said to His disciples, "The days will come, when ye shall desire to see one of the days of the Son of man, and ye shall not see it. And they shall say to you, See here; or, see there: go not after them, nor follow them. For as the lightning, that lighteneth out of the one part under heaven, shineth unto the other part under heaven; so shall also the Son of man be in his day. But first must he suffer many things, and be rejected of this generation."[18]

Again, Jesus said "this generation" as opposed to "that generation." Looking at Paul's reference to "that generation," we see that it had to do with those who tempted God in the wilderness. "As the Holy Ghost saith, To day if ye will hear his voice, Harden not your hearts, as in the provocation, in the day of temptation in the wilderness: When your fathers tempted me, proved me, and saw my works forty years. Wherefore I was grieved with that generation, and said, They do alway err in their heart; and they have not known my ways. So I sware in my wrath, They shall not enter into my rest."[19]

I believe William Miller was on the right track, but he possibly overlooked a connection between these passages and the time prophecies that he and others charted so accurately. Jesus blended the signs of three different periods: (1) the fall of Jerusalem, (2) the time of the end, which should not be confused with the end of time, (3) and the end of time (the former referring to the end of the time prophecies, and the latter with the close of probation and the second coming of Christ).

We must carefully study the prophecies in context. It was while with His disciples that Jesus remarked, "Verily I say unto you, There be some standing here, which shall not taste of death, till they see the Son of man coming in his kingdom."[20] Scoffers quickly point out that all who surrounded Jesus at the time the remark was spoken are now dead, and yet we still await Christ's promised coming. Yet the earnest Bible student recognizes the fulfillment of this statement in the event of the transfiguration.

---

16 1 Peter 2:9
17 Miller, *Miller's Works Exposition of the Twenty-fourth of Matthew*, vol. 1, p. 37.
18 Luke 17:22–25
19 Hebrews 3:7–11
20 Matthew 16:28

The Saviour has seen the gloom of His disciples, and has longed to lighten their grief by an assurance that their faith has not been in vain. Not all, even of the twelve, can receive the revelation He desires to give. Only the three who are to witness His anguish in Gethsemane have been chosen to be with Him on the mount. Now the burden of His prayer is that they may be given a manifestation of the glory He had with the Father before the world was, that His kingdom may be revealed to human eyes, and that His disciples may be strengthened to behold it. He pleads that they may witness a manifestation of His divinity that will comfort them in the hour of His supreme agony with the knowledge that He is of a surety the Son of God and that His shameful death is a part of the plan of redemption.

His prayer is heard. While He is bowed in lowliness upon the stony ground, suddenly the heavens open, the golden gates of the city of God are thrown wide, and holy radiance descends upon the mount, enshrouding the Saviour's form. Divinity from within flashes through humanity, and meets the glory coming from above. Arising from His prostrate position, Christ stands in godlike majesty.[21]

Again the skeptics read into Jesus' words another statement of apparent prophecy, "If I will that he tarry till I come, what is that to thee? follow thou me." John himself immediately corrects their misconception: "Then went this saying abroad among the brethren, that that disciple should not die: yet Jesus said not unto him, He shall not die; but, If I will that he tarry till I come, what is that to thee?"[22] Further study reveals that John indeed saw the second advent when Jesus revealed the future to him on Patmos.

The point is that Jesus prophesied by faith to the disciples, predicting that a generation would not pass away until these events were fulfilled. The disciples misunderstood its application, even at the time of Christ's ascension. Still looking for an immediate establishment of temporal reign, they queried, "Lord, wilt thou at this time restore again the kingdom to Israel? And he said unto them, It is not for you to know the times or the seasons, which the Father hath put in his own power. But ye shall receive power, after that the Holy Ghost is come upon you: and ye shall be witnesses unto me both in Jerusalem, and in all Judaea, and in Samaria, and unto the uttermost part of the earth."[23]

By His answer, it is clear that Jesus well understood a timeframe that would have unnecessarily discouraged the disciples until they had received power to hope, and patiently wait, for that period of time to elapse. Later, Paul gave insight to the length of time as he understood it from his study of Scriptures while in the desert of Arabia receiving instruction from Christ.[24]

---

21   White, *The Desire of Ages*, pp. 420, 421.
22   John 21:22, 23
23   Acts 1:6–8
24   Galatians 1:16, 17

Now we beseech you, brethren, by the coming of our Lord Jesus Christ, and by our gathering together unto him, That ye be not soon shaken in mind, or be troubled, neither by spirit, nor by word, nor by letter as from us, as that the day of Christ is at hand. Let no man deceive you by any means: for that day shall not come, except there come a falling away first, and that man of sin be revealed, the son of perdition; Who opposeth and exalteth himself above all that is called God, or that is worshipped; so that he as God sitteth in the temple of God, shewing himself that he is God. Remember ye not, that, when I was yet with you, I told you these things?[25]

The secret to understanding the generation to which Jesus referred, and that William Miller apparently overlooked even as he taught the prophecy timelines to which I am referring, is found in Leviticus 26:

And if ye will not yet for all this hearken unto me, then I will punish you *seven times* more for your sins. And I will break the pride of your power; and I will make your heaven as iron, and your earth as brass: And your strength shall be spent in vain: for your land shall not yield her increase, neither shall the trees of the land yield their fruits. And if ye walk contrary unto me, and will not hearken unto me; I will bring *seven times* more plagues upon you according to your sins…. And if ye will not be reformed by me by these things, but will walk contrary unto me; Then will I also walk contrary unto you, and will punish you yet *seven times* for your sins…. Then I will walk contrary unto you also in fury; and I, even I, will chastise you *seven times* for your sins.[26]

Seven times is another way of stating seven years. Accepting the biblical practice of prophesying a literal year for each prophetic day, seven multiplied by 360 days (in a Jewish year) equals 2,520 years.[27] It is very possible that Ezekiel prophesied about this time period when proclaiming the end of Gog and Magog.[28] It is equally important to note that Daniel wrote of two separate prophetic periods that, when combined together, equal 2,520 literal years. The extant of those two periods mentioned are "time, times, and an half."[29] Two multiplied by three and a half equals seven. So, how does this play out in history?

From the fall of Jericho to the time it was rebuilt, the children of Israel staggered at the promises and threats of God. Despite the warnings and exhortations of prophets, the majority eventually fell to such a level of unbelief and disobedience that God no longer restrained the

---

25   2 Thessalonians 2:1–5
26   Leviticus 26:18–28
27   Numbers 14:34; Ezekiel 4:5, 6
28   Ezekiel 39:9
29   Daniel 12:7; see also Daniel 7:25

judgments pronounced in Leviticus. From 722 BC we see the beginnings of the threatened dispersion among the many nations of the world with the capture of Samaria. Even as good a king as Josiah was, we read:

> Notwithstanding the Lord turned not from the fierceness of his great wrath, wherewith his anger was kindled against Judah, because of all the provocations that Manasseh had provoked him withal. And the Lord said, I will remove Judah also out of my sight, as I have removed Israel, and will cast off this city Jerusalem which I have chosen, and the house of which I said, My name shall be there.[30]

> And I will cause them to be removed into all kingdoms of the earth, because of Manasseh the son of Hezekiah king of Judah, for that which he did in Jerusalem."[31]

The fall of Jerusalem and the destruction of the temple took place in Nebuchadnezzar's third campaign against the city, which occurred in 677 BC. Herein are two starting points for computing the generational period to which Jesus was referring by His words, "this generation."

Time, times, and half a time, being a rephrase of three and a half years—with 360 days in each year—amounts to 1,260 literal years. Subtracting 722 from 1,260 leaves us with 538. Thus, the first half of the 2,520 years is marked from 722 BC to AD 538. This timeframe anchors the period from which the pagan kingdoms ruled over God's people who were dispersed among the nations.

From the fall of Jericho to the time it was rebuilt, the children of Israel staggered at the promises and threats of God.

However, in AD 538 a new power (the little horn) emerged with the uprooting of three kingdoms. Five years earlier, Justinian wrote to the bishop of Rome a most flattering letter that at that time was unenforceable because of the resistance of two remaining kingdoms of the three to be uprooted—the Vandals of Africa and the Ostrogoths in Italy—but still "proceeded, without delay, to the full establishment of the catholic church":[32]

> Rendering honor to the apostolic chair, and to your Holiness, as has been always and is our wish, and honoring your Blessedness as a father, we have hastened to bring to the knowledge of your Holiness all matters relating to the state of the churches. It having been at all times our great desire to preserve the unity of your

---

30 2 Kings 23:26, 27
31 Jeremiah 15:4
32 Gibbon, *The Decline and Fall of the Roman Empire*, vol. 4, p. 146.

apostolic chair, and the constitution of the holy churches of God which has obtained hitherto, and still obtains.

Therefore we have made no delay in subjecting and uniting to your Holiness all the priests of the whole East.

For this reason we have thought fit to bring to your notice the present matters of disturbance; though they are manifest and unquestionable, and always firmly held and declared by the whole priesthood according to the doctrine of your apostolic chair. For we cannot suffer that anything which relates to the state of the church, however manifest and unquestionable, should be moved, without the knowledge of your Holiness, who are the head of all the holy churches; for in all things we have already declared, we are anxious to increase the honor and authority of your apostolic chair.[33]

With the capture of Gelimer, completing the destruction of the Vandal kingdom in AD 534, Justinian's victorious and intrepid general, Belisarius, went on to subdue Sicily in AD 535, and captured Naples in AD 536. Upon hearing that a feeble garrison of 4,000 soldiers were all that defended Rome, Belisarius proceeded there next. He entered the city on December 10, but this did not conclude the conquest for power over the region. The Ostrogoths returned to besiege Rome the following spring—a campaign that lasted one year and nine days—only to end in a tumultuous retreat that soon after culminated in the destruction of the Ostrogoth kingdom.

So we have the year AD 538 to effectively establish the temporal clericalism of the Roman church, thus marking the transfer of persecuting power from paganism to papacy. The addition of 1,260 years culminates in AD 1798 when Marshal Berthier broke the political power of the papacy by arresting Pope Pius VI and imprisoning him in Valence, France. However, the fulfillment of 2,520 years not only fits the span of 722 BC to AD 1798, but it also fits the span of 677 BC to AD 1843, which marked the beginning of a great disappointment as foretold in the symbolism of John eating a book that tasted like honey in his mouth but was bitterness in his belly.[34]

We can then more fully appreciate the fulfillment of Christ's prophecy within the timeframe of "this generation." "Immediately after the tribulation of those days shall the sun be darkened, and the moon shall not give her light, and the stars shall fall from heaven, and the powers of the heavens shall be shaken."[35] "And I beheld when he had opened the sixth seal, and, lo, there was a great earthquake; and the sun became black as sackcloth of hair, and the moon became as blood; And the stars of heaven fell unto the earth, even as a fig tree casteth her untimely figs, when she is shaken of a mighty wind."[36]

---

33 Croly, *The Apocalypse of St. John,* pp. 167, 168; as quoted in Jones, *The Two Republics,* pp. 548, 549.
34 Revelation 10:9, 10
35 Matthew 24:29
36 Revelation 6:12, 13

The tribulation of those days of papal persecution ended in the mid 1700s, at which time the signs of the time of the end commenced.

> In fulfillment of this prophecy there occurred, in the year 1755, the most terrible earthquake that has ever been recorded. Though commonly known as the earthquake of Lisbon, it extended to the greater part of Europe, Africa, and America. It was felt in Greenland, in the West Indies, in the island of Madeira, in Norway and Sweden, Great Britain and Ireland. It pervaded an extent of not less than four million square miles. In Africa the shock was almost as severe as in Europe. A great part of Algiers was destroyed; and a short distance from Morocco, a village containing eight or ten thousand inhabitants was swallowed up. A vast wave swept over the coast of Spain and Africa engulfing cities and causing great destruction.[37]

Twenty-five years later the next sign was displayed in such a manner that many thought the end of the world had come. May 19, 1780, started out normal enough in New England, but a supernatural darkness descended on the region with a density, duration, and extent never recorded since the time of the Exodus from Egypt. When the full moon shone, it gave the appearance of blood, and did not give her full strength.[38]

About fifty-three years later, on the night of November 13, 1833, the heavens displayed yet another sign—the last—fulfilling Christ's prophecy.

> That was the most extensive and wonderful display of falling stars which has ever been recorded; "the whole firmament, over all the United States, being then, for hours, in fiery commotion! No celestial phenomenon has ever occurred in this country, since its first settlement, which was viewed with such intense admiration by one class in the community, or with so much dread and alarm by another." "Its sublimity and awful beauty still linger in many minds.... Never did rain fall much thicker than the meteors fell toward the earth; east, west, north, and south, it was the same. In a word, the whole heavens seemed in motion.... The display, as described in Professor Silliman's *Journal,* was seen all over North America.... From two o'clock until broad daylight, the sky being perfectly serene and cloudless, an incessant play of dazzlingly brilliant luminosities was kept up in the whole heavens."—R. M. Devens, *American Progress; or, The Great Events of the Greatest Century,* ch. 28, pars. 1-5....
>
> In the New York *Journal of Commerce* of November 14, 1833, appeared a long article regarding this wonderful phenomenon, containing this statement: "No

---

37   White, *The Great Controversy*, p. 304.
38   Ibid., pp. 307, 308.

philosopher or scholar has told or recorded an event, I suppose, like that of yesterday morning. A prophet eighteen hundred years ago foretold it exactly, if we will be at the trouble of understanding stars falling to mean falling stars, ... in the only sense in which it is possible to be literally true."[39]

The signs of the nearness of Christ's second coming have been fulfilled, and are still being fulfilled. As Christians professing to keep the commandments of God and having the faith of Jesus, we should be sharing the truth regarding Christ's prophecies. Yet how many of us are prepared for what is about to break over our heads even though warned as often as the disciples were about the glorification of Jesus?

Before his crucifixion, the Saviour explained to his disciples that he was to be put to death, and to rise again from the tomb; and angels were present to impress his words on minds and hearts. But the disciples were looking for temporal deliverance from the Roman yoke, and they could not tolerate the thought that he in whom all their hopes centered should suffer an ignominious death. The words which they needed to remember were banished from their minds; and when the time of trial came, it found them unprepared. The death of Jesus as fully destroyed their hopes as if he had not forewarned them. *So in the prophecies the future is opened before us as plainly as it was opened to the disciples by the words of Christ. The events connected with the close of probation and the work of preparation for the time of trouble, are clearly presented. But multitudes have no more understanding of these important truths than if they had never been revealed.* Satan watches to catch away every impression that would make them wise unto salvation, and the time of trouble will find them unready.[40]

Everywhere we turn there are strange winds of doctrine countering the faith of Jesus.

Heresies are now arising among the people of God, and they will continue to arise. As we near the end of time, falsehood will be so mingled with truth, that only those who have the guidance of the Holy Spirit will be able to distinguish truth from error. We need to make every effort to keep the way of the Lord. We must in no case turn from His guidance to put our trust in man. The Lord's angels are appointed to keep strict watch over those who put their faith in the Lord, and these angels are to be our special help in every time of need. Every day we are to come to the Lord with full assurance of faith, and to look to Him for wisdom. The ministers who teach

---

39   Ibid., pp. 333, 334.
40   White, "The Scriptures a Safeguard," *The Review and Herald*, June 7, 1906, emphasis added.

the truth for this time are to strengthen their hearts by studying the word of God. "It is the spirit that quickeneth," Christ said, "the flesh profiteth nothing: the words that I speak unto you, they are spirit and they are life" (John 6:63). Those who are guided by the word of the Lord will discern with certainty between falsehood and truth, between sin and righteousness.[41]

Many seek to modify or remove portions of the truths we have been led to believe in order to accommodate their attempts to have a form of godliness while denying the power thereof. If doctrine condemns their lifestyle, they choose to change it rather than be the object of discipline. Ellen White wrote to one such person:

> You must never, never seek to lift one pin, [or] remove one landmark, that the Lord has given to His people as truth. You can manipulate matters to suit your own plans and devices. But just as soon as you allow your influence to lead away from the strait and narrow path that the Lord has cast up for His people, in order to accommodate yourself, your prosperity will cease; for God will not be your guide…. Never seek for popularity. Never let the banner be lowered or drop from your hands in order to blend in the wording of the message for these last days anything but that which will keep the features of our faith prominent. "Here are they which keep the commandments of God, and the faith of Jesus" [Revelation 14:12].[42]

We must contend, to strive, to obtain for ourselves that faith once delivered to the saints in order to have defense against those who creep in unawares to corrupt the faith of Jesus and make it of no effect.[43] Otherwise we will awaken too late to the realization that:

> Satan has a large confederacy, his church. Christ calls them the synagogue of Satan because the members are the children of sin. The members of Satan's church have been constantly working to cast off the divine law, and confuse the distinction between good and evil. Satan is working with great power in and through the children of

"Never seek for popularity."

disobedience to exalt treason and apostasy as truth and loyalty. And at this time the power of his satanic inspiration is moving the living agencies to carry out the great rebellion against God that commenced in heaven.[44]

---

41   White, *Manuscript Releases*, vol. 7, pp. 359, 360.
42   White, *Manuscript Releases*, vol. 21, p. 53.
43   Jude 1:3, 4
44   White, *Testimonies to Ministers and Gospel Workers*, p. 16.

Now at the present time God designs a new and fresh impetus shall be given to His work. Satan sees this, and he is determined it shall be hindered. He knows that if he can deceive the people who claim to believe present truth, [and make them believe] that the work the Lord designs to do for His people is a removing of the old landmarks, something which they should, with most determined zeal, resist, then he exults over the deception he has led them to believe. The work for this time has certainly been a surprising work of various hindrances, owing to the false setting of matters before the minds of many of our people. That which is food to the churches is regarded as dangerous, and should not be given them. And this slight difference of ideas is allowed to unsettle the faith, to cause apostasy, to break up unity, to sow discord, all because they do not know what they are striving about themselves. Brethren, is it not best to be sensible? Heaven is looking upon us all, and what can they think of recent developments? While in this condition of things, building up barriers, we not only deprive ourselves of great light and precious advantages, but just now, when we so much need it, we place ourselves where light cannot be communicated from heaven that we ought to communicate to others.[45]

From the time of Daniel we have known that a power would arise which thinks to change times and laws. We see regularly some other fulfillment of the brazen attempts to make the papal sabbath the day of rest and worship. The leopard-like beast of Revelation has already had its forty-two months (another way of saying 1,260 years) of persecution power. It received its deadly wound (1798), and has been healed (the Lateran Pacts of 1929). I cannot help but believe that the image to the beast is being formed before our very eyes.[46] Still many have yet to be warned of the coming dilemma of which mark to receive: the seal of God or the mark of the beast. We barely show interest in the fact that Israel has had a law to protect a work-free Sunday since 2007. The pope is pushing for greater reverence on Sundays even as the European Union parliament is gaining support to legislate work-free Sunday protection. Soon, very soon, the matter will be pressed upon us!

> *"The faith of Jesus and the testimony of Jesus are blended. They are to be clearly presented to the world."*

So the question arises, do we have the faith of Jesus? Are we united upon that faith as evidenced in the Scriptures and the testimony of God's prophets? If we do, then we will demonstrate it! "God is leading a people out from the world upon the exalted platform of eternal truth,

---

45   White, *The Ellen G. White 1888 Materials*, pp. 518, 519.
46   Revelation 13:5, 6, 15

the commandments of God and the faith of Jesus. He will discipline and fit up His people. They will not be at variance, one believing one thing and another having faith and views entirely opposite, each moving independently of the body. Through the diversity of the gifts and governments that He has placed in the church, they will all come to the unity of the faith."[47] "The testimony of Jesus is the spirit of prophecy."[48]

We have been told that:

> The faith of Jesus and the testimony of Jesus are blended. They are to be clearly presented to the world. But in God's word we are shown the consequences of proclaiming this message. "The dragon was wroth with the woman, and went to make war with the remnant of her seed, which keep the commandments of God, and have the testimony of Jesus Christ." A refusal to obey the commandments of God, and a determination to cherish hatred against those who proclaim these commandments, leads to the most determined war on the part of the dragon, whose whole energies are brought to bear against the commandment-keeping people of God. "He causeth all, both small and great … to receive a mark in their right hand, or in their foreheads." Not only are men not to work with their hands on Sunday, but with their minds are they to acknowledge Sunday as the Sabbath. "And that no man might buy or sell, save he that had the mark, or the name of the beast, or the number of this name."[49]

Then let us have the faith of Jesus as given to us by the testimony of His mouth, which is the Spirit of Prophecy.

---

47 White, *Testimonies to Ministers and Gospel Workers*, p. 29.
48 Revelation 19:10
49 White, *Special Testimony to Battle Creek Church*, pp. 6, 7.

Chapter 14

Uncompromised Faith Strengthens Hope

Christmas of 1978 is especially memorable to me because of a trick my mother intended to play on me. If anyone else had tried to pull it off, I might have responded differently.

As usual, we all got up early to open gifts around the Christmas tree. First, there was the devotional thought to remind us of God's great gift to us and how we should return our lives to Him in gratitude. And then followed the orderly issuance of varied gifts purchased for our loved ones. The very last gift to be opened was one my mother gave me. I hastily tore the decorative wrapping from the box, pulled up the top, and saw a colorful tie that matched nothing in my wardrobe.

I could have thought, grudgingly, oh well—another tie I will never wear to hang up in my closet. But I didn't have that kind of relationship with my mom. Somebody else? Maybe. But not my mom. Instead, I held it up high, smiled really big, and said, "Thanks, Mom, for the new suit!"

Now, this response was not motivated by an inclination to put the most favorable construction upon what otherwise amounted to be a useless gift. I knew my mother well enough to comprehend that in buying me a tie—for which she would need no measurements—she would afterward take me to the department store to buy me a suit at which time I could be measured for the necessary alterations. I had not thought, nor did I express concerns about any need for a suit. But I almost instantly recognized that the tie was indicative of the greater gift that she wanted to bestow. Looking back on that experience reminds me of how faith can strengthen hope.

The relationship between faith and hope is inseparable. Paul wrote of three things that will last when all others dissipate. "And now abideth faith, hope, charity, these three; but the greatest of these is charity."[1] In fact, we may go so far as to conclude that "of faith hope is born."[2] But

---

1   1 Corinthians 13:13
2   White, "How to Meet Trial and Difficulty," *The Review and Herald*, May 30, 1912.

if hope is to emerge, abide, and be strengthened, then faith must be uncompromised. God has made this relationship quite clear in His word.

When Adam compromised his faith by yielding to the temptation presented by his fallen wife, he placed us all in a rather hopeless condition—except for the intervention of God through the gift of His Son. But the condition of life in that covenant of love was obedience by faith. By taking our place—our penalty—God shows us that under the new covenant, the covenant of grace, the condition remains unchanged. If we do not obey by faith, we can only expect the wages of sin—death.[3] We cannot rightfully hope that the gift of eternal life will be given to those who continue in transgression of the law of love that governs the whole of God's kingdom.

Noah obeyed by faith when building an ark of gopher wood to the precise specifications revealed by God. Though the storm winds howled and the waters rolled over them in mighty waves and torrents, his obedient faith strengthened hope and secured the survival of his household.

> *We cannot rightfully hope that the gift of eternal life will be given to those who continue in transgression of the law of love that governs the whole of God's kingdom.*

When Joseph was sold as a slave by his brothers, then wrongfully accused by an adulterous wife and imprisoned by her jealous husband, he did not compromise faith. He did not have Scripture as we now do. All he had was the teaching of his father and two dreams. Yet he refused to compromise faith, which would result in endangering his hope in God. Therefore, when he was elevated to prime minister after interpreting Pharaoh's dreams, he obeyed by faith in gathering enough grain to save not only Egypt and his family but the surrounding nations when the famine struck. Even in the midst of unprecedented disaster, he had strong hope.

Job did not sacrifice his integrity or his faith despite enormous losses of wealth and family. Job said to his friends, "He hath destroyed me on every side, and I am gone: and mine hope hath he removed like a tree."[4] "For there is hope of a tree, if it be cut down, that it will sprout again, and that the tender branch thereof will not cease. Though the root thereof wax old in the earth, and the stock thereof die in the ground; Yet through the scent of water it will bud, and bring forth boughs like a plant."[5] He didn't understand why the trials were permitted in his life, but he refused to let go of his faith or hope in God. In the end, he glorified God and was restored abundantly.

Remember the sorrow Naomi suffered at the loss of a husband and two sons? She tried to prevent her daughters-in-law from returning to Judea with her, saying, "Turn again, my daughters,

---

3   Romans 6:23
4   Job 19:10
5   Job 14:7–9

go your way; for I am too old to have an husband. If I should say, I have *hope*, if I should have an husband also to night, and should also bear sons; Would ye *tarry* for them till they were grown? would ye stay for them from having husbands? nay, my daughters; for it grieveth me much for your sakes that the hand of the Lord is gone out against me."[6] The Hebrew for tarry (*sabar*) can also be translated "hope." Orpah eventually returned to her people. But Ruth persevered in her hope that the God of Naomi—now Ruth's God—would provide for both of them. That persistence resulted in a marriage to Boaz and a place in the lineage of King David and of Christ.

As we seek to obtain the faith of Jesus for ourselves, we recognize that it is by grace we are saved through faith.[7] But we also acknowledge the role of hope in our salvation as we patiently wait for it.[8] If we are as King Saul, impatient and rash, we can expect nothing good, for faith is compromised. Hope will dissipate just as his army did while he sat lamenting his lost prestige under the pomegranate tree.[9] Fear and disappointment led Saul to make a severe oath, which caused many soldiers to pass by a store of honey God provided to strengthen them. Jonathan nearly lost his life for eating the honey. Yet it was the hope of Jonathan and his armor bearer that prompted the battle. But because the people heard and obeyed the command of Saul, they were inclined to so hastily prepare their suppers that care was not taken to remove all the blood from the meat they ate.[10]

Though David led the life of a fugitive for many years, his psalms contain many passages about hope:

> Be of good courage, and he shall strengthen your heart, all ye that hope in the Lord.[11]

> Behold, the eye of the Lord is upon them that fear him, upon them that hope in his mercy…. Let thy mercy, O Lord, be upon us, according as we hope in thee.[12]

> For in thee, O Lord, do I hope: thou wilt hear, O Lord my God.[13]

> And now, Lord, what wait I for? my hope is in thee.[14]

---

6   Ruth 1:12, 13
7   Ephesians 2:8
8   Romans 8:24, 25
9   1 Samuel 14:2
10   1 Samuel 14:24–32
11   Psalm 31:24
12   Psalm 33:18, 22
13   Psalm 38:15
14   Psalm 39:7

Why art thou cast down, O my soul? and why art thou disquieted in me? hope thou in God: for I shall yet praise him for the help of his countenance.[15]

What is to be the basis of this hope? The common theme we see, again in the psalms, is grounded in the word of God and keeping His commandments:

That they might set their hope in God, and not forget the works of God, but keep his commandments.[16]

And take not the word of truth utterly out of my mouth; for I have hoped in thy judgments.... Remember the word unto thy servant, upon which thou hast caused me to hope.... They that fear thee will be glad when they see me; because I have hoped in thy word.... My soul fainteth for thy salvation: but I hope in thy word.... Thou art my hiding place and my shield: I hope in thy word.... Uphold me according unto thy word, that I may live: and let me not be ashamed of my hope.... I prevented the dawning of the morning, and cried: I hoped in thy word.... Lord, I have hoped for thy salvation, and done thy commandments.[17]

I wait for the Lord, my soul doth wait, and in his word do I hope.[18]

Paul concurred with the psalmist when he wrote, "For we through the Spirit wait for the hope of righteousness by faith."[19] Here is where the principle of hope becomes practical. Hope involves waiting. Faith involves working. We do all that we can by faith, and then hope for the promised salvation as we wait on God to provide.

> *Here is where the principle of hope becomes practical. Hope involves waiting. Faith involves working.*

Consider the very first Passover. The day had been spent in removing leaven from the dwelling, slaying a perfect, spotless lamb, and taking a branch of hyssop dipped in the blood and striking the lintel and doorposts. Then they roasted the lamb and hastily ate it with bitter herbs while standing around the table fully garbed as though they were going to eat and run.[20] But having done all these things by faith, they then waited in hope that the destroying angel would indeed pass over them and that Pharaoh would

---

15   Psalm 42:5
16   Psalm 78:7
17   Psalm 119:43, 49, 74, 81, 114, 116, 147, 166
18   Psalm 130:5
19   Galatians 5:5
20   Exodus 12:11, 22

indeed let them go. Uncompromised faith strengthens hope in the face of imminent personal danger.

Unfortunately, not all who left Egypt left Egypt. There were some who had lingering doubts about the Promised Land. Ten times they provoked God with compromised faith and weakened misplaced hope. They didn't completely forsake what they liked about Egypt—the fleshpots, the leeks, the onions, the gravesites, etc. The lesson to us is that love of the world is enmity to God.[21] Yet the lukewarm Laodicean is no different from those children of Israel swayed by the influences of the mixed multitude. Indeed, "many who profess to be looking for the speedy coming of Christ, are becoming conformed to this world, and seek more earnestly the applause of those around them, than the approbation of God."[22]

> In the Laodicean state of the church at the present time, how little evidence is given of the direct, personal guidance of God! Men place themselves in positions of temptation, where they see and hear much that is contrary to God, and detrimental to spirituality. They lose their warmth and fervor, and become lukewarm Christians, who are, in a great measure, indifferent to the glory of God, and the advancement of his work. If God calls his servants to positions where the influence is of a worldly character, he will give special grace that they may be enabled to overcome the evil consequent upon their circumstances. There should be religious fervor corresponding to the faith and doctrines we have accepted as truth. If this were the case, how earnestly would prayers be offered to know the will of God, and how diligently would the heart be kept, out of which are the issues of life! The servants of God become estranged from the truth by associating with the world, and by partaking of its spirit. When this is done, the truth is not appreciated as a sacred and sanctifying truth.[23]

It is Satan's desire to compromise our faith and weaken our hope. "Satan besets the pathway of every one of us. If he can get you to love yourselves, to indulge inclination, to compromise your faith, then you are his servants. You cannot afford this. You do not want your names enrolled as those enlisted in his army."[24]

One of the ways that Satan best accomplishes such a compromise is when those who are raised as believers of Christ marry or develop business relations with unbelievers.

---

21   James 4:4; 1 John 2:15
22   White, "To the Brethren and Sisters," *The Review and Herald*, June 10, 1852.
23   White, "The Work at Fresno, California," *The Review and Herald*, June 19, 1888.
24   White, *Manuscript Releases*, vol. 21, p. 222.

Remember, you have a heaven to gain, an open path to perdition to shun. God means what He says. When He prohibited our first parents from eating the fruit of the tree of knowledge, their disobedience opened the floodgates of woe to the whole world. If we walk contrary to God, He will walk contrary to us. Our only safe course is to render obedience to all His requirements, at whatever cost. All are founded in infinite love and wisdom....

[All] are under the most sacred obligation not to belittle or compromise your holy faith by uniting with the Lord's enemies. If you are tempted to disregard the injunctions of His word because others have done so, remember that your example also will exert an influence. Others will do as you do, and thus the evil will be extended. While you profess to be a child of God, a departure on your part from His requirements will result in infinite harm to those who look to you for guidance.[25]

But if we will set our hearts upon God, the promises of His Word, and wait for His bestowment of blessing or salvation from trial, then we will be filled with great joy.

One of the best defenses of faith and bulwarks of hope is diligent labor for God. As He opens our eyes and ears to Christian duty, our willing and cheerful response will exercise faith and hope.

The soul that is indolent falls an easy prey to temptation; but in the life that has a noble aim, an absorbing purpose, evil finds little foothold. The faith of him who is constantly advancing does not weaken; for above, beneath, beyond, he recognizes Infinite Love, working out all things to accomplish His good purpose. God's true servants work with a determination that will not fail because the throne of grace is their constant dependence.

God has provided divine assistance for all the emergencies to which our human resources are unequal. He gives the Holy Spirit to help in every strait, to strengthen our hope and assurance, to illuminate our minds and purify our hearts. He provides opportunities and opens channels of working. If His people are watching the indications of His providence, and are ready to co-operate with Him, they will see mighty results.[26]

In all that we think, say, feel, and do, we are to keep our eyes off of self. We must behold Jesus standing within the Most Holy Place interceding on our behalf, constantly reminding us that "for all the promises of God in him are yea, and in him Amen, unto the glory of God by

25 White, *Testimonies for the Church*, vol. 5, pp. 365, 367.
26 White, *Prophets and Kings*, p. 660.

us."[27] "That by two immutable things, in which it was impossible for God to lie, we might have a strong consolation, who have fled for refuge to lay hold upon the hope set before us: Which hope we have as an anchor of the soul, both sure and stedfast, and which entereth into that within the veil; Whither the forerunner is for us entered, even Jesus, made an high priest for ever after the order of Melchisedec."[28] "The Lord is good unto them that wait for him, to the soul that seeketh him. It is good that a man should both hope and quietly wait for the salvation of the Lord."[29]

By beholding Jesus, seeing how He lived by faith and strengthened His hope in the Father, how He overcame temptation by faith in using the Word of God as the basis of His hope, we can overcome as He did. The promises to the faithful are rich and well worth the discipline. Acknowledging the joy set before Jesus, we can move forward—enduring the shame of the cross and entering into His suffering—then seeing the travail of His soul and ours, we will share in His satisfaction.

Trials will come. But it is God's purpose to remind us of our constant dependence upon Him.

> It is the will of the Lord that the heart shall be tried. He would see whether it will turn to the Stronghold for strength and sympathy. We need to cultivate faith, hope, and courage. Let our tongues be educated to speak forth His praise at all times.
>
> We need to frame the promises to God, and hang them up in the chambers of the mind, then we can communicate to others the comfort wherewith we are comforted. Here we are to learn the language of heaven, whose inhabitants will be our companions through eternity.[30]

The time of the end with an eternity in heaven is nearer to us than we can imagine.

What we need is a steadfast hope that will endure every temptation—every trial—and carry us through the great test of the time of trouble. We all need to heed the counsel given to the youth:

If you would have a religion that will stand the test of the last great day, or that will not fail you when you are brought face to face with death, you must not take as your standard public opinion even in the Christian world. When the

"Cherish no uncertain faith, no unsound hope. Move understandingly, in a sure path."

27 2 Corinthians 1:20
28 Hebrews 6:18–20
29 Lamentations 3:25, 26
30 White, "Praise the Lord," *The Bible Echo*, November 6, 1899.

shadows gather about the soul, you will not regret that you attended so few places of amusement, that you took part in so few jovial scenes, and knew so little of worldly dissipation. In that solemn hour, how will your life-work be revealed in the light of eternity! Be careful, dear youth, to make no mistake where eternal interests are concerned. Cherish no uncertain faith, no unsound hope. Move understandingly, in a sure path. Avail yourselves of every means that will help you to become acquainted with Him in whom your hopes of eternal life are centered.[31]

In following this counsel we will not need to experience by degrees the accompanying despair of opportunities lost which may overwhelm our hope.

Hope, strengthened by uncompromised faith, will give confidence and assurance despite the almost overwhelming trial of the final test. Yet we must comprehend the need to submit to a disciplined faith. Faith must be founded upon the Word of God.

When the testing time shall come, those who have made God's Word their rule of life will be revealed. In summer there is no noticeable difference between evergreens and other trees; but when the blasts of winter come, the evergreens remain unchanged, while other trees are stripped of their foliage. So the falsehearted professor may not now be distinguished from the real Christian, but the time is just upon us when the difference will be apparent. Let opposition arise, let bigotry and intolerance again bear sway, let persecution be kindled, and the half-hearted and hypocritical will waver and yield the faith; but the true Christian will stand firm as a rock, his faith stronger, his hope brighter, than in the days of prosperity.[32]

It is my sincere hope that all who read this entreaty will have a greater appetite to pursue even further study into our need for the faith of Jesus. Together, as we continue to grow in grace and knowledge of the Lord Jesus Christ, we will be able to magnify His character before the world. Only let us "sanctify the Lord God in [our] hearts: and be ready always to give an answer to every man that asketh [us] a reason of the hope that is in [us] with meekness and fear."[33]

---

31   White, "Be Ye Followers of Christ," *The Youth's Instructor*, May 14, 1884.
32   White, "The Scriptures a Safeguard," *The Review and Herald*, January 10, 1907.
33   1 Peter 3:15

Bibliography

Anderson, Roy Allan. *Unfolding the Revelation*. Mountain View, CA: Pacific Press Publishing Association, 1974.

Bobrick, Benson. *Wide as the Waters: The Story of the English Bible and the Revolution It Inspired*. New York, NY: Simon and Schuster, 2001.

Burnside, George. *The New International Version or The King James Version*. Payson, AZ: Leaves-Of-Autumn Books, 1988, 1991, 1993.

Carson, D. A. *The King James Version Debate: A Plea for Realism*. Grand Rapids, MI: Baker Book House Company, 1979.

"Clinical Death." Wikipedia. http://1ref.us/3 (accessed June 1, 2014).

Clough, Shepard B. *European History in a World Perspective: Ancient Times to 1715*. 3rd ed. Lexington, MA: Heath, 1975.

Croly, George. *The Apocalypse of St. John*. St. John's Square, London: R. Gilbert, 1827.

Cumming, John. *Apocalyptic Sketches: Lectures on the Book of Revelation*. 9th ed. London: Hall and Co., 1849.

De Rosa, Peter. *Vicars of Christ: The Dark Side of the Papacy*. New York, NY: Crown Publishers, 1988.

Di Bruno, Joseph Faa. *Catholic Belief*. 3rd edition. London: Burns and Oates, 1880.

Foster, Lewis. *Selecting a Translation of the Bible*. Cincinnati, OH: Standard Pub, 1983.

Foxe, John. *Book of Martyrs*. Hartford, CT: Philemon Canfield, 1830.

Gibbon, Edward. *The Decline and Fall of the Roman Empire*. Vol. 4. New York, NY: Peter Fenelon Collier, 1899.

Gibbons, James Cardinal. *Faith of Our Fathers*. Baltimore, MD: John Murphy Company, 1917.

Gilbert, F. C. *Practical Lessons From the Experience of Israel for the Church of To-day*. South Lancaster, MA: South Lancaster Printing Company, 1902.

Heppenstall, Edward. *The Man Who Is God: A Study of the Person and Nature of Jesus, Son of God and Son of Man*. Washington, DC: Review and Herald Publishing Association, 1977.

Jones, A. T. *The Consecrated Way to Christian Perfection.* Mountain View, CA: Pacific Press Publishing Company, 1905.

———. *The Two Republics.* Battle Creek, MI: Review and Herald Publishing Co., 1891.

Josephus, Flavius. *The Genuine Works of Flavius Josephus.* Translated by William Whiston. New York, NY: William Borrodaile, Johnstone and Van Norden, 1824.

Leone, Jacopo. *The Jesuit Conspiracy: The Secret Plan of the Order.* London: Chapman and Hall, 1848.

Mauro, James. "Bright Lights, Big Mystery." *Psychology Today.* http://1ref.us/1 (accessed January 18, 2014).

Miller, William. *Miller's Works Exposition of the Twenty-fourth of Matthew.* Vol. 1. Joshua V. Himes, 1842.

Priebe, Dennis. "Is It Essential or Nonessential?" Dennis Priebe Seminars. http://1ref,us/4 (accessed January 12, 2014).

"Proverbs 26:10." NET Bible Study Environment. http://1ref.us/5 (accessed January 12, 2014).

"Questions and Answers About Ellen G. White." The Ellen G. White Estate, Inc. http://1ref.us/6 (accessed January 12, 2014).

Smalley, Gary, and John Trent. *The Gift of Honor.* Nashville, TN: Thomas Nelson, 1987.

Smith, G. Vance. *Texts and Margins of the Revised New Testament.* London: British and Foreign Unitarian Association, 1881.

Sweigart, Jon. "Jesus' IDEA for Evangelism." Sermon, Nebraska City, NE, February 21, 2009.

Unger, Merrill F. *The New Unger's Bible Dictionary.* Chicago, IL: Moody Press, 1988.

Waggoner, E. J. *General Conference Bulletin.* Vol. 4, April. 22, 1901. Battle Creek, MI: Review and Herald Publishing Association, 1901.

Whidden II, Woodrow W. *Ellen White on the Humanity of Christ.* Hagerstown, MD: Review and Herald Publishing Association, 1997.

White, Ellen G. *The Acts of the Apostles.* Mountain View, CA: Pacific Press Publishing Association, 1911.

———. "Ask, and It Shall Be Given You." *The Signs of the Times*, September 5, 1900.

———. "Be Gentle Unto All Men." *The Review and Herald*, May 14, 1895.

———. "Be Ye Followers of Christ." *The Youth's Instructor*, May 14, 1884.

———. "A Call to Service." *The Southern Watchman*, June 18, 1907.

———. "The Character That God Approves." *The Youth's Instructor*, August 3, 1899

———. "Christ May Dwell in Your Hearts by Faith." *The Review and Herald*, October 1, 1889.

———. "Christ's Example in Prayer." *The Signs of the Times*, July 15, 1908.

———. *Christ's Object Lessons.* Washington, DC: Review and Herald Publishing Association, 1900.

———. "Christ's Prayer for Unity." *The Signs of the Times*, November 26, 1902.

———. "The Conference in Sweden." *The Review and Herald*, October 5, 1886.

———. *Confrontation*. Washington, DC: Review and Herald Publishing Association, 1971.

———. *The Desire of Age.* Mountain View, CA: Pacific Press Publishing Association, 1898.

———. "Divinity in Humanity." *The Signs the Times*, March 5, 1896.

———. *The Ellen G. White 1888 Materials.* Washington, DC: Ellen G. White Estate, 1987.

———. *Evangelism.* Washington, DC: Review and Herald Publishing Association, 1946.

———. "Evidences of Genuine Faith." *The Review and Herald,* March 6, 1888.

———. "Faith and Good Works." *The Signs of the Times*, May 19, 1898.

———. "Farewell Words—Words of Comfort." *The Signs of the Times*, November 18, 1897.

———. "The Father, Son, and Holy Ghost." *Bible Training School*, March 1, 1906.

———. "Filled With the Fruits of Righteousness." *The Review and Herald*, May 17, 1906.

———. "The Foreigners in America." *The Review and Herald*, October 29, 1914.

———. "From Persecutor to Disciple." *The Youth's Instructor*, November 22, 1900.

———. "Go Work Today in My Vineyard." *The Signs of the Times*, April 1, 1897.

———. "Go Ye Therefore, and Teach All Nations." *The Signs of the Times*, August 5, 1903.

———. *Gospel Workers.* Washington, DC: Review and Herald Publishing Association, 1915.

———. "Grace and Faith the Gifts of God." *The Review and Herald*, December 24, 1908.

———. *The Great Controversy.* Mountain View, CA: Pacific Press Publishing Association, 1911.

———. "How to Meet Trial and Difficulty." *The Review and Herald*, May 30, 1912.

———. "Humility and Faithfulness in Laborers." *The Review and Herald*, April 8, 1884.

———. "Importance of Right Associations." *The Signs of the Times*, December 7, 1882.

———. "In Gethsemane." *The Signs of the Times*, December 9, 1897.

———. "Lessons from the Christ-Life." *The Review and Herald*, March 12, 1901.

———. "The Living Testimony." *The Signs of the Times*, February 7, 1895.

———. "The Love of Christ." *The Signs of the Times*, February 15, 1883.

———. "Luther at Wittenberg." *The Signs of the Times*, June 7, 1883.

———. "Luther's Source of Strength." *The Signs of the Times*, June 21, 1883.

———. *Manuscript Releases*. Vol. 7. Silver Spring, MD: Ellen G. White Estate, 1990.

———. *Manuscript Releases*. Vol. 16. Silver Spring, MD: Ellen G. White Estate, 1990.

———. *Manuscript Releases*. Vol. 17. Silver Spring, MD: Ellen G. White Estate, 1990.

———. *Manuscript Releases*. Vol. 21. Silver Spring, MD: Ellen G. White Estate, 1993.

———. "The Ministry Is Ordained of God." *The Review and Herald*, May 12, 1903.

———. *The Ministry of Healing.* Mountain View, CA: Pacific Press Publishing Association, 1905.

———. "Missionaries for God." The Review and Herald, April 10, 1888.

———. "Missionary Nurses." *The Review and Herald*, December 24, 1914.

———. "Missionary Work at Home." *The Health Reformer*, October 1, 1876.

———. "The Need of Earnest Effort." The Review and Herald, February 11, 1904.

———. *Notebook Leaflets From the Elmshaven Library.* Vol. 1. Payson, AZ: Leaves-Of-Autumn Books, 1985.

————. "Obedience the Path to Life." *The Review and Herald*, March 28, 1893.

————. "The Obedient Approved of God." *The Review and Herald*, August 28, 1894.

————. *Patriarchs and Prophets*. Washington, DC: Review and Herald Publishing Association, 1890.

————. "Praise the Lord." *The Bible Echo*, November 6, 1899.

————. "Pray for the Latter Rain." *The Review and Herald*, March 2, 1897.

————. "Prayer." *The Signs of the Times*, June 18, 1902.

————. *Prophets and Kings*. Mountain View, CA: Pacific Press Publishing Association, 1917.

————. "Redemption—No. 1." *The Review and Herald*, February 24, 1874.

————. *Reflecting Christ*. Hagerstown, MD: Review and Herald Publishing Association, 1985.

————. "Resisting Temptation." *The Review and Herald*, February 20, 1913.

————. "The Resurrection of Lazarus." *The Youth's Instructor*, March 30, 1899.

————. "Return to the First Love." *Special Testimony to Our Ministers*, no. 2.

————. "The Righteousness of Christ." *The Review and Herald*, August 19, 1890.

————. "The Risen Saviour." *The Youth's Instructor*, August 11, 1898.

————. "Sacrificed for Us." *The Youth's Instructor*, July 20, 1899.

————. "Sanctification Through the Truth." *The Review and Herald*, April 12, 1892.

————. "The Scriptures a Safeguard." *The Review and Herald*, June 7, 1906.

————. *The SDA Bible Commentary*. Vol. 1. Washington, DC: Review and Herald Publishing Association, 1953.

————. *The SDA Bible Commentary*. Vol. 6. Washington, DC: Review and Herald Publishing Association, 1956.

————. *The SDA Bible Commentary*. Vol. 7. Washington, DC: Review and Herald Publishing Association, 1957.

————. "The Second Adam." *The Youth's Instructor*, June 2, 1898.

————. *Selected Messages*. Book 3. Washington, DC: Review and Herald Publishing Association, 1980.

————. "Sin Condemned in the Flesh." *The Signs of the Times*, January 16, 1896.

————. *Special Testimony to Battle Creek Church*. No imprint: 1896.

————. "The Spirit of Christ." *The Review and Herald*, June 22, 1886.

————. *The Spirit of Prophecy*. Vol. 2. Battle Creek, MI: Seventh-day Adventist Publishing Association, 1877.

————. *The Spirit of Prophecy*. Vol. 4. Battle Creek, MI: Seventh-day Adventist Publishing Association, 1884.

————. *Spiritual Gifts*. Vol. 1. Battle Creek, MI: Seventh-day Adventist Publishing Association, 1858.

————. *The Story of Redemption*. Hagerstown, MD: Review and Herald Publishing Association, 1947.

———. "Sufficiency in Christ." *The Signs of the Times*, March 17, 1898.

———. "The Temptation of Christ." *The Review and Herald,* July 28, 1874.

———. "Tempted in All Points Like as We Are." *Youth's Instructor,* December 21, 1899.

———. "To Our Missionary Workers." *The Review and Herald*, December 8, 1885.

———. "To the Brethren and Sisters." *The Review and Herald*, June 10, 1852.

———. *Testimonies for the Church*. Vol. 3. Mountain View, CA: Pacific Press Publishing Association, 1875.

———. *Testimonies for the Church*. Vol. 4. Mountain View, CA: Pacific Press Publishing Association, 1881.

———. *Testimonies for the Church*. Vol. 5. Mountain View, CA: Pacific Press Publishing Association, 1889.

———. *Testimonies for the Church*. Vol. 8. Mountain View, CA: Pacific Press Publishing Association, 1904.

———. *Testimonies to Ministers and Gospel Workers*. Mountain View, CA: Pacific Press Publishing Association, 1923.

———. "The Vine and the Branches." *The Review and Herald*, November 16, 1897.

———. "Wise or Foolish, Which?" *The Youth's Instructor*, January 16, 1896.

———. "Words of Warning—No. 3." *The Review and Herald*, December 27, 1898.

———. "The Work at Fresno, California." *The Review and Herald*, June 19, 1888.

Wilkinson, Benjamin G. *Our Authorized Bible Vindicated*. Payson, AZ: Leaves-Of-Autumn Books, 1996.

———. *Truth Triumphant*. Brushton, NY: Teach Services, 1994.

"Woman Declared Dead, Still Breathing in Morgue." Fox News. http:/1ref.us/7 (accessed January 18, 2014).

We invite you to view the complete
selection of titles we publish at:

www.TEACHServices.com

Scan with your mobile
device to go directly
to our website.

Please write or e-mail us your praises, reactions, or
thoughts about this or any other book we publish at:

P.O. Box 954
Ringgold, GA 30736

info@TEACHServices.com

TEACH Services, Inc., titles may be purchased in bulk for
educational, business, fund-raising, or sales promotional use.
For information, please e-mail:

BulkSales@TEACHServices.com

Finally, if you are interested in seeing
your own book in print, please contact us at

publishing@TEACHServices.com

We would be happy to review your manuscript for free.